Tirpitz:
The Halifax Raids

by

Nigel Smith

Air Research Publications

First published 1994 by
Air Research Publications
PO Box 223, Walton-on-Thames,
Surrey, KT12 3YQ
England

Typeset in Great Britain by
A.C.E.Services,
Radlett, Herts, WD7 8LU

Printed in Great Britain by
MBA Group Ltd,
London N17 0HW

ISBN 1-871187-27-3

Tirpitz:
The Halifax Raids

The Bomber Command attacks
on the battleship *Tirpitz* in 1942

by

Nigel Smith

Air Research Publications

Dedicated to my father-in-law,
Vic Stevens,
Flight Engineer of Halifax W1048 'S-Sugar,'
who first told me the story of the Tirpitz Raids

CONTENTS

Acknowledgements		6
Foreword		10
Prelude		13
Chapter One	The Tirpitz.	16
Chapter Two	The January raid.	36
Chapter Three	Under Observation.	54
Chapter Four	The March Raid.	68
Chapter Five	The April Raids - Plans and Preparations.	96
Chapter Six	The Final Briefing.	109
Chapter Seven	Over the North Sea.	121
Chapter Eight	The Main Attack.	141
Chapter Nine	'S-Sugar' Under Fire.	163
Chapter Ten	The German Defence and the Aftermath.	
Chapter Eleven	The Second Raid.	188
Chapter Twelve	Survival.	208
Chapter Thirteen	Evasion and Capture (I).	228
Chapter Fourteen	Evasion.	249
Chapter Fifteen	Evasion and Capture (II).	261
Chapter Sixteen	Internment and Return.	270
Chapter Seventeen	In Memoriam.	275
Chapter Eighteen	Closing the Circle.	283

Appendices

Appendix I	Memories of a Young Girl.	290
Appendix II	The Impossible Mission?	293
Appendix III	Photographic Reconnaissance.	303
Appendix IV	The Raising of Halifax W1048 'S-Sugar'.	305
Appendix V	The Manufacture of W1048.	314
Appendix VI	Failed to Return.	319
Index		324

Acknowledgements

This book was born from my desire to know more about Halifax W1048-S 'Sugar', which I first laid eyes on in 1973. This was shortly after she had been brought back to England across the North Sea by a tank landing craft and when she lay covered in dust-sheets in a hangar at RAF Henlow in Buckinghamshire. Fascinated as I was in learning more about the aircraft and the series of raids in which she had taken part, I waited 'for the book to appear'. When no book was forthcoming, I realised that if I were to know what had happened to W1048-S 'Sugar', I was going to have to find out for myself.

In 1987 I began to interview my father-in-law, Vic Stevens, about his wartime experiences. We continued these conversations over a period of three years and, as Vic talked, I realised that, intriguing though his recollections were, they told only part of the story. With the assistance of a growing number of correspondents from the United Kingdom, Canada, South Africa, Australia, Germany, France and Norway, I began to discover the details of the events of the spring of 1942. To my delight I realised that these events had made such an impression on my informants that they could recall the details with considerable clarity and in a style of language that revealed their training. Aircrew were trained to report facts clearly and concisely. There was no room in a combat situation for men to express themselves other than with precision and my informants wrote to me expressing themselves clearly and concisely. They took considerable pains to be accurate and to show where they were not sure of the reliability of their memory. The 'truth', though, was harder to come by. Many of my correspondents survived one or even two tours (a tour was thirty operations over enemy territory) and clearly recalled many different incidents that had happened to them. Remarkably enough there was no instance when details of other raids were confused with details of the raids on the *Tirpitz*, such had been the impact of these raids. Sometimes, though, there was

6

confusion about which of the raids a particular incident belonged. However, corroboration of personal recollections, with details of the planning and results of the raids obtained from the Public Record Office at Kew, generally established the facts, also adding a wealth of detail. On the very few occasions when recollections have conflicted with the recorded facts, or when crews' recollections have differed, I have chosen to present what seems to me to have been the most logical and/or likely sequence of events.

I have had the great privilege to have met and spoken to some of the men involved, usually more than once. This, for me, has been one of the most rewarding aspects of the project. They were most hospitable, showed great interest in the project and supported it wholeheartedly, sharing with me many of their memories, some of them painful, some of them humorous, for the aircrew of the Second World War are a special breed. I owe all those who corresponded with me and/or allowed me to record my conversations with them, a great debt. I have done my best to render their story in a way that satisfies their own desire for accuracy in the telling of the tale. Indeed, it was the immediacy of the recorded spoken word that prompted me to tell the story as far as possible in the words of those who took part, while I took on the role of compiler and researcher of the linking details. On a very few occasions, I have chosen to 'tidy up' the spoken or written words of my informants to make their meaning clear. Otherwise the words quoted are as they were written or recorded.

I am most grateful for the help of the staffs at the Public Record Office at Kew, the Imperial War Museum, the Air Historical Branch of the Ministry of Defence, the Research Library at the RAF Museum, Hendon, the Bundesarchiv in Germany, the Air Photo Library at the University of Keele, the staff of Sawbridgeworth Library who made so many books available for me on seemingly 'indefinite' loan. Also for the author and researcher Alan Cooper's assistance at the PRO on the day I bumped into him quite by chance at the beginning of my quest for information. Peter Cornish, the civilian diver who formulated the strategy that was used to recover Halifax W1048-S 'Sugar', encouraged me to write the book, giving freely of his own knowledge and observations. I am particularly grateful to my father-in-law, Vic Stevens, whose lively telling of his story captured my imagination. His tireless assistance in answering my many queries over a long period of time kept me on track. He and his wife Gwen have been a constant source of advice and support throughout the project, even when I felt that the task would never be completed. Throughout the five years of work on the book my wife Patsy has selflessly provided the deepest possible support, as well as illustrating the chapter headings and drawing the maps. Without the assistance of the many people with whom I have corresponded over several years, the story could never have been pieced together. To them I extend my warmest gratitude, in the hope that this book will go some way to satisfying their curiosity about what transpired concerning the *Tirpitz* during the spring of 1942. My thanks are offered in particular to those whose words (reproduced either from their letters or from transcriptions of interviews I held with them) appear in the story that follows. They gave most generously of their energy, enthusiasm and time.

Correspondents and Contributors:

10 Squadron: Peter Bell; Chris W Charlton; Doug Dent; Philip Ellison; "Phil" Eyles; Ben Gibbons; Charles E Harrison; George Kent; G E ("Dusty") Miller; R H Saunders; George Smith; Harry Walmsley; Brig Gen J V Watts; Dennis Windle

15 Squadron: Peter Boggis; Don Fink; Don Jeffs; R ("Robbie") Roberts; Ian Ryall; B D Sellick; Stan Smith; Roy Stamp; Arthur D Stobbs; R A Strachan; I C K Swales

35 Squadron: Pierre Blanchet; Peter Cribb; Glenn Gardiner; Dr W (Bill) Grierson; Ian Hewitt; Don MacIntyre; Vic Stevens; Ron Wilson

76 Squadron: Hank Iveson; W (Bill) Lawes; Alex E Oram; R Radford; G Waddington; W R Waite; Roy Williams

97 Squadron: Brian Hallows

102 Squadron: H E (Batch) Batchelder

210 Squadron: John G Walker

No.1 P.R.U.: Richard Cussons; Roy Kenwright

Norway: Magnhild Aabakken; Bernhard Bergersen; Einar Borvik; Trygve Dalanes; Arne F Egner; Hans Flaamo; S Frigaard; Anton Gjorve; Karsten Granlund; Asbjørn and Gudmund Heggdal; Birger Hernes; Karl Hernes; Ivar Hoel; Oddmund Holmen; Paula Juliussen; Trygve Lian; Bjørn Olsen; Johan E Øyan; Paul Øyum; Bjørn Rørholt; Leif Rostad; Arne Sivertsen; Solveig and Lars Skjeldstad; Peter Trætli; Rolf Trøite; Aasmund Vinje.

Other Correspondents: Bert Aggas; Roger Anthoine & J -L Roba; Sir Alfred Ball; Mrs Ly Bennett; W Balderson; Miss E (Lettice) Curtis; Arthur Day; A ("Bert") De V Leach; Miss Jackie Gimson; Ron Gough; J A Hall; Walter Henry; Harry Jacques; Edmund Kuhnen; Charles Lambert; John A Macbean, Wing Commander (Retired); R Massey; D J P Milne; John Murray; R J Nelson; Roy C Nesbitt; Robert M Owen; Charles C Pallett; G Panichelli; Dr Alfred Price; Wally Rouse; Ernest Schofield; Tony Southern; E Whittles.

Other Assistance: Bernhard Bergersen; Rennie Chambers; Eva & Robin Cherry; Trevor Clifford; Mike Grace; Karin Keddy; Ulla Murray; Bjørn Rørholt; Adrian Wright.

It has been the intention of the author to acknowledge all help received and to provide the names of the sources of all written and pictorial material. If any person or organisation has been omitted either inadvertently or through lack of knowledge, the author extends his apologies to them and would be pleased to hear from them.

Sources for photographs are given, where available, with each photograph.

I am grateful for permission from the following publishers to use quotations from their publications.
William Kimber, an imprint of Harper Collins Publishers Ltd. (*Terror by Night*, by Michael Renaut 1982); Newton Publishers (*Death or Decoration*, by Ronnie Wait 1991); W.R.Chorley (*To See the Dawn Breaking - 76 Squadron Operations* by W. R. Chorley 1981); Key Publishing (*The Saving of S-Sugar* in *FlyPast* Magazine October 1982); *World War II Investigator* magazine (*Norway's Anonymous Radio Spies.* - Article by Bjørn Rørholt May 1988).

Foreword

On a sunny and cold morning early April 1942 I boarded a little train at the Trondheim Central station. In a hand bag I carried a German *Retina-II* camera and I was on my way, with a special German permit, to visit my father at the Falstad concentration camp just north of Trondheim. The real object of my trip was, however, to take pictures from the train, of the brand new battleship *Tirpitz*, which had just arrived from Germany. There was nothing heroic about this operation, but it was to turn out to be a prelude to the dramatic events in the coming weeks. Norway was about to enter its third year of German occupation and this winter was the hardest during the whole war. Food and clothing were desperately short. For most people their homes had to be kept unheated through a bitterly cold winter. And the war went on badly for the Allies. From all over the world the news only told of defeat and disaster. For most individuals, however, the German terror was even worse. Nobody knew what the next day would bring, as death and torture was the way the Germans thought they could conquer the Norwegian opposition against their brutal occupation. This was the way they thought they could get the Norwegians to accept the 'new order'. The people were in fact prisoners in their own country. All radios had been confiscated. Listening to the BBC was to be punished by death. The newspapers were full of German propaganda. And through the streets of Trondheim German troops paraded with their brass bands arrogantly demonstrating their victories 'on all fronts'. For most people this was the end, they had no hopes for the future - everything was just despair. Then, by the end of January, British reconnaissance 'planes began to turn up, on nearly every day of clear sky. I am deeply moved when I think back on these days as I vividly remember how people stopped in the streets, looking up at the vapour trails with tears in their eyes. And I can also remember an old lady whispering: 'God bless them - they are *our* boys - the Royal Air Force.' Thus the British 'planes came to be symbols of freedom and also visual signs of hope and help from the outside world. And then - when the real thing started - with low-flying 'planes, a hell of exploding bombs, ferocious flak fire and raining shrapnel, then the strange thing happened that people ran to the shelters with excited smiles and laughter, wishing the boys up there luck. Thus - the Royal Air Force came to be a symbol of freedom for the population throughout the whole war. Although the raids on the *Tirpitz* were unsuccessful, it was clear evidence that the Germans were not as undefeatable as one had thought.

The audacity, determination and skill shown in these raids thus was an enormous inspiration to the people of Norway, giving it new hopes for an end to their despair. Nigel Smith has told the story of these raids in a magnificent way and he has used a lot of time having a large number of Norwegians tell their story. The story he was told by the local population was one of devotion to the common cause and about their willingness to risk their lives for the gallant British warriors, who they looked upon with boundless admiration. Nigel Smith's book therefore is an important contribution to the history of the people who lived and experienced the raids against the *Tirpitz* from March to April 1942. Being one of them, I am deeply thankful for him writing this book.

Bernhard Bergersen
Trondheim, November 1991

A MESSAGE FROM THE A O C-in-C

DATE ... 3. 5. 42

SPECIAL ORDER BY GROUP CAPTAIN S. GRAHAM, M.C.
COMMANDING RAF STATION, LEEMING

The following message has been received from the Air Officer Commanding-in-Chief, Bomber Command

"The courage and determination shown by your crews in the attacks on Tirpitz was indeed worthy of immediate and outstanding success. Moreover, undismayed by their first experience of the full fury of the defences, they returned with undiminished ardour to the charge. Never was more asked, and never was more given of outstanding devotion to duty. We shall I hope yet find that their efforts have not been in vain but be that as it may your crews have set an example unsurpassed in the annals of British Arms".

The message received from Air Marshal Arthur T. Harris, the AOC-in-C Bomber Command

Prelude

Lake Hoklingen, Norway, 30th June 1973

It occurred before anybody was really aware of what was happening. For eleven days now, out near the centre of the lake, the makeshift raft had dipped and risen as divers slid over the side or climbed aboard after their twenty minute stint ninety feet down in the cold, murky waters. For days the normally quiet lake surrounded by tree-clad hills had throbbed and pulsated to the insistent clatter of the air-compressor on the raft. Equipment of all descriptions lay scattered on the shore - diving and lifting gear - and visitors and camera crews came and went or stood waiting for something to happen.

It was ten minutes past two in the afternoon. One moment the surface of the lake was rippling in the sunlight as it had done for the last few exhausting days. The next moment the surface surged and erupted as, with a plunging heave the jutting jaw and nose of the bomber thrust upwards in a flurry of water. Water cascaded from the shattered and opaque perspex windscreen as the aircraft settled and lay still, surrounded incongruously by the bobbing, air-filled, oil-drums that had drawn her from the bottom of the lake.

Entombed for 31 years beneath the surface of Lake Hoklingen, Halifax W1048 'S-Sugar' had risen at last into the light of day. She carried no bombs and no dead crewmen lay in her mud-filled fuselage. She would fly no more.

But she had a story to tell. How had she reached this lake all those years ago? What was the purpose of the operation in which she had been taking part? And what had happened to her crew?

This book tells the story of the men and aircraft who, despite the hazards of wartime flying, bad weather and great distances, gave their utmost (and some their lives) in the attempts to cripple or sink the German battleship *Tirpitz* by attacking her in the spring of 1942. As Phil Ellison, a Canadian Flight Sergeant who took part in the raids in April 1942, remarks about the last two attempts:

> "It was a great and valiant effort to try and sink the *Tirpitz* in April 1942 and no one ever got to know about it due to wartime secrecy. It was a most difficult type of attack to be made by regular squadron crews and aircraft. We were not trained for this type of operation. Most of our crews had only recently converted from Whitleys and were not experienced on the Halifax. If we had been successful in sinking the *Tirpitz* it would have been a feather in the cap of the RAF. The raid could easily have been the turning point in the Battle of the Atlantic.
>
> "This was an outstanding example of the skill and the courage of our young men in the Royal Air Force, Royal Canadian Air Force, and Royal Australian Air Force - no one turned back off the second night, after the first terrible experience."

Flight Sergeant Phil Ellison of 10 Squadron, who completed a total of 56 operations.

(E. Ellison)

It is a sobering reflection that, had the RAF been successful in disabling the *Tirpitz* by the end of April 1942, then the ill-fated merchantmen of Convoy PQ17, threatened by the emergence of the *Tirpitz* during the convoy's run across the northern Atlantic to Archangel two months later, would never have been ordered to scatter on the evening of July 4th, thus losing the protection of their escorting cruisers and destroyers. They would not have been molested with such

After thirty-one years submerged beneath Lake Hoklingen the last Halifax, W1048 'S-Sugar' ,surfaces like a Leviathan from the deep.

terrible consequences by the German *U-boats* and aircraft that were able to pick them off one by one. Twenty-three out of thirty-six merchant vessels of that convoy were lost to enemy action. The mere presence at sea of the *Tirpitz* had compelled the Admiralty to order the convoy to scatter to prevent the cruisers and destroyers accompanying it being overwhelmed by a superior German naval force.

Had the *Tirpitz* been put out of action by the RAF at that time it is likely that the nature of these daring raids of 1942, and the exploits of the crews who took part, would have attracted the acclaim accorded to those who breached the dams in May 1943, or to those who finally sank the *Tirpitz* with *Tallboy* bombs in November 1944.

Had the efforts of these airmen been successful the course of the war at sea would probably have been different. The fact that they failed in their objective, that the prize eluded them, must not be allowed to conceal the fact that they lacked nothing in the attempt.

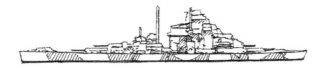

Chapter One
The *Tirpitz*

Across some of the most inhospitable and dangerous seas in the world, slow-moving merchant ships laboriously punched their way. They moved through mountainous seas, spray that froze as it touched the ships' rigging and superstructure and gales that howled around them for unrelenting days at a time. But these were not what the merchant crews feared most on their desperate winter voyages across the North Atlantic to the northern ports of Russia, their holds crammed with supplies and military equipment. It was on the surface of the sea and beneath the waves that their most deadly enemies lurked. The German *U-boats* and the warships of the German *Kriegsmarine*. The only protection for the merchantmen lay in keeping up with the remainder of the other vessels in the convoy, a gaggle of ships spread out across the sea as far as the eye could see, anxiously patrolled by British warships and aircraft of Coastal Command.

The advent of 1942 seemed to bring little hope for the British in their island stronghold. They were still in a state of siege. The thin and stretched lifeline of merchant convoys from the United States was being strangled all too effectively by German surface and underwater forces and the situation was becoming increasingly grave. The number of Allied merchant ships sunk by the *U-boats* prowling the waters of the North Atlantic was rising and would continue to do so for much of the year. Although the German capital ships, *Gneisenau*, *Scharnhorst* and *Prinz Eugen* lay inactive in the docks at the French port of Brest, they could, almost at any moment, break out into the

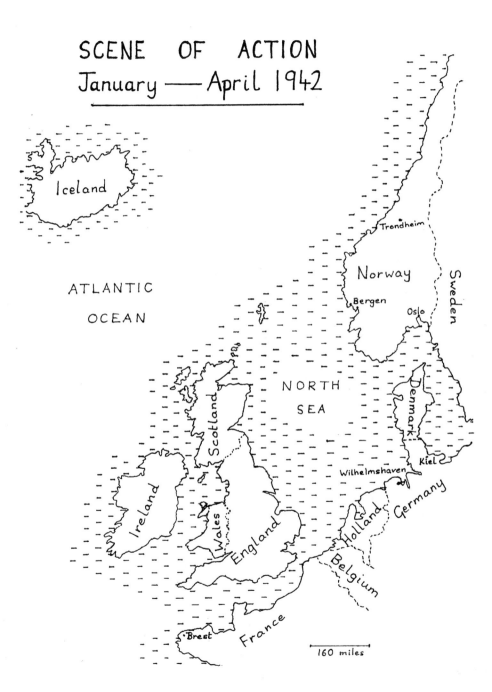

SCENE OF ACTION
January — April 1942

North Atlantic where their considerable might, added to that of the *U-boats*, could well turn the tide of the war at sea against the Allies. And now a new threat was emerging. The new giant battleship *Tirpitz*, sister-ship to the now-vanquished *Bismarck*, her sea trials in the Baltic concluded, was now fully operational. But where would she strike?

It was imperative that the convoys of merchant ships continue to reach the Russian ports of Archangel and Murmansk. Churchill's commitment to Stalin, to maintain a regular supply to meet essential war-needs, had to be honoured to enable the German forces to be engaged more effectively on the Eastern Front. This supply-line would be broken if German naval units were allowed to roam the freezing waters off the north of Norway unmolested.

Among the escort vessels available for the protection of these convoys were three *King George V* class battleships. Despite the fact that these vessels were desperately needed in the war in the Pacific, they had to be stationed in northern waters in case the German surface fleet, and in particular the *Tirpitz*, chose to emerge and hunt down both the Russia-bound convoys and those outward-bound with troops for North Africa and the Middle East. These three vessels would be free to fight in the Pacific if only the threat from the *Tirpitz* were to recede.

The threat to the Allies posed by her mere presence in Northern waters had to be met, preferably by her destruction. Failing that, damage sufficient to prevent her taking to the high seas needed to be inflicted. The Allies believed that the build-up of German naval forces in central Norway was in preparation for an offensive. In fact Hitler, believing at this time that the war would be decided in Norway and that an Allied invasion of Norway was either imminent or likely in the near future, was deploying his forces in a defensive rôle. As far as he was concerned, any battleship not in Norway was 'in the wrong place'. It was this prime concern of his that was to lead to the mustering of several of Germany's most powerful warships, including the new *Tirpitz*, in Norway during the early part of 1942.

As for the part to be played by Bomber Command, Harry Walmsley, one of the airmen who was to be shot down over the *Tirpitz* in April, has this to say of his own, No 10, Squadron.

"In January 1942 the squadron was ready to resume the offensive against the German fatherland. But, quite unexpectedly, we were diverted from that course, at a time when Bomber Command was the only fighting force actually striking at the German based targets.

"What happened was a request from Royal Navy 'top brass' for assistance in meeting the threat of U-boats, Luftwaffe fighter planes and enemy battleships. Although C-in-C Bomber Command (who at this period was Acting C-in-C, Air Vice-Marshal J.E.A. Baldwin) tried to resist the switch to these new targets he was over-ruled by the War Cabinet which was committed to reducing the disastrous losses of merchant ships in convoys crossing both the Atlantic and the Northern Waters to Russia.

"So, as a consequence of this new strategy, I was to operate with my regular Halifax crew on raids to:- St Nazaire U-boat pens; Brest Naval Dockyard; Lista airfield in Southern Norway (Bf109 base); *Scharnhorst* and *Gneisenau* (battlecruisers in the English Channel); and *Tirpitz*. There were two German-based targets in between, but all these operations, except *Tirpitz*, were carried out within a few weeks by the end of March 1942."

On 12th January 1942, on orders from Admiral Raeder and the German Naval Staff, the new battleship *Tirpitz* sailed from the Baltic where she had been undergoing extensive sea trials. Passing through the Kiel Canal, she arrived at the port of Wilhelmshaven on the coast of Germany. On 14th January, sailing through thick weather with an escort of four destroyers and led by an ice-breaker, she set out to negotiate the dangerous coastal minefields off Norway. Two days later, on 16th January, she steamed up Trondheim Fjord, past the city of Trondheim and into a berth at the head of Fætten Fjord. Despite the efforts of the Photographic Reconnaissance Unit, it was the following day, the 17th, before the British were aware that she had even sailed from Wilhelmshaven.

Hitler, against the advice of his Admirals, had vetoed the suggestion that *Tirpitz* should be moved to Brest, from where she could wage war on the Atlantic convoys with impunity. He ordered that she should instead be stationed in Norway. Accepting the inevitable, Hitler's Admirals put *Tirpitz's* forthcoming move to Norway on a reasoned footing. Her presence in Norwegian waters would protect the small vessels that supplied the German army in Norway. Trondheim, situated mid-way between the south and north of Norway, provided an excellent .

base from which to protect the entire German position in Norway. This menacing naval presence in Trondheim could threaten the North Atlantic convoys and effectively tie down the Allied forces both at Scapa Flow in the Orkneys and in the North Atlantic.

The knowledge that the *Tirpitz* was no longer at Wilhelmshaven immediately alerted the British Admiralty to the threat of a German naval strike on the convoy route from the north of England and from Iceland to the northern ports of Russia, along which supply ships had been regularly transporting essential war materials to the beleaguered Russians. The imminent departure of convoy PQ9 was immediately delayed until February 1st. It was essential that the *Tirpitz* be located as soon as possible.

As the Prime Minister, Winston Churchill, said of her:

> "The destruction or even crippling of this ship is the greatest event at sea at the present time. No other target is comparable to it. ... The entire naval situation throughout the world would be altered and the naval command in the Pacific would be regained." [1]

What was it about the vessel herself that made her such a threat? The 42,900 ton *Tirpitz*, launched at Wilhelmshaven, Germany, on April 1st 1939, was the pride of the German Navy when she was commissioned in January 1941. She was a highly sophisticated floating gun-platform, armed with eight enormous 15-inch guns and an impressive display of other weaponry, including eight twin 37mm. anti-aircraft guns. She could out-gun any ship in the British Navy and carried four Arado seaplanes that could be catapulted into the sky. Capable of reaching a speed of 31 knots and with a range of nine thousand miles at nineteen knots, she was the most powerful battleship afloat in Western European waters.

Once it was realised that the *Tirpitz* had left Wilhelmshaven, the British made strenuous efforts to find her, although they had little information to go on. Their only chance of locating her quickly lay in the use of aircraft, with the additional hope that she be sighted by the Royal Navy. However, the first clue to her whereabouts was a broken-off radio message from an agent in Norway. Bjørn Rørholt, a trained radio operator who was to be sent out to Norway in February, recalls how the battleship was located:

The Tirpitz, photographed in Fætten Fjord in 1942. (via Author)

The quadruple 20mm Rheinmetall C/38 mountings fitted aboard Tirpitz in 1941 for anti-aircraft defence. On the right can be seen the rangefinder. (via Author)

"In Bergen on Norway's west coast, Jan Dahm had an efficient intelligence group, but had no radio. 19-year-old Bjarne Thorsen braved the North Sea to get one. As a result, station *Theta* was operative in Bergen by New Year 1942. Dahm had a scout on a coastal steamer, who observed the *Tirpitz* coming into Trondheim Fjord, as the steamer emerged in the evening of 16 January en route to Bergen. A message went out over *Theta* late on the 17th. Due to electricity rationing, local power was cut at midnight, amputating almost half the message. Probably, Home Station at Bletchley Park reconstructed the contents. With the double-transposition we used, it would not take long. Later, *Theta* added the information that *Tirpitz* was moored east of Trondheim, camouflaged as a small island. It took reconnaissance aircraft days to spot her." [2.]

Although her general whereabouts was known, her exact location was still a mystery. One of the Photographic Reconnaissance Unit pilots, Flying Officer Richard Cussons of 'B' Flight 1 PRU, who took part in photographic sorties over the *Tirpitz* from April to July 1942, recalls the events of the time:

"In January 1942 'C' Flight of No 1 PRU, commanded by Flight Lieutenant Tony Hill, was detached from its base at RAF Benson in Oxfordshire, to RAF Wick, specifically to look for, and watch the movements of, the *Tirpitz*...

"The Spitfires were based at Wick simply because it was the nearest mainland RAF station to Norway, but the disadvantage was its distance from PRU's base at Benson and the Central Interpretation Unit at Medmenham, near Henley. However the newly arrived Mk P.R.IV Spitfires had an operational range of about 1,800 miles at an altitude of 28-30,000 feet and a cruising speed of about 320 knots, and so could reach far enough to cover Trondheim fairly easily so long as there was no strong upper wind. In order to stretch the range as far as possible it was our practice to take off from Wick with the wing tanks 'filled to overflowing' and the main tanks also full, fly at low level to Sumburgh using main tanks only, land there and have the main tanks topped up to the brim. With all this fuel on board it was just possible to get airborne and climb out of Sumburgh. We then set course, as worked out before take-off, using a forecast wind from the Met. man; with 400 miles or so of nothing but sea, the navigation was entirely by dead-reckoning (and hope that the Met. man was right), until one could see the Norwegian coast and pick up a recognisable point on the map; very often there was a good deal of cloud cover which made life even more difficult."

The Coastal Command operation to observe and track the movements of the *Tirpitz* was known under the code-name *Chamberlain*. It was Flight Lieutenant Peter Fane, one of the PRU pilots involved in this operation, who was the first to spot and photograph the *Tirpitz* in her new berth.

Above: Flying Officer Richard Cussons (centre, with cap) on the nose of a PRU Spitfire. (R. Cussons)

Right: A Spitfire PR IV of No.1 PRU. (R. Cussons)

On the afternoon of Friday 23rd January 1942, flying PR IV Spitfire R7035 back from a reconnaissance patrol to Trondheim (the fifth reconnaissance sortie over Trondheim since the search for *Tirpitz* had begun), Fane landed at RAF Wick to report that he had taken photographs at 12.50 hours of a 'suspected large naval unit' in Åsen Fjord. The film was removed from the camera and the developing process begun, while the Photographic Interpreter stood by.

The job of photographic interpreters was to interpret the photographs taken by reconnaissance aircraft. There were three phases in this process. In the first, the film negative was examined as soon as it was developed and a brief on-the-spot report made, without recourse to printing it. This was carried out at Benson, or an out-station if a unit was on detachment to somewhere like St Eval or Wick. Within maybe thirty minutes of the aircraft landing it was thus possible to report urgent information gleaned from the negative, still wet from the developing and rinsing tanks. The second stage was carried out by the interpreters at the Allied Central Interpretation Unit at Medmenham, where a detailed report comparing photographs taken within the previous twenty-four hours was made. A third and final phase report was then made, if necessary, by experts from the appropriate forces - land, sea or air - who had a special interest in the subject of the photographs. The interpreters would use stereoscopic viewers to enable them to see the images in three-dimensions and thus to be able to establish extremely detailed information and measurements. Sometimes, as in the attacks on the *Tirpitz* in Fætten Fjord, an accurate model could be made from this information.

The photographic interpreter, who had been sent from RAF Benson to Wick with the PRU detachment to make the first phase interpretations of reconnaissance photographs, was a Dane by the name of Hauch. His English was excellent and his knowledge of the Norwegian coastline remarkable. Richard Cussons recalls that, later in the war when the PRU was trying to discover the whereabouts of the German pocket battleship *Lützow*, he himself was despatched on a reconnaissance sortie, at maximum range, to cover Stettin. On the way there the dense cloud beneath his Spitfire suddenly cleared and he saw below him six vessels, sailing in a protective formation at a good speed. He hurriedly photographed them, sure that they were none other than the *Lützow* and five attendant destroyers. He immediately turned for home. Not bothering to land for fuel at Sumburgh as normal (for he had not flown his full sortie), he made straight for Wick, landing there in great excitement. Hauch, when he saw the wet negatives, was able to confirm Cusson's identification. Equally importantly and quite remarkably, he was able to identify the exact location of the enemy vessels from a small strip of land visible in a corner of the photograph.

As the wet strip of negative emerged from the rinsing tank under Hauch's careful scrutiny, he announced that the 'naval unit' that Fane had photographed was the battleship *Tirpitz*. She had been located again after a seven-day search. The photographs showed her lying close inshore on the north side of an inlet at the head of Åsen Fjord, known as Fætten Fjord. She

*A PRU low-level obli-
que photo of the Tir-
pitz, taken in Faetten
Fjord in 1942. Note the camouflage rafts and the anti-torpedo boom.
Just visible onshore are the concrete plinths to which she was moored.*
(via Sqn Ldr D.Iveson)

*Inset: Tirpitz photographed by Peter Fane of the PRU on 20th March
1942, showing the hostile terrain and the narrowness of the Fjord.*
(Air Photo Library)

lay up against a towering hill-side, partially protected by an
incomplete anti-torpedo boom. It was evident from the photographs that the crew was busy constructing camouflage netting

around her bows. The search was over and the planning of how to deal with the menacing presence could begin.

Some Norwegians living in the Åsen area at the time, mostly

━━━━━━━━━━━━━━━━━━━━━━━━━━━━━━━━━━━

fishermen and farmers, still remember the huge vessel creeping for the first time into the berth that had been prepared for her, on that January afternoon in 1942, coming to rest next to the cliffs near the head of Fætten Fjord. She was secured, alongside staging that had been built at the edge of the fjord, to mighty mooring chains concreted into the hillsides so securely that they remain there to this day.

It was not long before members of her crew were seen hard at work camouflaging the ship. Rafts were placed at bow and stern. From these and from the deck of the ship herself, great camouflage nets were spread to the shore in an effort to conceal the distinctive outline of the battleship. Small fir trees cut from the woods on the shore were secured to the guard rails. More were poked into the links of the great anchor chains that lay along her decks, while the distinctive protruding barrels of her huge guns were draped with white canvas. To protect her from underwater attack, anti-submarine netting was hung from floats in the water within 100 yards of her. Small working boats also appeared and were moored nearby, while anti-aircraft guns and searchlights were erected on concrete bases let into the hillsides on both banks of the fjord. That first month or so was a busy time for the battleship's crew, as they worked to create the protection their ship needed.

The narrow fjord and the high cliffs looming above afforded the *Tirpitz* a considerable degree of natural protection and, protected as she was from aerial attack by her own anti-aircraft guns, by gun emplacements on the surrounding hills and islands and by *Flak* ships moored in the surrounding waters, she was virtually invulnerable. A large area in the vicinity of Trondheim Fjord, containing a concentration of enemy shipping (submarines, tankers, small warships etc.), was dotted with searchlight posts and anti-aircraft batteries. A number of *Flak* ships and destroyers were also at anchor in the roads. Additionally, there was a *Flak* battery at the head of Fætten Fjord itself, a

Top: Crewmen lay out camouflage netting over the Tirpitz.
(via Author).
Bottom: The fore-deck of the battleship, with netting over the guns
and fir trees on deck. (via Author)

few hundred yards from where *Tirpitz* lay.

Tirpitz was to remain a familiar sight in her secluded lair for the next year. She only occasionally left her berth for exercises in Trondheim Fjord or a foray into the open waters of the North Atlantic. Her presence dominated the life of the people in the district all the time she was there. Military installations of all kinds - anti-aircraft guns, searchlights, smokescreen apparatus - were scattered around both sides of the fjord. At several carefully selected positions on shore, powerful lamps were erected. These were the 'leading lights' that guided *Tirpitz* through the deep-water channel as she threaded her way past Saltøya (Salt Island) and on up the narrowing fjord into her berth.[3]

Isolated as they were on their parents' small-holdings and farms, the advent of the *Tirpitz* into their little world was nothing short of a wonder to the local children. Birger Hernes later recalled:

"For us children, it was an exciting time when the *Tirpitz* came slowly into the Fjord sometime during the winter of 1942. I was eight years old. I lived together with my parents and two siblings on a small holding called Aavikstykket, which lies a short distance up in the hills. We were too young to understand the problems the ship of war brought. Suddenly there were people everywhere and we stared at the ship with fright and wonder. The closest we ever dared go was up to the side of the ship. The only Norwegian person to go aboard was my father. He demanded to speak to the ship's captain about the sailors' annoying football games in our field. He was invited aboard and the football games seemed to stop.

"Days and weeks passed by, and we soon got used to the new way of life. The Germans built smoke-screen equipment up in the hills and down by the beach. Another was built on Saltøya and here, as in many places, they built gun emplacements. They practised a lot. Thick disgusting smoke poured out over the fjord and up into the Vududalen (the steep-side valley at the head of Fætten Fjord). A dense carpet of smoke covered the arm of the fjord and I remember that I felt ill from the smoke. Afterwards they practised rifle shooting. We heard the noise of machine guns and cannons, especially when they echoed round the mountainsides. But we got used to it after a while."

Odin Lovtangen who, on the nights of the two attacks in April was to take shelter in the cellar of his nearby hillside farm, remembers that the Germans did not interfere with the daily life of the local people. They were allowed to move freely about the fjord. Lovtangen even rowed out to collect pigswill every day from the battleship, although he never went on board. He also

Surrounded by Arctic sea smoke, the battleship Tirpitz in Fættenfjord.
(via Author)

Tirpitz in Fætten Fjord in January 1942. Note the camouflage rafts and the proximity of the wooded slopes. (via Author)

recalls that the German sailors occasionally carried out shooting practice:

> "I remember once I was driving a horse in the farmyard. All of a sudden splinters rained all around me, and one of them hit the earth only a few centimetres from the horse." [4.]

Such events must have brought variety to the rather dull existence the sailors led aboard the *Tirpitz*. They were mostly young men who had joined the *Kriegsmarine* to see the world and to take part in some action, not to be confined to an inactive, 'floating barracks'. But, the most mighty ship of the German Navy was trapped. Not by the fjords and islands of Norway, but by the fear of the German High Command that should she venture out into the Atlantic with an inadequate number of support ships she might be outnumbered by the British Navy and go the same way as her sister ship *Bismarck*, sunk, to Hitler's dismay, in May 1941. There was also a severe shortage of fuel-oil.

Two miles down the fjord towards Trondheim lay Salt Island. In the attacks that took place against the *Tirpitz*, this island was to provide an essential navigational landmark. It had been requisitioned and developed by the crew of the *Tirpitz* as a leave centre (known by them as 'Tipito'). The crew could not be expected to remain cooped up on the battleship for months on end without respite. The distance back to Germany was too great for a short leave, but at 'Tipito' the sailors were able to relax. In the event of an alert two motor boats were available to ferry those on leave back to the *Tirpitz*, while shelters were available if they were caught by an air-raid. For the ship's officers a chalet, standing at the head of Fætten Fjord, had been adapted as a mess. It was known as 'Perrig Heim' and was reached by a track that led up from the boat landing place at the head of the fjord. In a field near the fjord a number of wooden buildings were constructed, to be used as workshops.

Within a very short time of her arrival in Trondheim Fjord, Allied aircraft were seen flying over the hills and inlets of the area. The local people realised that they must be photo-reconnaissance aircraft. It was obvious that, since the *Tirpitz* was a ship of great importance, it would have to be disabled or destroyed. Therefore she, and the land around her, would soon

Tirpitz turning with the aid of tugs at the entrance to Fætten Fjord with Saltøya (Salt Island) to the right of her. She is on her way out into Trondheim Fjord. (via J. Øyan)

be under attack - an alarming realisation for those who lived in the small-holdings and farms not far from her mooring-place.

The stationing of the *Tirpitz* at Trondheim, coupled with enemy naval activity at the French harbour of Brest, gave rise to British fears that the Germans were planning a major fleet operation. They believed that it would probably be a voyage into the waters of the North Atlantic to attack the sea-borne supply route from North America to Britain and Russia. On Sunday 25th January, two days after the first sighting of the *Tirpitz*, Major-General Hastings Ismay, the Secretary to the Chief of Staffs Committee, received a minute from the Prime Minister, Winston Churchill. He presented copies to that Committee at its meeting later that day; it read as follows:

"Prime Minister to General Ismay, for C.O.S. Committee 25 Jan 42

1. The presence of *Tirpitz* at Trondheim has now been known for three days. The destruction or even crippling of this ship is the greatest event at sea at the present time. No other target is comparable to it. She cannot have ack-ack protection comparable to Brest or the German home ports. If she were even only crippled, it would be difficult to take her back to Germany. No doubt it is better to wait for moonlight for a night attack, but moonlight attacks are not comparable with day attacks. The entire naval situation

throughout the world would be altered and the naval command in the Pacific would be regained.

2. There must be no lack of co-operation between Bomber Command and the Fleet Air Arm and aircraft-carriers. A plan should be made to attack both with carrier-borne torpedo aircraft and with heavy bombers by daylight or at dawn. The whole strategy of the war turns at this period on this ship, which is holding four times the number of British capital ships paralysed, to say nothing of the two new American battleships retained in the Atlantic. I regard the matter as of the highest urgency and importance. I shall mention it in the Cabinet to-morrow, and it must be considered in detail at the Defence Committee of Tuesday night. [5.]

It was thus clear that, having been tracked down, the *Tirpitz* must be contained in her Norwegian hide-away. She should either be sunk or, at the least, damaged without delay.

At a meeting of the War Cabinet the following day (Monday 26th January) the following minute was recorded:

"The *Tirpitz*: In answer to a question by the Prime Minister, the First Sea Lord and the Chief of the Air Staff said that the possibility of attacking the *Tirpitz*, now in Trondheim Fjord, had been exhaustively examined and it was hoped that an attack would be made as soon as weather conditions were favourable.

The Prime Minister said that it was of the utmost importance strategically that the *Tirpitz* should, if possible, be disabled or sunk." [6.]

Bomber Command had by now gained considerable experience of attacking enemy warships in harbour. A series of costly raids on Brest, La Rochelle and La Pallice had shown them that battleships in harbour were stoutly defended. They were also notoriously difficult to hit, so small a target did they present to even low-flying bombers. However, when attacking battleships in harbour the entire port, with its dockside facilities, storage depots and so on, became a useful target for bombs failing to hit the ships. With the *Tirpitz*, however, near-misses would be of no value.

It was self-evident that the longer *Tirpitz* lay at anchor in Fætten Fjord the more formidable would the shore-based anti-aircraft defences become. Time was of the essence. The planners were also up against the two problems of range and effectiveness. Aircraft had to be able to fly the considerable distance to Trondheim carrying an effective bomb-load. The task required a bomb that was capable of penetrating *Tirpitz's* thick armour-plating before exploding below decks. In 1942 there was no bomb with such capability. Even had such a bomb been

The Air Officer Commanding-in-Chief, Bomber Command, Air Marshal Sir Arthur Harris.
(via V. Stevens)

available, there was no way, other than by chance, that an aircraft with the currently available bomb-sight could aim accurately enough from a sufficient height for such a bomb to be effective. The only action that could be taken was to attempt to disable her in some way, perhaps by damaging her superstructure. The 2,000lb bombs in service, if they struck her deck, could do considerable damage, enough to keep her in port for a time.

Churchill believed that carrier-borne aircraft of the Royal Navy had a part to play. The Admiralty was consulted and it was suggested that carrier-borne aircraft carry out an attack timed to take place at first light following a night attack by Bomber Command.

However, despite the fact that they could easily be brought to within range, it was realised that an attack by Naval torpedo-carrying aircraft would be impossible to carry out. It seemed that only heavy bombers of Bomber Command had any chance of success.

The only two aircraft types available to Bomber Command at this stage of the war that were capable of flying the distance and carrying a useful weight of bombs were the Short Stirling and the Handley Page Halifax. Both were four-engined heavy bombers equipping Nos 3 and 4 Groups respectively. The Stirling had been flying operationally since February 1941 and the Halifax since March. The Avro Lancaster Mk 1, which took part in later attacks, did not become operational until March 1942. With its top speed of 275 mph at 14,500 feet, its perfomance was comparable with the Halifax, although the Halifax could reach a greater altitude and could also carry a greater weight and variety of bombs. The better bomb-carrying capacity was to be crucial in the operations that were to follow.

The heavy bombers of 3 and 4 Group were all based in Yorkshire and Norfolk, all out of range of the *Tirpitz*. However, if the bombers were detached from their home bases to advanced bases in the North of Scotland, they should be just within striking range of their target. All that remained to be settled was the date and the time of the intended operation. The question now was, should the attack be made in daylight or at night?

The Prime Minister's minute of 25th January had raised one of the major difficulties that beset Bomber Command throughout the war. Daylight bombing, although giving aircrews the best chance of finding and hitting a target, also led to an intolerably high crew and aircraft loss-rate to enemy action. Night-bombing, although safer for the crews, inevitably reduced the accuracy of target-finding and subsequent bombing. By the spring of 1942 Bomber Command was carrying out very few daylight operations. Therefore, at a conference held by the Chief of Air Staff, the decision was made to attack the *Tirpitz* at night. A pitch-black night, which would give attacking bombers the sure defence of darkness against the guns of the enemy, would also make it virtually impossible for them to find the target. Consequently the most suitable conditions would consist of a bright moonlit night, with minimal cloud cover and no more than a light wind. Good visibility would enable aircrews to navigate with reasonable ease and afford the bomb-aimers the best chance of hitting their target, while the absence of strong winds would ease the navigators' task of guiding their aircraft to and from the target. They would also alleviate the problem of the aircraft operating at a great distance from base at the limit of their fuel capacity. Minimal cloud cover would also help with the navigation, particularly over the Norwegian coast when landmarks would need to be recognised, and would reduce the danger of searchlights picking out aircraft against a pale backdrop of clouds, giving the German anti-aircraft gunners easy targets.

A period of reasonably full moon lasts about a week, but the next available moon period was fast approaching. If there was to be the least possible delay in this attack taking place, the planners had no more than a few days before the operation must occur.

The first opportunity would be the night of 29/30th January, although it could be delayed for a few days if the weather proved unsuitable. It was to take Bomber Command only four days to mount and carry out this, the first of four operations against the *Tirpitz* in Fætten Fjord.

NOTES

1. Public Record Office, Kew.
2. *World War II Investigator*, May 1988.
3. See map on page 17
4. From a story reported in a local Norwegian newspaper in the 1980s.
5. *The Second World War Vol IV.* - Winston S. Churchill
6. PRO CAB 65-25 WM (4) 11a Conclusions.

Chapter Two
The January Raid

Plans were made hurriedly and, just after midnight, in the early hours of Monday 26th January, at the Headquarters of No 3 Group at Mildenhall in Suffolk, the details of *Operation Oiled* were dispatched to the Squadrons involved. The plan required the detachment of a small force of Stirlings and Halifaxes to divert their current bombing efforts over Germany to a small target tucked into a Norwegian fjord. Heavy bombers of 3 and 4 Groups were to assemble on 28th January at an advanced base, RAF Lossiemouth, in the far north of Scotland, from where they would carry out their bombing attack on the *Tirpitz*. The attacking force was to carry a mixture of 2,000lb Armour-Piercing (AP) bombs and 500lb Semi-Armour-Piercing (SAP) bombs. The 2,000 pounders were intended to damage parts of the vessel's superstructure, while the SAP were intended to deal with the defences. No.3 Group was to provide a total of sixteen Stirlings from 15 and 149 Squadrons, while 4 Group was to provide ten Halifaxes from 10 and 76 Squadrons. In the event thirteen Stirlings and eleven Halifaxes reached the advance base, a total of twenty-four aircraft. Wing Commander J. C. Macdonald, the Officer Commanding 15 Squadron (3 Group), was to command the whole operation. Since this operation was considered to be very urgent, crews on leave were to be recalled if necessary. It was also regarded as a highly secret operation, for radio silence was to be maintained except in emergency, even during the flight up to Lossiemouth. Flight Lieutenant 'Hank' Iveson, who flew on three out of the four raids that took place at this time against the *Tirpitz*, comments on this period

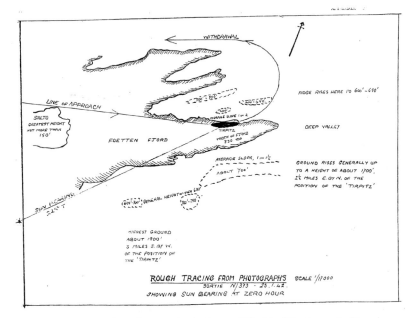

A contemporary 'rough tracing' from Flight Lieutenant Fane's reconnaissance photograph of 23rd January 1942, onto which was drawn the proposed attack and withdrawal route used later for the April raids. The inclusion of the sun's declination may indicate that this tracing was prepared to meet the original demands for a daylight raid. (PRO)

in the life of 76 Squadron:

"Morale at this time (1941/42) was very high indeed. The Halifax aircraft was very new and a great improvement on previous aircraft (Whitleys, Wellingtons, etc.). Crews were very pleased and proud to have it. It was a great morale booster. The other squadron on the same base still had Whitley aircraft. The level of experience on the squadron was unusually high; most of the crews having previously operated over Germany in Whitley aircraft. Leadership was good. As a very junior officer in December 1941, I was particularly impressed by the Squadron Commander, Wing Commander David O. Young."

Since the location of a naval target could change at short notice it was essential that the *Tirpitz's* position be closely monitored. Coastal Command was tasked with keeping the *Tirpitz* under constant observation by daily reconnaissance, a job carried out by the aircraft of No.1 Photographic Reconnaissance Unit (No. 1

PRU). It was in fact impossible to maintain a daily watch on the *Tirpitz*. Bad weather conditions, mechanical failures and the occasional appearance of enemy aircraft meant in practice that the battleship was observed and photographed only about once a week throughout the Spring of 1942. The responsibility for the operation had passed from Headquarters Bomber Command to 3 and 4 Groups and finally to the Squadrons. Now it was down to the aircraft crews to carry it out. On Wednesday, 28th January, through low cloud, sleet and rain, and with the assistance of a southwesterly wind, the twenty-four aircraft from the four squadrons involved in *Operation Oiled* took off from their various bases and set course for Lossiemouth. That afternoon, as the Stirlings and Halifaxes and the occasional transport Harrow circled over Lossiemouth and came in to land, the Control Tower recorded their arrival. At 10.30 hours Wing Commander McDonald had taken off from Wyton leading the ten crews of 15 Squadron (Stirlings) detailed for this attack. All these aircraft carried their 2,000lb A.P. bombs and, while some of the ground crews were taken in the Stirlings, most flew north in Harrows. By 16.00 hours they had all arrived safely at Lossiemouth. Only three of the planned four Stirlings of 149 Squadron from Mildenhall reached Lossiemouth that afternoon, also accompanied by a Harrow carrying ground personnel, for the fourth Stirling detailed for the operation had become unserviceable. From Leeming, Wing Commander Tuck had led a detachment of six 10 Squadron Halifaxes, while five Halifaxes from 76 Squadron led by Wing Commander Young had flown in from Middleton St. George. The Stirlings carried as many bombs as possible, six 2,000 pounders apiece and just enough fuel for the three hour flight. The flight up to Scotland was not without incident; the aircraft flew at low-level up the coast of the North Sea in order to avoid being tracked by the enemy RDF, but this led to an unexpected problem, as several crew-members recall. Ex-Warrant Officer wireless operator/air gunner Don J. Jeffs, of 15 Squadron, remembers that,

"On the way up to Lossiemouth, on a cold but brilliant morning, somewhere around Whitley Bay we overflew a small convoy of coasters etc., and these 'friendly' ships immediately banged away at us with all manner of light *Flak*. There were quite a few planes around flying as a loose gaggle, and for a few minutes there was panic stations whilst we found the colours of the

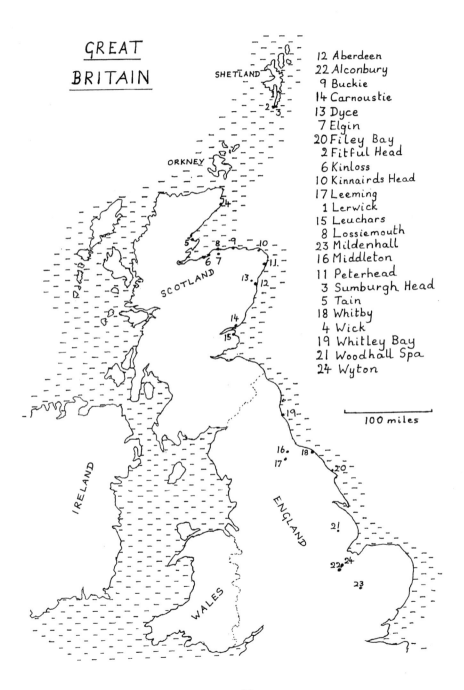

GREAT
BRITAIN

SHETLAND

ORKNEY

SCOTLAND

IRELAND

ENGLAND

WALES

12 Aberdeen
22 Alconbury
9 Buckie
14 Carnoustie
13 Dyce
7 Elgin
20 Filey Bay
2 Fitful Head
6 Kinloss
10 Kinnairds Head
17 Leeming
1 Lerwick
15 Leuchars
8 Lossiemouth
23 Mildenhall
16 Middleton
11 Peterhead
3 Sumburgh Head
5 Tain
18 Whitby
4 Wick
19 Whitley Bay
21 Woodhall Spa
24 Wyton

100 miles

day and waggled wings etc. Considering the sunny day and the fact that we were at 2/3,000 feet., aircraft recognition did not seem to be the Navy's strong suit."

Don Fink, pilot of Stirling N3676:U, of 15 Squadron, recalls that one aircraft was shot down during this encounter, as he noted at the time in his Log-book:

"... one Halifax shot down in the sea on our way to Lossiemouth by our Navy, even though he gave the colours of the day. Crash landed on beach. All crew got out."

This was the first of a number of aircraft that were to be lost even before the raid began. Things continued to go wrong as soon as some of the aircraft arrived at Lossiemouth, as corporal fitter Arthur Stobbs of 15 Squadron, who serviced Stirling N6098:G, recalls:

"One NCO and two airmen ground crew for each aircraft flew to Lossiemouth in Transport Command Harrows, with Flight Sergeant H. Warne in charge of all ground crew. Although Lossiemouth was reasonably clear there were fairly large patches of frozen snow lying about. One aircraft hit one of these on landing - damaged the tail plane and reduced the operational strength to nine."

For some aircrew the trip north was a flight into well-known territory, as R.A. Strachan, observer on Stirling N6094:R remarks:

"On flying north to Lossiemouth we circled low over Carnoustie - my parent's home - twice. Probably the first time the locals had seen a four-engined bomber!"

Pilot of the last Stirling to arrive, N3674:T, Flying Officer I.C.K. Swales, remembers the trip:

"On 28 Jan 42 I took off from Alconbury in Stirling N3674 around lunch-time and flew at low-level around the coast to avoid radar detection by the Germans to Lossiemouth in North Scotland. We were told we were going on detachment for a special operation and carried with us 6 x 2,000lb armour-piercing bombs and just sufficient fuel for the 3 hour flight to Lossiemouth. We arrived at Lossiemouth, which was then an all-grass airfield, home to a Wellington O.T.U. (Operational Training Unit), in the late afternoon.

Warrant Officer wireless operator/air gunner Don J. Jeffs, 15 Squadron, comments:

"Most of the crews looked forward to being on detachment, and away from the grind of bombing Germany and the Ruhr. I don't think the RAF in general were very enthusiastic about attacking ships in harbour. We had too many bad memories of *Scharnhorst, Gneisenau, Prinz Eugen* etc., at Brest,

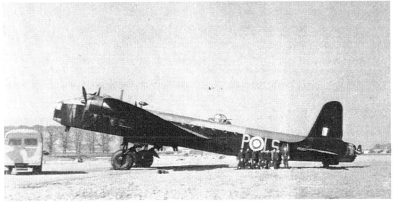

Top, Mark II Halifaxes of 10 Squadron in flight. (via Author)
Lower: 'The Stirling I flew at Wyton, good old P-Peter' Flying Officer
Ian Swales' aircraft. (I. Swales)

and in particular the daylight raid on 18th December when Stirlings, Halifaxes and Manchesters took part. 15 Squadron lost two good crews on that one, and Squadron Leader Boggis won his DFC there."

Sergeant Stan Smith, instrument maker with 15 Squadron:

"The conditions at Lossiemouth were far from ideal, although they had their compensations: When we arrived at Lossiemouth on a cold, bleak winter's day, and had bedded down the aircraft, we went to our billets. They were very basic: an annexe to the Sergeants' Mess, with no heating, just a bed and locker in each bunkroom. The food was reasonable. We had no time for recreation as we were concerned with the serviceability of the aircraft."

Warrant Officer wireless operator/air gunner Don J. Jeffs, 15 Squadron, who flew in 'F' Freddie:

"The accommodation at Lossiemouth was not intended for such a large influx of people including aircrew, ground crew, support people etc., so things were pretty primitive. The people of Scotland, however, were very good to us and. as we waited for the weather to clear, we visited Elgin, a lovely town with lovely people."

The presence of twenty-four heavy bombers taxed the facilities at Lossiemouth to the limit. Working conditions there in the middle of winter were very trying for both air and groundcrew. Corporal R. H. Saunders of the 10 Squadron groundcrew detachment, remembers that it was not easy to obtain the necessary pieces of servicing equipment at the base. The Fleet Air Arm was using the base and their ground crews were reluctant to lend pieces of equipment to the new arrivals from Bomber Command. Saunders recalls working from a small hut and 'scrounging' the odd ladder or two when needed. He spent many hours one night servicing one of the aircraft and vividly recalls the cold and the hoar-frost that covered everything,

"Even the men: I can tell you Lossiemouth in winter was pretty horrible, and we looked like Eskimos after an hour or two servicing aircraft with any piece of equipment we could borrow."

On 29th January a photographic reconnaissance flight confirmed that the *Tirpitz* was still in her berth and additional camouflage rafts were being arranged at her bow and stern in an attempt to disguise the tell-tale outline of a battleship. Ironically, in fact, the presence of both camouflage rafts and (in particular) an anti-torpedo boom (both clearly visible in reconnaissance photographs), were unmistakable indications of the presence of a capital ship. In this instance they also showed that she had no intention of leaving her berth in the immediate future. The target's position assured, the operation could commence. Flying Officer I.C.K. Swales:

"The following morning (the 29th) the panic started. We learnt that our target was the *Tirpitz* in Trondheim Fjord and Met. were forecasting the best conditions of the winter over Norway, with clear skies that night but a front with snow arriving over Lossiemouth early in the morning. This meant that there was a latest time for take-off, and some sixteen four-engined aircraft to be refuelled with some 2,000 gallons of fuel each by 3 small fuel bowsers. As I had been the last to land the previous day I was the last in the queue, but hoped to make it in time."

Corporal R.H. Saunders (front row, second from left) with air and ground crew at Leeming in 1942. (R.Saunders)

R.A. Strachan DFC, observer in Stirling N6094:R:

"The weather conditions at Lossiemouth that evening were poor, but, despite the forecasting of icing conditions on the outward journey, since it promised to be excellent over Norway, the operation was 'laid on'. Of the twenty-four aircraft that had arrived at Lossiemouth the previous afternoon, a total of eight were unable to take part in the operation for a variety of reasons. The crews viewed the forthcoming operation in the prevailing conditions with some trepidation and those crews who were prevented by aircraft mechanical failure from taking part were understandably not that dismayed: Two engines showed bad mag. drops on running up the engines and we were scrubbed from the operation. Just as well, with hundreds of miles of sea, and icing conditions forecast - we were not unhappy!"

Eventually, despite the difficulties of maintaining and operating aircraft in sub-zero temperatures, nine Halifaxes and seven Stirlings were able to take off. The Stirlings, which were to set off first, began to leave the ground at 00.30 hours on January 30th. They took off into a sea of cloud that stretched from sea-level to 20,000 feet. As they flew on, condensation developing on their fuselages, wings and flying control surfaces, began to turn into ice, making the aircraft unwieldy and difficult to fly. It also prevented most of them from gaining enough height to fly into the clearer atmosphere above the clouds. Flying aircraft in icing conditions was a frightening experience, as Ian Ryall, who flew with 15 Squadron, although he did not take part in *Operation Oiled*, explains:

"A Stirling was a heavy aircraft to handle at the best of times. Controls were manual with no power assistance as they are today. I seem to remember it had a fairly ineffective de-icing system which consisted of pumping de-icing fluid over the wings. The supply of fluid didn't last long however and, if one was not able to get out of icing conditions pretty quickly, ice started to build up fast, the aircraft became very heavy and sluggish, speed dropped off fast and it began to sink. If there was room between the bottom of the icing conditions and the ground, you got out of it, if not you didn't. It was a bit frightening really."

Squadron Leader B.D. Sellick, pilot of N6092:O, must have broken through the clouds at some point, for he still vividly recalls the sight of the silvery clouds beneath his aircraft as they laboured on under a full moon.

"I think it was on that operation that I first saw at night a halo around the shadow of the aircraft on the clouds, more or less full moon, I think, something to do with ice crystals and very pretty!"

To the Stirlings that had been unable to leave the ground were now added those that could not remain long in the air. Indeed, none of the crews were to see the target, although some of the aircraft did come within sight of the Norwegian coast. Stirling N3676:U of 15 Squadron suffered from severe icing at 11,000 feet and, being unable to climb any higher into the murk, her pilot, Pilot Officer Fink, jettisoned his bombs 'safe' in the sea, turned his aircraft round, and returned to base. Pilot Officer 'Red' King, in 'MacRobert's Reply', N6086:F, also failed to get far, having to turn back early with an overheating engine. Squadron Leader Wilson, piloting Stirling N3673:D, was more fortunate however, for he was able to fly on until his aircraft reached the Norwegian coast where, with no break in the cloud cover, he finally turned for home. Flying Officer I.C.K. Swales, the pilot of the last Stirling to arrive at Lossiemouth the previous day, who had been worried that his aircraft (N3674:T) would not be ready in time, only just made it:

"As I remember, I took off five minutess after the latest time and decided I could make up time en route. We climbed up through cloud, base 2,000 feet and tops about 4,000 feet with a bright moon on top, much as met. forecast. The cloud was forecast to break completely about half way over the North Sea, which was after about two hours flying, but from 10,000 feet there was no sign of a break ahead. We flew on for about three and a half hours, which

Squadron Leader B.D.Sellick (fifth from left) and crew in front of their 15 Squadron Stirling, pictured at Wyton in 1941. All but two of them took part in the abortive January raid. (B. Sellick)

took us almost to the Swedish border, and there was not a hole in the cloud sheet anywhere. We could see the tops of some of the Fjord hills poking up through the cloud so it was pretty low and we needed a minimum 8,000 feet bombing height for our armour-piercing bombs to be effective, so we brought them back."

Two Stirlings from 149 Squadron also took part, but also failed to locate their target. They both returned safely, although one, W7462:T, overshot on landing and ran into a trench where its undercarriage collapsed. This bomber was 'written off'. And so, despite a tremendous effort, the Stirling crews had been unable to achieve their objective, as ex-Warrant Officer Don Jeffs remarks:

"As to the raids on the *Tirpitz*, these were a fiasco, due to the terrible weather both at Lossiemouth and also en route. ... it was impossible to continue, and we turned back just short of Norway. The outside temperature reached minus 58 degrees at times and we were very lucky to have survived these sorts of conditions."

The nine Halifaxes fared little better in the appalling weather conditions, although their problems were not due to ice forming on their wings and control surfaces. The Halifaxes of 10 Squadron simply ran short of fuel. They had taken off from Lossiemouth a couple of hours later than the Stirlings, between 02.10 and 02.34 hours that morning. All four Halifaxes from 10

Squadron turned back early when they realised that their petrol consumption was such that they would be unable to reach the target and make the return journey. Wing Commander Tuck, flying Halifax R9369:D pressed on further than the others, reaching Bremanger Island, about 230 miles short of the target area, before turning for home, landing at 08.10 hours. Each crew, having made the decision to turn back, managed to make their way back to the advanced base safely, although Flight Lieutenant Miller, flying Halifax V9985:V, had to put down at Wick before flying on to Lossiemouth later in the morning. The five Halifaxes of 76 Squadron had all taken off between 02.04 and 02.27 hours, led by Wing Commander David O. Young in Halifax L9617:A. However, they too were robbed of their chance to attack the *Tirpitz*. Flight Lieutenant 'Hank' Iveson pilot of Halifax L9561:H, remembers feeling extremely disappointed at having come so far only to be foiled by the clouds that persisted from the Norwegian coast all the way to the target area. He recalls:

"Without sighting anything we flew north where gradually the cloud could be seen to be breaking up. I estimate that within two hours the area around Trondheim would have been clear, for there was a strong northerly wind blowing. Feeling extremely disappointed we flew home via the Shetlands, remaining above the worst of the weather."

Although the records do not make it clear, it is probable that all five Halifaxes of 76 Squadron actually reached the target area, but four of them, being unable to pinpoint the *Tirpitz* through the local 5/10ths cloud cover, were unable to attack, fearing that indiscriminate bombing would be more likely to injure Norwegians than Germans. Most of these aircraft jettisoned their bombs over the sea on their return flight in order to lighten their load and thus make their fuel last just that little longer. One pilot, however, apparently did manage to carry out an attack. Sergeant Herbert, pilot of Halifax L9617:V, was the only one of the entire force to release his bombs over what he believed to be the target area. On return to Lossiemouth he reported that:

"The target was not observed, but a barrage of light *Flak* indicated the position of the target. Bombs were dropped from a height of 8,000 feet at 06.05 hours and bursts were seen between the ship and shore. Visibility was good but 10/10ths cloud cover over the target." [7.]

There is no doubt that the *Tirpitz's* crew was aware of the attack. Between 05.12 hours and 06.45 hours that morning, in temperatures of -17 degrees Celsius, the air-raid sirens sounded in Trondheim and the *Flak* crews were ordered to their posts on board the battleship. At 05.57 hours the Officer of the Watch aboard the *Tirpitz* reported about six four-engined aircraft, which flew into the Trondheim Fjord area from the south and west, banked over the outer fjords and flew towards the city of Trondheim and the entrance to Åsen Fjord. Anti-aircraft batteries opened up into the 5/10ths cloud cover above Vaernes Aerodrome and Trondheim itself, while the batteries around the Åsen area fired intermittently into the darkness of the early morning sky. The sound of aircraft was heard occasionally for the next fifteen minutes, then it died away. The abortive attempt was over. Despite the fact that some crews had been unable to take off, they had all demonstrated their ability, determination and steadfastness to get on with the task in hand, despite the fact that they were well aware of the difficulties and risks to which they were exposing themselves by taking off in conditions that common sense indicated were just too dangerous. Although they were disappointed at having failed even to reach or see the target, all the crews were utterly relieved that they had got back safely. Flying Officer I.C.K. Swales:

"We just managed to get back into Lossiemouth as the snow started and found that one Stirling had crashed on landing and one Halifax was down in the sea. No one had seen the target. So much for Met!."

The one aircraft that had failed to make the return flight successfully was Sergeant Harwood's Halifax, L 9581:Q. During her journey home her port inner engine failed and Harwood ordered her bombs to be jettisoned. Just before 10.00 hours three aircraft, an Anson from Kinloss and two Spitfires (one from 416 Squadron at Peterhead and the other from 603 Squadron at Dyce) were scrambled with the intention of finding and escorting 'Q - Queenie' to the airfield at Dyce, but arrived too late. Despite lightening her load and, having strayed from her homeward course by only a few miles, off Kinnairds Head - about 60 miles to the east of Lossiemouth - 'Q - Queenie' ran short of fuel. With tanks virtually dry, she made a successful ditching in the sea off the coast of Scotland, about three miles from Gregness near Aberdeen. Although two of the crew were slightly injured in the ditching they all scrambled to safety in the dinghy while the Spitfire from Peterhead established visual contact and circled overhead. At the time there were eight patrol vessels in the vicinity and it was not long before the crew was rescued by one of these. Other patrol vessels attempted to salvage the aircraft, but at 10.34 hours she sank. All the remaining Halifaxes landed back at base between 05.40 hours and 08.10 hours and were parked in the dispersals with the Stirlings. Then their crews were debriefed. However, not all was gloomy; A. D. Stobbs, a member of 15 Squadron ground crew, remembers a comic incident at the return of the crews from the abortive operation:

> "All the ground crew were billeted together irrespective of rank at Lossiemouth and I well remember that when the aircraft returned from the abortive raid because of bad weather there was ice several inches thick on the tailplane leading edges - a piece about 18 inches long was brought into our billet by one of the pilots 'Titch Basson' and reverently laid on Flight Sergeant Warne's chest - Flight Sergeant Basson, as he was then, was often ribbed by Flight Sergeant Warne because of his small stature - but there was a great rapport between the two." [8.]

But, despite the failure of his small force even to reach their target, Wing Commander Macdonald was determined that they should try again. The following morning the aircraft were prepared and the crews were sent out on night flying tests in preparation for a second attempt that evening. Sergeant Stan Smith, instrument maker with 15 Squadron, has a vivid recollection of that day:

> "All the day we spent servicing the aircraft, as we hoped to get another crack at the *Tirpitz*, and this was when we had a fire on N6098."

Stirling N6098:G was written off by an incident that happened all too frequently when aircraft were being refuelled. Corporal fitter Arthur Stobbs of 15 Squadron, who serviced this aircraft, also recalls what happened:

> "During refuelling to full petrol load my mechanics overfilled No 2 tank in the starboard wing - petrol flooded the ground adjacent to the undercarriage and some ran down the main spar into the fuselage."

Sergeant Stan Smith, who was on board the aircraft at the time, continues the story:

"I was in the nose section, a fitter was monitoring the fuel going into the tanks, and an electrician was somewhere in the fuselage, when someone put his head through the rear hatch and yelled out 'Fire!'. As we hurtled out of the rear hatch, the Electrician pulled out the plug on the trolley acc-to-aircraft and ran. When I got out an armourer ran to me and said, 'Let's jettison the bombs', so, as he entered the aircraft, I plugged in the trolley acc to restore power and he jettisoned the bombs 'safe' and then unplugged the trolley acc and we both ran as the fire engine arrived. The fire by this time was engulfing the port wing and the undercarriage. I can still see in my mind the thump as 10,000lb of bombs hit the ground flat and the aircraft rising as the undercarriage extended and the tail units on the bombs bent when they hit the ground."

Flying Officer I.C.K. Swales comments:

"The most likely cause of this fire on board N6098 was static ignition caused by a static spark which occurred when the refuelling hose was removed from the aircraft tanks. Wing Commander Macdonald's hopes for a second stab at the *Tirpitz* were short-lived. The weather never cleared, and in the end the whole attempt had to be called off. In fact, it was to prove difficult enough just to get the aircraft back to their own bases. If my memory serves me right, a similar op. was laid on for that night but cancelled owing to bad weather, more snow, over Lossiemouth. This proved to be right as it snowed, on and off, for the next five days. The North of Scotland froze up and the O.T.U. students were used each day to try and keep a runway clear on the airfield."

The weather clamped down and it was clear that there would be no more attempts on the *Tirpitz* during the current moon-phase. No one knew when the aircraft would be able to take off and return home, so the crews amused themselves, as Flying Officer I.C.K. Swales recalls:

"While we were snow-bound in Lossie for five days, morale was getting pretty low, and Squadron Leader Sellick, our Flight Commander, and Wing Commander McDonald, the C.O. (Commanding Officer), borrowed a small Hillman staff car each and nineteen of us piled into them to go out to a small village called Buckie. The roads were thick with broken ice and with all the weight in the cars, the tyres were rubbing on the wheel arches and we had to stop at various pubs to let them cool down! You can imagine the look on the landlord's face when two cars pulled up and nineteen people got out and ordered nineteen pints of beer! They probably hadn't seen anyone else for a week."

Bomber Command could not afford to have any of its force lying idle. When, on February 6th, a thaw set in and the weather conditions improved sufficiently for flying again, attempts were made immediately to bring the aircraft home. At that time the runway at Lossiemouth consisted of grass sown on sand and, although this surface was satisfactory in its frozen condition, when a thaw came it brought with it considerable difficulties for the take-off of heavy bombers. If the aircraft did not get off as soon as possible there was every likelihood that they would be bogged down where they stood for a month or more. However, since the bad weather had closed their bases in Cambridgeshire and Yorkshire, the only course left to them was to fly the aircraft to airfields with concrete runways. It was decided that the Stirlings would divert to Peterhead, the Fighter Command runway on the coast north of Aberdeen, while the Halifaxes were to go to Wick, further north still. The difficulty now was the simple matter of taking off. Desperate measures were required, as Flying Officer I.C.K. Swales recalls:

> "We were faced with the problem of being full of fuel and with bombs on board; we were way over our maximum loading weight. There were few bowsers to suck out the fuel, and 2,000lb A.P. bombs were in very short supply. Eventually some of the aircraft had fuel removed and the rest of us jettisoned our bombs on the airfield and prayed they wouldn't go off."

For those watching from the ground, this somewhat desperate exeunt from Lossiemouth was an unforgettable sight, to say the least, as the heavy bombers took off through huge puddles on the sand-based grass runway. The patches of frozen snow had now become small lakes and through these the Stirlings had to plough, at maximum revs and boost. In some cases water cascaded over the engines and wings as the aircraft, with agonizing slowness, lumbered into the air. Fortunately no water found its way into the intakes or engines of the aircraft and all of them managed to take off successfully. Once the bombers had taken off and climbed into the lowering skies, it was time for the ground-crews to gather together their belongings and equipment and return home too. The lightly laden Harrows carrying their groundcrew passengers to Alconbury had little difficulty taking off and the crews were surprised to find their home base frostier and snowier than the north of Scotland.

The saga of the diverted bombers was still being played out; Flying Officer I.C.K. Swales continues the account of his aircraft and of the ensuing events at Peterhead:

> "I eventually landed at Peterhead in the late afternoon, last but one, followed by 'MacRobert's Reply' (N6086:F). Peterhead had two runways at right angles, cleared of snow, with snow packed about five feet high on each

Flying Officer Ian Swales and his crew that took part in the raid pose in front of their Stirling at RAF Wyton. (I.Swales)

side of the runways. The nine Stirlings were parked nose to tail on the cross-wind runway. At dawn on 7th February a Ju88 recce aircraft made two runs over Peterhead, which was ominous with nine of Bomber Command's four-engined aircraft nose to tail on a runway (what a target!). Some of us were damaged by ice on take-off from Lossiemouth and were in need of repair (I had a badly dented tailplane). Peterhead scrambled a Spitfire to try and get the Ju88, but no joy. As always happens on these occasions, the runway on which all the Stirlings were parked was now into wind and the clear runway was across a fairly strong wind. The Spitfire, on landing, swung and ran off the runway through the wall of snow which collapsed its undercarriage, and was sitting on its belly just off the runway. It was reckoned that we had very little time before we could expect a German bomber raid from Norway, so if we could fly with our damage, as the weather had cleared at our bases in England, we were to get off as soon as possible, using the cross-wind runway. 'MacRobert's Reply', which I think still had bombs on board, swung on take-off in the cross-wind, over-corrected, and went through the hole in the snow-wall made by the Spitfire, hit the Spitfire which collapsed its undercarriage and it finished up sitting on its belly on top of the Spitfire. What a nice mess I had to follow; fortunately there was no fire. Eventually the rest of us got airborne O.K. and we had a nice relaxing low-level flight down the coast and in to Alconbury, near Wyton."

Sergeant Stan Smith, instrument maker, had good reason to be grateful that there was no fire when MacRobert's Reply crashed - he was one of those aboard, hitching a ride home from Peterhead:

> "We were the second of four taking off on the morning of the 8th. Just before airborne, we lost power on both port engines and slewed off the runway at about 70 knots, crashing through a Spitfire dispersal, and we finished up with our nose in the mud, the port undercarriage bent and half buried, with the port wing tip on the ground and a Spitfire jammed under our tail, which we had dragged off dispersal. Luckily, no one was hurt, only a few bruises. We jettisoned the upper hatch and ran down the port wing to the ground, released the dinghy, and all had a good swig of rum from the survival pack. The aircrew took off in the remaining two aircraft when all the fuss had died down, and I was left behind with the bent aircraft with instructions to remove the MacRobert's crest, the clock and bombsight, and they would call and collect me in a few days. I was glad of that, as I did not fancy lugging my heavy toolkit and kitbag etc. back by train."

'MacRobert's Reply' was subsequently recovered and repaired, finishing its life at a conversion unit.

However, the attempt to deal with the menace of the *Tirpitz* was far from over. As the moon period ended, the heavy bombers and their crews found themselves operating over the more usual German targets, including the city of Essen. 'It was of course an over-ambitious venture in terrible weather conditions,' was the comment made by R.A. Strachan many years after the event. Indeed it was a sorry result after such effort. Only sixteen aircraft had actually taken off from a total of twenty-four that had flown up to the advanced base at Lossiemouth. One aircraft only had dropped her bombs 'over the target', but in fact the *Tirpitz* had suffered no damage whatsoever. The stakes had been high, but nothing had been achieved, other than the mercifully safe return of the crews. The operation had been conceived in haste and with a sense of desperation and urgency. It had been an operation that had put the crews at considerable risk. It is remarkable that, given the unsuitable weather conditions, all came safely home. Regardless of the optimistic met. forecast, the weather had been appalling. Not only had it made the flight out difficult (even impossible for some), but having arrived in the target area the notoriously fickle weather over the Norwegian coastline had blanketed the target in cloud at the most inopportune moment. The inadequacies of the aircraft, too, had been shown up. The Stirlings had been unable to climb high enough to rise above the icing conditions, while the Halifaxes had found that the considerable distance they had had to travel had left them with the narrowest of safety margins as regards fuel. Despite the fact that all crews had returned safely, there had been a total of six aircraft lost. Of the Stirlings, one from 149 Squadron had crashed on landing back at base, one had damaged its tail plane in the take-off from Lossiemouth to Peterhead, one had been destroyed by fire at the dispersal on the morning of the raid and 'MacRoberts' Reply' had been severely damaged when she swung off the runway at Peterhead. The Spitfire into which she crashed was a total write-off. Finally one Halifax had been lost at sea, although all her crew had been saved. And what conclusions could have been reached concerning this failure?

First, the weather conditions had to be good enough for crews to reach Trondheim and find the *Tirpitz*. Secondly, in adverse wind conditions the aircraft would need a greater fuel-range and greater engine-power to enable them to climb out of the worst of the weather and so evade icing conditions. Thirdly, the aircraft had to be capable of carrying a more effective weapon than 2,000lb bombs that would, even if they struck the battleship, do little lasting damage. The Stirling, the first of the four-engined heavy bombers to come into service, was not designed to carry bombs larger than 2,000 lbs and so was not used again in the attacks on the *Tirpitz*. In the next attempt the job was given to the Mk II Halifax bomber alone, with its greater bomb capacity and its more powerful Merlin engines.

NOTES

7. Operations Record Book entry for Halifax L9617:V.
8. Note: Flight Sergeant Basson was not one of the pilots who took part in the raid and, presumably, went out to one of the aircraft when it landed.

Chapter Three
Under Observation

On 11th February a trained Norwegian radio operator, Bjørn
Rørholt crossed the North Sea on the renowned 'Shetland Bus',
a system that had been devised to transport agents, resistance
equipment and the occasional refugee, between Norway and
Britain in fishing boats. He sailed from the Shetland Islands on
the Norwegian fishing boat *Arthur* and was landed on one of the
offshore islands that cluster off the Norwegian coastline. Three
weeks earlier he had sailed over to Norway in the *Feie*, but after
difficulties in contacting England by radio he had had to return.
Now he was safely ashore in his homeland and was soon in
touch with the Scandinavian section of the SIS (the Secret
Intelligence Service). Bjørn Rørholt explains why he was sent in
to Norway:

> "My job in Norway on that particular occasion was not primarily to report
> on the position of the *Tirpitz*, but it was to organise a system of
> radio-stations to continue to keep watch on the *Tirpitz*. Now of course they
> had no-one else in the Trondheim area at that time, so I had to combine the
> reporting function with this planning function, and it was the intention that
> I should only spend a month - in actual fact I spent about three. I was only
> sent over as a sort of a panic measure because *Tirpitz* broke out from
> Germany to Trondheim."

He took up this work at great risk to his own life, for, as a
member of the Norwegian resistance movement, he had earlier
had to flee from Norway after he had shot his way out of a
confrontation with the Gestapo who had surrounded his home,
leaving behind his family and other members of the 'gang' to
which he belonged; the Germans knew who he was. Within a
short time of his arrival, Rørholt reached Trondheim, where:

'The Shetland Bus'. Bjørn Rørholt (in duffel coat) on board the 'Arthur', en route for Norway in February 1942.

(Norges Hjemmefrontmuseum)

"My contact was the Director of the shipyard in Trondheim, and he had this great facility that he could phone around to anywhere where there were ships, and he had already set up a code whereby his people could tell him which ships were where, and so on. So he provided me with the information that I needed to send - Birger Grønn is his name - and he kept this service going. The first day I came into Mr Grønn's office, *Tirpitz* came out on the Fjord and was doing target practice. That was quite an impressive sight. The targets were way out towards Agdenes, but *Tirpitz* came from an easterly direction, came gliding out on the Fjord, and then she put on full speed and speeded up and shot, under full speed, at these targets. Whether she hit or not I can't tell you because these targets were way out of my sight. Grønn had a big window on the Fjord (in his office), a large picture window - being the Director of the shipyard he did a lot of his inspections from just looking out - it was the first and also the only time that I was in his office."

A man named Lian, who lived on Salt Island, and two brothers, Jan and Georg Høgsve, who kept watch on the *Tirpitz* from the hill overlooking her mooring from the east, reported what they could. But information concerning movements the battleship made from her mooring in Fætten Fjord was inevitably ambiguous, as Rørholt explains:

> "An agent near *Tirpitz's* mooring, 25 miles east of the town, reported by telephone code, but we could not know if the ship was going to sea or merely exercising in the fjord. A radio was needed at Agdenes, the narrow inlet at the mouth of the Trondheim fjord, where the Germans had a strong fortress. It seemed hopeless. Then a true patriot, Magne Hassel, who ran a flour mill inside the fortified area, agreed to take the enormous risk of operating a radio transmitter. Disguised as an insurance salesman, I went out there and set up the station. Hassel kept it going for two years, sending 'blind' but most important messages." [9.]

In setting up his radio-reporting network Rørholt acted with commendable coolness, steely determination and was prepared to take considerable risks. One of his biggest problems was that:

> "I was so well known locally that I could only go out at night, and even that was risky. In order to establish a continuous watch on the *Tirpitz* I had to devise a plan, not involving myself. I hit on the 'watchdog' plan by which five picked men would go to Britain on the 'Shetland Bus' for a crash course on technicalities, and return with radio sets."

He set about selecting and recruiting men suitable for this difficult and dangerous job, but it was not until 12th May (nearly a fortnight after the final raid of the series of four carried out by the RAF at this time) that the first 'watchdog' was in place and able to report back on the *Tirpitz*. Until then, it was up to Hassel to keep watch on the entrance to the fjord at Agdenes by reporting on ship movements. Rørholt spent some of his time in Trondheim during this period. His willingness to take risks is apparent in an amusing and ironical story he tells about visiting the Britannia Hotel (the largest hotel in Trondheim) with a group of three friends. While sitting at a table in the dining room they were somewhat alarmed to see several very senior German naval officers from the *Tirpitz* enter the room and make for the spare table next to Rørholt's. As they sat down, one of the officers rather ostentatiously removed his dress-sword and laid it on the empty chair between himself and Rørholt. Rørholt responded immediately by carefully taking out his pocket-knife and laying that alongside the officer's sword.

Tirpitz moored alongside the cliffs overlooking Fætten Fjord and protected by its torpedo boom. It was secretly photographed from a passing train by a Norwegian agent, probably in October 1942.
(Oskar A. Johansen)

Both groups shared the joke. This was the closest Rørholt came to the men of the battleship whose surveillance he had been sent to arrange.

The main north-south railway line, running from Trondheim to Levanger and beyond, happens to run right along the eastern shore of Fætten Fjord, passing within a few hundred yards of the battleship's cliff-side berth. In the spring of 1942 this railway line provided an excellent vantage point from which travellers could see the ship across the waters of the fjord. It also gave anyone with nerve and determination the opportunity to photograph her. Such photographs, taken by Norwegians and delivered to the Allies could, when examined by experts, add useful detail to the knowledge already obtained of the ship. Rørholt was one of the agents who managed to photograph her from a carriage-window as the train ran past Fætten Fjord, although, as he explains, it is now impossible to be quite certain which of a number of surviving photographs of the battleship is his:

"I took a photo with my *Leica* camera from the train on the morning of the 28th April, in other words the morning after the big raid in April 1942. This picture went through the Swedish control, was delivered to the British Embassy in Stockholm, and was speeded to England, where it was developed. I saw it no more. Unknown to me at the time, quite a few photos were taken of the *Tirpitz* round about the same time, also from the railway. One of my unknown colleagues, Rolf Kahrs Baardvik, had arranged to take one from a covered freight wagon with a hole in it."

After the war Rørholt met another agent, Bernhard Bergersen, who had been keeping watch on the *Tirpitz* at much the same time. Rørholt discovered that Bergersen had also taken a photograph of the battleship from a train as it passed Fætten Fjord! Bergersen's job, as he himself recalls, was:

"... to report movements in the Trondheim harbour, not take pictures, although I on some occasions did. I had my observation post on the roof of my grandfather's warehouse overlooking the harbour - a most suitable place, well hidden from all sides. I went up on this roof every day and thus got an excellent view of German movements. I worked for the naval intelligence surveilling German shipping in the Trondheim harbour and the fjord generally, and thus kept a close eye on the *Tirpitz* when she turned up for her trials in the Trondheim Fjord. And I then got the question from London if I could take a picture of her."

He remembers photographing the *Tirpitz*, not when she appeared in Trondheim harbour, but when she lay in Fætten Fjord:

"I took a picture of the *Tirpitz* from the train in April 1942 and had the negatives sent to Sweden by courier. Apparently this was also done by Bjørn at approximately the same time. When I came to Sweden eight months later I went to work with the naval intelligence at the Norwegian naval attache's office in Stockholm before I was sent to England and joined the Royal Norwegian Navy. In Stockholm a picture turned up and I always believed it to be mine, although I never saw a copy of it as I sent the undeveloped film away. So Bjørn and I don't know whose picture belongs to who.

"Having lost my camera in another action I had, by the way, to 'borrow' one from a German officer who was lodging in the house I lived in at the time. The picture is not up to today's standard, but one should not forget the circumstances under which it was taken - from the train - with German soldiers facing it with their sharp loaded guns every fifty yards. It is rather hair-raising, thinking back on it."

As for the German soldiers, Bergersen explains that:

"... these were stationed along the fjord to operate the smoke canisters. They were by the way operated by army soldiers, stangely enough."

It was not only agents who photographed the *Tirpitz*. Eighteen and-a-half year old Karl Hernes lived with his younger brother Birger and his family in a small-holding on the western side of Fætten Fjord. Armed with determination, daring and some skill, he managed to take two photographs of the battleship whose

Top, the German pocket-battleship 'Admiral Scheer', photographed secretly from the roof-top of a warehouse in Trondheim by Sub-Lieutenant Bernhard Bergersen in 1942. Bottom, Tirpitz moored in Fætten Fjord. Bernhard Bergersen took this picture from a passing train in the spring of 1942. The line across the hillside is a fault in the film. (via B.Bergersen)

berth was a mere 500 yards away at the foot of the steep slope beyond his house:

"I had an old camera. We didn't live far away from *Tirpitz*. I spied on it and hoped to get a picture. I hid the camera in a paper bag, I had already made a hole in it so everything was ready for taking a photograph. I had it all under a jacket I wore. I went to a place with a good view and sat down after I made sure there were no Germans. I opened my jacket and adjusted the bag so that the *Tirpitz* came into view. I took a picture and did my jacket up and went calmly from the place. I also took a picture when the *Tirpitz* went on a shooting (firing) exercise in the Trondheimfjord. The film wasn't developed until 1945 as I didn't dare risk it during the war."

Towards the end of February, on the 23rd, the cruiser *Prinz Eugen* and the pocket-battleship *Admiral Scheer*, accompanied by three destroyers, reached berths in Trondheim Fjord, to join the *Tirpitz*. The cruiser *Admiral Hipper* joined them later still, on 21st March. This build-up of enemy Naval strength in northern waters was a cause of great concern to the Allies and it was imperative that they knew as much as possible of the movements of these vessels. Of course, the aircraft of the Photographic Reconnaissance Unit were an essential element in this surveillance. Both Wick and Leuchars, the two bases used by PRU Spitfires and Mosquitos during the sorties against the *Tirpitz* at this time, were not many miles from Lossiemouth, from where some of the bombers took off for each of the four raids on Fætten Fjord. From 15th January to the end of April 1942, over one hundred sorties were flown by the PRU over Trondheim and its neighbouring fjords. Not all of these sorties were intended to reconnoitre the *Tirpitz* herself and not all produced useful results. Bad weather (usually cloud cover over the target), failure of equipment, or, occasionally, enemy interception, were the reasons that aircraft failed on occasion to bring back photographs. But when cover was brought back it provided the most detailed and useful information upon which Bomber Command could act. As Flying Officer Richard Cussons of 'B' Flight 1 PRU recalls:

"The general idea was to fly fast and high to nip in, take the photos and nip out again before the enemy realised what was happening. Our defence against enemy action depended mainly on 'rubber necking' - i.e. keeping a very good lookout in all directions! The general technique was to climb as high as possible until one was leaving a vapour trail (this appeared in a rear-view mirror as a black smudge) and then descend 500 feet so as not to leave a tell-tale streak across the sky; the aircraft itself was painted a special P.R. Blue which made it invisible from the ground at heights at which we operated. If an enemy fighter climbed above, to get the advantage of height, he would be leaving a trail and we could see him coming, in which case one would 'open up all the taps' and dive slightly, when our Spitfires could outpace the Me109 easily; the long-nosed FW190 (sic), which appeared in 1942, was faster and we lost quite a few aircraft until the PR Mk XI came when we once again had the advantage, but with a reduced operational range. *Flak* was, in general no problem as we flew above accurate shooting range, but the German 88mm A.A. gun could be very 'unfriendly'."

Roy Kenwright, a PRU Spitfire pilot who flew Photographic

The photograph that Karl Hernes took of Tirpitz in Fætten Fjord, 1942. (K.Hernes)

Reconnaissance sorties over the *Tirpitz* when she was lying in Kaafjord in 1943, recalls:

"The photos were taken out of the aircraft after it landed. They were sent to RAF Medmenham, which is not very far from RAF Benson. There they were printed and interpreted. The interpreters used stereoscopes in examining the photographs in order to give a sense of perspective. The findings of the photographic interpreters were relayed back to the branch of the forces which had orinally made the request."

It took a special courage to fly at great altitude in freezing conditions for hours at a time over the featureless expanse of the North Sea. Spitfire flights to reconnoitre the *Tirpitz* at this time lasted between four and five and-a-half hours. Not only had the pilot's navigation to be accurate, but as he either had no radio, or had to maintain radio silence, he had no one with whom to share the responsibilities of his lonely flight. The PRU Mosquito, on the other hand, had a crew of two, a pilot and an observer, and an increased endurance of up to nine hours. It had two pairs of vertical cameras, the controls for which were operated by the observer from his position in the nose of the aircraft, and one oblique camera operated by the pilot from his cockpit, using a sighting ring in the port side of his perspex canopy. Unlike the bomber pilot, whose job ended when he reached his target and bombed it, the PRU pilot not only had to reach his target, but he also had to return to his base afterwards with his exposed film for his flight to have any value at all. Inevitably, not all the pilots who flew reconnaissance flights over Norway at this time returned. In all, five crewmen were lost from the one Mosquito and the three Spitfires that failed to return from recconnaisance sorties between 15th January and the end of April 1942. Although most PRU flights took place at high altitude, occasionally a low level pass would be made over a target, the pilot relying entirely upon speed and surprise to avoid being attacked by the defences. The PRU Spitfires and Mosquitoes involved over Norwegian 'targets' were all unarmed. Instead of guns they carried cameras and extra fuel. In fact, the first Spitfires able to reach Trondheim were known as 'bowsers' since they carried so much fuel, even the leading edges of the wings being pressed into service for fuel storage. Although the *Tirpitz* spent most of the next few months secure at moorings in Trondheim Fjord (consuming every month 1,200 tons of the German fuel oil that was in such short supply), she sometimes shifted her berth for the night to an anchorage in Vaena-sund; and on a number of occasions she was photographed from the air carrying out exercises in the open waters of the larger arms of Trondheim Fjord. On 5th February she was seen under way with no escort, heading northeast up Norvik-sundet, about 30 miles from the city of Trondheim. Four days later she was back in her berth. Six days later, on 15th February, low oblique aerial photographs taken from 15,000 feet, showed her 15-inch gun barrels camouflaged white and fine camouflage netting draped from the shore to the side of the ship. Four days later she was seen speeding at 26 knots in a northeasterly direction up Trondheim Fjord, returning to her moorings a few days later. On 24th February it was deduced from aerial photographs that she was ammunitioning and, the following day, she set out once again to carry out three days of exercises in the main fjord.

A PRU Mosquito. (via Author)

The *Tirpitz* was back in her usual berth again on the morning of 28th February, taking on fuel from a tanker secured alongside, at about the time the next attempt on the battleship was due to take place. Towards the end of February, 217 Squadron, a Beaufort unit based at Thorney Island on the south coast of England, flew up to the north of Scotland to take part in a somewhat desperate operation. Arriving at Skitten, near Wick, a detachment was sent on to Sumburgh, the most northerly aerodrome in the U.K. On arrival the squadron ground crews set about stripping the aircraft of as much weight as possible - they were to carry bombs, not equipment, out to Norway. They did not have sufficient fuel capacity to reach the Trondheim area and return - they would have run out of fuel about 60 miles short of the British coast. Having delivered their bomb-loads, the crews were instructed to fly eastwards until they were well over the Swedish border where they were to bale out, leaving their aircraft to crash. Alternatively they could fly for home, bale out when their aircraft ran out of fuel and wait to be rescued! As Roy Conyers Nesbit, a navigator with 217 Squadron, points out in his book *Torpedo Airmen*, this gave the operation something of the nature of a suicide attack; men adrift in the North Sea at that time of year were unlikely to survive more than about twenty minutes. However, just before take-off the operation was cancelled, no doubt much to the relief of the crews! It seems that, although Bomber Command was not willing to sacrifice heavy bombers on such a 'one-way' mission, it was felt that Beauforts were expendable in the critical situation that the *Tirpitz* created from her lair in Fætten Fjord. The PRU recconnaisance photographs made available just before the operation was due to begin showed the *Tirpitz* refuelling and the camouflage rafts all drawn out of her way. This was sufficient indication that she might leave her berth as soon as refueling was complete and, in such an uncertain situation, no raid could be carried out. In fact she did not leave her berth until 6th March, four days after the tanker had departed, when she remained away until the 13th. There was at this time a critical shortage of heavy bombers and the recently appointed Air Officer Commanding-in-Chief, Sir Arthur Harris, needed what forces he could muster to carry out his bombing campaign over the industrial areas of Germany. By 1st March, a week after Harris had taken up his new appointment, out of a total of 547 bombers in the Command, 29 were Halifaxes, 29 were Stirlings and only four were the new Lancasters. It is further evidence of the importance of the *Tirpitz* that by the end of the month Harris was prepared to hazard 31 Halifaxes and twelve Lancasters in a determined effort to damage or sink her.

On 5th March there occurred the first aircrew casualty of the RAF raids on the *Tirpitz*. At 08.07 hours, Pilot Officer Gunn took off on a routine photographic reconnaisance flight to Trondheim in Spitfire AA810. He failed to return. It is briefly recorded in the war diaries of *XXXIII Armeekorps*, that on 5th March a Spitfire was shot down by fighters in the Sunndalsøra area, about 180 miles southwest of Trondheim. The pilot, who was slightly wounded, was taken prisoner. Heinz Knoke, the German pilot who shot down Pilot Officer Gunn, recalled the details of how this reconnaissance flight ended in his book *I Flew for the Führer*, published after the war. That day, the duty officer at the fighter airfield at Lade ordered the interception of an intruder that had been located over Trondheim Fjord. Heinz Knoke, a German fighter pilot who, since arriving in Central Norway in February, had made several unsuccessful attempts to locate and attack PRU Spitfires, took off in his Messerschmitt

A Bristol Beaufort of No.42 Squadron. This unit regularly flew anti-shipping patrols across the North Sea to Norway. (via Author)

109 at 12.02 hrs. (local time). Fifteen minutes later he was at 25,000 feet, scanning the skies for his target. A dark speck in the distance, trailing a short smudge of vapour and silhouetted against the glaring white snowy landscape, could only be the intruder. Pilot Officer Gunn was flying in circles over his objective, presumably taking photographs, as Knoke positioned his aircraft about 3,000 feet above the Spitfire. Either because his work was complete, or because he had spotted Knoke, Gunn then set course to the west. Knoke dived in pursuit and began to open fire. His first tracers pierced the unarmed Spitfire's fuselage and Gunn, at full throttle, threw his aircraft into a series of twists and turns in a desperate effort to outwit the Messerschmitt on his tail. But as Gunn straightened out of a dive it was clear to Knoke that the Spitfire had been damaged. He fired once again as the smoke streaming from the Spitfire grew thicker and oil from its shattered oil-cooler splashed onto Knoke's own windshield. Although Gunn was still in control of his damaged aircraft he was evidently in difficulties: the smoke was thinning, but he was flying slower. Suddenly another Messerschmitt appeared and within seconds had opened fire. Gunn's starboard wing was shot away and fluttered earthwards, as the remains of his aircraft burst into flames and hurtled towards the snowfields below. Almost too late, Gunn managed to bale out and Knoke watched with great relief and a sense of fellow-feeling as his parachute opened and slowly drifted, carrying Gunn to safety. Upon landing at Lade, Leutnant Dieter

Flying Officer Gunn on the snow-covered runway at RAF Wick in February 1942. (via Author)

Gerhard (the pilot of the second Messerschmitt, who had fired the final shots at the smoking Spitfire), flew off into the mountains in a Fiesler Storch fitted with skis and brought back the Spitfire pilot. Knoke was very proud of the fact that this was his first successful 'kill' and celebrated by sharing with Dieter and his victim a bottle of brandy that had been put up as the prize for the first pilot to bring down the British intruder. After this brief exhibition of cameraderie between airmen of opposing sides, Gunn was taken away as a prisoner-of-war. He was taken to Germany, to Stalag Luft III at Sagan, in Silesia. He was murdered by the Germans after taking part in the mass escape from there in March 1944. He was the first aircrew lost from the PRU flights reconnoitring the coastal districts of Norway in *Operation Chamberlain*.[10]

The loss of Flying Officer Gunn coincided with a loss of contact with the *Tirpitz* at a crucial moment, as Bjørn Rørholt recalls:

> "*Tirpitz* went out on the 6th of March and on the 6th of March my transmitter unfortunately was out of action, either because I was moving or because it was under repair. I know that when *Tirpitz* came back again on the 13th after this PQ 12 foray I was on the air and reported that."

In fact, it was the submarine *Sea Wolf*, lying outside Trondheim Fjord, that sent back a report that the *Tirpitz* was making for the open sea. At last, after cooping herself up in Trondheim Fjord since her arrival there in the third week of January, the great battleship was setting out on her first operation.

NOTES

9. From *World War II Investigator*, May 1988.
10. Although Heinz Knoke claimed the victory, it was actually credited to Dieter Gerhard (*Jagdgeschwader 1 / 11* -Jochen Prien)

Chapter Four

The March Raid

The *Tirpitz* had left the shelter of Norway for the North Atlantic to attack a convoy (Convoy PQ12) as it steamed from Reykjavik in Iceland to Murmansk and Archangel in Russia. During these first few days of March a number of 10 Squadron Halifaxes were sent on a series of exercises to test out a new method of attacking the battleship. Work had been under way for some time to remedy the fact that the bombs carried by the Stirlings and Halifaxes in January (2,000lb AP and 500lb SAP), even had they been dropped accurately on their target, would have done little lasting damage. The weapons and the tactics would have to change and with them, the aircraft and the squadrons that would be involved. Stirlings, which did not have a bomb-bay wide enough to hold the explosives that were to be carried, were no longer to be used, while a third Halifax squadron, 35 (which incidentally had been the first squadron to fly Halifaxes operationally) was called into the game. In addition, there were to be Lancasters from 97 Squadron, Lancasters having only just become operational.

The only sure way to sink a battleship is to blow a hole in her hull to let the water in, but there is more than one way to do this. The first method was with torpedoes. These were of no use in attacking the *Tirpitz* in Fætten Fjord for a number of reasons. Not only was she protected on the offshore side by an anti-torpedo netting, but, since torpedoes are best launched at the side of a vessel to give them the most chance of hitting her, the position in which the *Tirpitz* lay prevented this kind of approach. Torpedoes needed to be dropped accurately. An

A Lancaster of No.44 Squadron (via Author)

aircraft carrying one had to be lined up on the target in the exact direction in which the torpedo was required to travel. The *Tirpitz*, moored alongside the edge of a narrow fjord no more than 330 yards in width at this point, and protected by steeply rising high ground, was thus an impossible target for air-launched torpedoes.

Secondly, there were bombs, but no Armour Piercing bomb was powerful enough at that time to penetrate the decks of the *Tirpitz*. Although 4,000lb H.C. bombs were used in all the three raids in March and April 1942 in order to cause superficial damage to the superstructure of the battleship, and injury to her crew, thus inhibiting her movements and even her ability to put to sea at all, they would not sink her.

Since both torpedoes and bombs would not do the job, there remained only the third option: mines. A mine, set to explode underwater, if dropped close enough to the side of the target, could cause considerable damage to the underwater part of the hull. It was decided that the Naval Mk. XIX anti-submarine mine was best suited for the job.

Thus one hundred of these spherical mines were supplied by the Royal Navy. Their adaptation included the removal of their sinker and mooring fittings and the use of a different explosive within the mine casing. Wing Commander J A MacBean, co-author of *Bombs Gone*, writes:

> "In both its original form (and the conversion), the mine was constructed with a fairly robust steel casing, 31 inches in diameter. As I understand it, the only strengthening done, was to the welding around the centre of the casing to make it more robust for air-dropping. The original mine, weighing 290 lbs., contained about 100 lbs of amatol (or TNT). When the guts were removed for air use it was filled with 770 lb of Minol (amatol + aluminium powder to increase blast)." [11.]

Unlike conventional mines that exploded on contact with the hull of a ship, these mines would be detonated automatically by a hydrostatic firing pistol at a depth of about fourteen feet. If such mines could be dropped from the air to land close enough to the *Tirpitz* and explode under water, then, it was believed, there was a good chance that the ship would either be sunk or the rudder and propellers, or even the turbines within her hull, would be severely damaged by the underwater shock waves and by the sudden displacement of the hull upwards and sideways. The closer they were dropped in the water around the hull of the ship the greater the damage they would inflict and, if they fell in the confined space between cliff-side and hull, the explosive effect would be greatly increased. Ideally, they were to be dropped as close as possible to the stern of the *Tirpitz*, between the ship and the fjord side 50 feet away. However, even without the hazard of attacking the *Tirpitz* under heavy defensive fire, it would require an extremely accurate or lucky shot for one of these mines to land close enough to the ship to blow a hole in the hull and sink her. There were no Naval aircraft able to carry mines of the size required, therefore an attacking force could not be launched from a carrier's deck off the coast of Norway. Heavy bombers were the only possible solution.

A number of 10 Squadron aircraft spent several days in the first fortnight of March carrying these mines from their base at Leeming up to the seas off the Outer Hebrides where they released them from a variety of heights in order to establish their effectiveness. Charles E. Harrison, a wireless operator

Halifax W7656 'P-Peter' provides the backdrop for this photograph of the men of 35 Squadron, Linton-on-Ouse, February 1942. 'P-Peter' was shot down on the raid of 28/29th April. (via G.Cranstone)

with 10 Squadron, who did not in fact take part in the raids as he was not crewed up with a regular crew, recalls the arrival of these mines at Leeming:

"In early 1942 a Naval Petty Officer came to the Station and was billeted in the Sergeants' Mess with us, and he was a mine expert from some Naval Station on the South Coast. At the same time the special mines, which were like huge round footballs, began arriving at the station disguised, I believe, in crates, as some entirely different equipment. It was this Petty Officer's job to organise these mines along with the armourers, ie. fusing, adapting the bomb bays etc, of the several aircraft which would be carrying them.

"Then came a period when these planes and crews had to practise dropping these mines, testing the equipment etc, and this was carried out in the sea off the Outer Hebrides. Two of my close friends, both wireless operators like myself, were in crews detailed, and I am sure I remember them telling me after dropping the first ones that the tail gunners were catching blast in their turrets because of the terrific explosive power, and the fact that they were being dropped too low and exploding virtually on impact."

There were other dangers, too, as Harrison recalls:

"It was during these practice sessions that a plane had a mine hang-up, and on landing the mine fell off and followed the plane along the runway, without exploding. It finished up at or near the intersection of two runways, so putting the airfield out of action until it was defused and removed."

Flight Sergeant Phil Ellison, a Canadian with 10 Squadron at the time, recalls having, from his seat in his aircraft's rear turret, 'a bird's eye view of the bods on the ground running in all directions!' This particular incident took place after a flight test over Filey Bay, as Flying Officer Jack Watts (flying as observer at this time) explains in his unpublished memoirs:

"We prepared two of our squadron Halifaxes for the test: one was ours and the other belonged to one of our experienced RAF NCO pilots, Sergeant Wyatt. We were detailed to fly to Filey Bay on the coast of Yorkshire where there was a firing range and to drop the weapon at 150 feet above the sea. Our task was to fly alongside the sergeant's aircraft while I photographed the results of his dropping the weapon at this altitude. The weapon resembled a gigantic football hanging halfway below the fuselage of the aircraft. It didn't appear that there would be any difficulty in following and photographing its fall.

"We made our bombing run together, and I began taking photographs as they called 'Bombs away', wondering at the same time whether I was going to witness and record their demise in a monstrous spout of water. But nothing happened! The great metal ball still hung in their bomb-bay. We made another run. Again I started photographing at the call 'Bombs away'. Again, nothing happened. That damned great ball still hung in their bomb-bay. As we circled for the third run, we heard the sergeant pilot say, 'To hell with it. If it hasn't gone by now, it isn't going to go, at least not with me flying it.' With that, he turned for home. We flew alongside him, perhaps equally relieved at the lack of results. We would have felt sick to have to witness their demise. When we reached base we allowed the other aircraft to precede us, figuring the sooner he was on the ground the happier he would be. We were absolutely horrified as we watched him touch down and saw the weapon fall from his bomb bay and roll in pursuit down the runway behind them!

"As soon as they had touched down, albeit a little hard, the tail-gunner had called on the inter-com, 'Hey, skipper, did we lose our tail wheel?' The captain had replied, a little caustically perhaps at this implied criticism of his landing, 'No. Of course we haven't, you bloody clot!' The tail-gunner quickly replied, 'Well something is chasing us.' The captain had realised immediately what had happened, and though he could not get airborne again by this time, pushed the throttles open to speed up his taxiing and to keep ahead of the mine which was trundling along behind him, at least until he could turn off to greater safety. Although the flight test had not worked out quite as planned, it did seem fairly certain that the mine would not explode on impact with the water (it appeared that the hydrostatic detonator had been driven into the centre of the mine by the impact on the ground), and that our chances of dropping it at low level, with safety, were fairly good."

In fact, the records indicate that during these tests, the mines were successfully dropped from a variety of heights ranging from 10,000 - 4,000 feet. In light of the fact that the plan for this raid - the first raid to use this weapon - called for the mines to be dropped from only 600 feet above the surface of the water, it is interesting to note that during the tests the mines were dropped from these much greater heights. Since they were spherical they had no ballistic capabilities that would allow the bomb-aimers to be able to predict their trajectory with any certainty. The only way they could be delivered with the necessary accuracy was from as low a level as possible. This would greatly increase the chances of sinking a mine within a few yards of the battleship, where the resultant explosion would wreak the maximum effect. However, it would mean that the bombers would have to make a steady and virtually suicidal approach at low-level right over the guns of the battleship. This, of course, is exactly what Sergeant Wyatt was practising and what was planned to take place during the March raid.

On 9th March, the day when the *Tirpitz* was sighted at sea and attacked by the Fleet Air Arm, a detachment of seven 10 Squadron aircraft with their crews flew up to Lossiemouth, 'in order to carry out a mission to be detailed by H.Q. Bomber Command'. One aircraft, Halifax R9371, was damaged when it crashed on landing at Lossiemouth with defective brakes. The pilot, Flight Sergeant 'Chick' Whyte, and his observer, Flight Sergeant Richards, were slightly injured. The damage to the brakes was caused, it seems, by anti-aircraft fire from Royal Naval vessels that were escorting a convoy along the coast - something that had occurred to the aircraft flying north to take part in the previous raid in January. The detachment of heavy bombers, flying low to avoid detection by enemy radar and following the coast, were easily detected by Naval vessels with anxious gun-crews escorting convoys that felt so vulnerable to enemy air attack. The Navy would have been told nothing of such aircraft movement and the gunners would therefore have assumed the worst. Flight Sergeant Chris Charlton was the first wireless operator on board and adds a little more detail to this incident:

"We set off for Lossiemouth on the 9th of March, and as we went out over the coast at Whitby we ran right over a coastal convoy, and the Navy started shooting at us plus the other five following us, scoring a direct hit on the port inner engine and damaging the propeller. We carried on quietly rather than return for a spare aircraft and have to go up the following day.

"When we got there we came in a little high because we had a 4,000 pounder on board. It had been a very high tide the previous night and we landed on a large wet patch on the airfield, and as the skipper applied the brakes we swung to starboard and headed for a large drainage ditch used to run high tides off the airfield quickly. We dropped into this which tore the undercarriage off, and our momentum carried us up the side of a submerged hangar which tore open the fuselage in front of the mainplane, and the 4,000lb unfused bomb off its carrier. When the W/O armourer crawled underneath it he found the bomb still locked to its carrying frame, so that was us for that trip."

Flying Officer Jack Watts was one of those who witnessed the remarkable escape of the crew from this disastrous landing:

"The air and the ground crews in the aircraft spewed out of the escape hatches and ran for safety, while the aircraft was still ponderously sliding across the field heading for a collision with the hangar, the last of them being the pilot out of the hatch over his head. His speed afoot made up for his later start as he overtook some of the slower escapees in their race across the field."

The aircraft was hurriedly replaced by another flown up by Squadron Leader Thompson, but in the event was not needed, along with the rest of the detachment's aircraft, as Chris Charlton remarks:

"The weather was never any good for us all, so we came home after our four days allowed for the trip - as passengers. The worst part was, we lost our faithful R9371 which we flew as our No 1 machine. The aircraft was put in a hangar for use as spares whilst we were at Lossiemouth, and later it was disposed of to a scrapyard at Forres, near Kinloss airfield."

Although not made clear in 10 Squadron's Operations Record Book, it would seem that this detachment was sent north in preparation for an attack on German naval units, presumably the *Tirpitz* herself, as Sergeant Harry Walmsley, a second pilot with 10 Squadron, recalls:

"My regular crew took off on 9th March for Lossiemouth, but the mid-upper gunner was replaced by a Royal Navy officer for ship recognition purposes. All other Halifaxes had this kind of replacement. However, the raid was cancelled after waiting four days at Lossiemouth for the weather to clear, so we returned to base."

Tirpitz had set out to attack convoy PQ12 on 6th March. It may reasonably be presumed that Bomber Command H.Q. had been preparing for an opportunity to attack the battleship at sea if she ventured within range of the Halifaxes waiting at Lossiemouth. However, the *Tirpitz* fled from the open sea after being attacked by torpedo-carrying Fleet Air Arm aircraft launched from the deck of the aircraft-carrier *Victorious*. She then slid into Vest Fjord, out of range of the bombers waiting in the North of Scotland. In any case, the weather had made an attack impossible and on 13th March, four days later, the aircraft of 10

Squadron returned to their base at Leeming. On the previous day the *Tirpitz* had left her anchorage off Bogen, near Narvik, and had slipped out of Vest Fjord, steaming south; for safety she had hugged the coast by taking the inner leads. By 22.00 hours on the following evening she lay once more up against the protection of the steep sides of Fætten Fjord.

The next Bomber Command attack on the *Tirpitz* was scheduled for the end of March but, during the evening of 27th March and the early hours of the 28th, hundreds of miles away on the French Atlantic coast, another operation with a bearing on the *Tirpitz* took place. In a raid combining secrecy with deception, great daring and courage, British commandos in a small flotilla of ships penetrated the German defences along the Loire estuary. The objective, to put out of action the only dry dock large enough to take the *Tirpitz*. This target, situated in the port at St Nazaire, was attacked with spectacular success. The destroyer *HMS Campbelltown*, her bows packed with high explosive, rammed the gates of the dock and later exploded, effectively closing the dry dock until after the war. The success of the raid now made it difficult for the Germans to carry out any necessary major underwater repairs to the *Tirpitz* and thus made a raiding voyage into the Atlantic too risky an enterprise for the Germans to put at risk their largest capital ship.

On 27th March, as the British commandos were steaming towards St Nazaire, bombers were gathering once again at several bases in the North of Scotland. Twelve aircraft from 76 Squadron landed at Tain, eleven from 10 Squadron landed at Lossiemouth and thirteen from 35 Squadron at Kinloss. All were Halifaxes. Strict secrecy about the presence of heavy bombers at bases in the North of Scotland was preserved at all stages. If the Germans became aware that such a force was assembling in that area they could deduce that it was intended to attack the *Tirpitz*. Such advance warning could enable them to reinforce the *Luftwaffe* presence at Værnes Aerodrome.

Consequently, R/T ground stations were not to broadcast in the period prior to take-off, while the wireless operators on the aircraft themselves were to preserve radio silence during the flight out to Norway. Peter Bell, an armourer with 10 Squadron, recalls several trips up to Lossiemouth in support of these operations and describes the journeys:

> "Most of the ground crew travelled by train from York - leaving in the evening and arriving at Lossiemouth in the following afternoon. It was a very tiring journey, and many hours were spent in blacked out compartments. Our journeys were broken at Aberdeen and Elgin. We travelled in working dress (including gum-boots) and a party of us was stopped by Redcaps in Aberdeen and reported for being 'improperly dressed'! Needless to say, when the charge sheets eventually arrived at Leeming the Squadron Commander consigned these to the proper place - the waste paper basket! Our stay at Lossiemouth was usually 5/6 days and once the aircraft were bombed up and the 'D.I.s' (Daily Inspections) carried out, we had very little to do. We were the scourge of the S.W.O. (Senior Warrant Officer) who was appalled at our standard of dress and the untidiness of our billets. Lossiemouth at that time was an O.T.U. with bags of 'bull'."

Thirty-four out of the thirty-five Halifaxes that had reached Scotland were to test themselves alone against the *Tirpitz*, for there were no Stirlings this time. They had the hopes of a new weapon (the modified Mk XIX Naval mine), although the crews may not have shared the enthusiasm for them that was no doubt felt by the planners. Although two Lancasters of 97 Squadron were scheduled to fly out of Tain and attack the German fighter aircraft known to be based at Værnes Aerodrome, in support of the bombing operation, they did not actually take part. They both set out on 26th March from Woodhall Spa, but only one arrived at Tain. As Flying Officer B. R. Hallows recalls:

> "On 26th March I had been told off to fly to Scotland on the first stage of a mission against the *Tirpitz*. Unfortunately, due to an error by my second pilot, who retracted the undercarriage prematurely, we did not get airborne, but slithered to an ignominious stop just off the end of the runway. It was rather exciting as we were carrying full tanks and a 4,000lb bomb. Luckily no fire or explosion."

Apart from injuries suffered by Hallows' second pilot, Flight Sergeant J. M. Smith, none of the remainder of the crew were hurt in this incident. Flight Lieutenant Coton flew on up to Tain in the other Lancaster, but on 28th March, according to the official records, 'returned from Tain today owing to operation being cancelled due to grounding of aircraft.' Quite why this aircraft did not take part is not made clear in the light of the Halifax raid two nights later. Perhaps there were second thoughts about sending a single Lancaster on a solo mission to attack the Norwegian airfields. However, the inclusion of Lancasters with a special rôle in the plan is significant, for it shows that increasingly complex tactics were being planned in order to cover every eventuality, thus giving these operations a greater chance of success as the early months of 1942 went by. This attack was not to rely on sheer desperate, brute force and the unpreparedness of the enemy, as had the attack in January. A new weapon had been prepared and the operation needed careful planning if it was to be delivered successfully against an enemy that had had plenty of time to prepare its defences. The tactics developed by the end of March in order to carry these mines to their target established a pattern that persisted throughout the aerial attacks on the *Tirpitz* during March and April 1942.

So what were the plans? The Leeming Station Commander, Group Captain S. Graham, was to take command of the entire operation, setting up his headquarters at Lossiemouth with 10 Squadron. Ten aircraft of 76 Squadron were each to carry one 4,000lb RDX filled H.C. bomb and four 500lb or 250lb general purpose bombs. These 4,000 pounders were the new and highly successful dustbin-shaped blast bombs designed to give maximum blast just above the surface. They were to be aimed at the ship herself in order to 'remove' the crews manning the ship's defences, while the 500 pounders were to be used against the anti-aircraft guns and searchlights set up close to the ship. Having dropped their bomb loads the Squadron was to cruise around the area, engaging the defences with their machine guns. Twenty aircraft from 10 and 35 Squadrons were to carry four 1,000lb mines each, as well as four small bomb containers (S.B.C.s, each holding ninety 4lb bombs), while two of the 35 Squadron aircraft were to carry 50lb incendiary bombs. The mine-carrying aircraft were to drop their mines as close as they could to the hull of the ship in the second, low-level, phase of the attack.

Flying to within 50 miles of the Norwegian coast, at a height of under 5,000 feet in order to remain undetected by the enemy RDF chain, the aircraft were to attack in two distinct waves. First the 76 Squadron aircraft were to drop their 4,000 pounders and flares, before the remaining aircraft dropped incendiaries and mines. The attack was to start at 21.45 hours.

Sergeant Gordon Cranstone, a wireless operator with 35 Squadron, recalls, with his wry sense of humour, one aspect of the preparations which he was to have good cause to remember. Before taking part in the operation the crews were given a demonstration of the technique of releasing and using the emergency survival dinghy. The "Type J" dinghy was stored inside a small hatch behind the inner engine on the port wing. When the manual release lever near the crew's forward upper escape-hatch was pulled the dinghy was ejected from the wing to inflate as an orange, roofless, doughnut-shaped dinghy large enough for the entire crew. But the demonstration did not go to plan:

> "It was supposed to instill confidence - instead of that it completely demoralised us, and in fact on the night my dinghy came out (after his aircraft had ditched during the night of 28th/29th April) I couldn't believe my luck! I think it was in March (they cut it out after that!). There were all these big-wigs standing around, and they gave us the old 'hype' about, you know, you've got to imagine that you've crashed into the drink out there, and you've got about two minutes or so before your kite goes down. They went all through the drill, and they said 'We've got Flight Sergeant So-and-so here tonight who is a dinghy expert, knows everything there is, and he's going to show you how easy it is.'"

But when the instructor pulled out the parcel-shaped dinghy from its stowage, as if it had been automatically ejected:

> "... out comes the parcel, and it was a parcel, 'Up it comes!', he said, 'and then it inflates!' Unfortunately, this one remained square that night. And they never did it again because everybody said 'That's good, isn't it?!' Giving us confidence! We're all now thinking 'Oh, bloody marvellous! If that stays as a square we ain't got no chance!' And they never did it again. That was the only time, and I think one or two heads rolled! I mean when they got rid of the aircrew they got into this poor Flight Sergeant who was the expert, and wanted to know why he'd got a dinghy that didn't come out like a dinghy! 'Cos you can imagine what the aircrew boys said, all a bit of a giggle, as they walked away, 'A lot of bloody good that was!' Or words to that effect! And so of course the poor man was paralysed. And so when I went down about a month later I thought 'Here we go again!', but actually it

The remarkable low-level oblique photograph taken by Flight Lieutenant Peter Fane. It was taken from about 200 feet. (via Author)

was marvellous, it worked, you know, so you got to be lucky. Well I tell you what, if it had been like that night up in Kinloss, we'd have never made it!"

All day preparations were made and the aircraft were 'bombed up' with the mines provided by No 77 Maintenance Unit. Two days earlier (on 28th March) the PRU had confirmed that the target was in her usual berth. The pilot who flew over her that day was the same Flight Lieutenant Fane who had been responsible for locating her for the first time in Fætten Fjord, two months earlier. In an audacious piece of flying he had taken a remarkable close-up of the ship. Taking her crew completely by surprise he had managed to fly his Spitfire (R7044) at very low-level straight over the ship's mast. So close was he to the *Tirpitz* that his photograph, which showed details of the centre of the ship, including the bridge, also showed the faces of astonished sailors looking up impotently as his aircraft flashed by above their unmanned guns. Earlier that day, in the middle of the afternoon, Mosquito W4061, flown by John Merifield on a reconnaissance flight to observe the *Tirpitz*, had been detected as it approached the coast, but despite the take-off of five Bf109s from Værnes, Merifield managed to beat a hasty retreat, aborting his mission and escaping.

Shortly after six o'clock on the evening of 30th March the bombers trundled around the perimeter track towards the down-wind end of the runway and began to take off, led by Wing Commander Young at 18.07 hours. For some of the crews this was their second stab at the *Tirpitz*. For some of them this was to be their final operation. At Kinloss, Flight Sergeant Glenn Gardiner and Pilot Officer Reggie Lane of 35 Squadron flipped a coin for the honour of first off. 'We carried liquid phosphorous, hopefully to 'light the *Tirpitz* up', Gardiner later remarked.

At Lossiemouth and Tain and Kinloss the groundcrews returned to their billets, to await the return of their charges. The sky was thickly overcast and they could only hope that the bombers would break through the cloud layer by the time they reached the Norwegian coast. It was not until some time after two o'clock in the morning, when the first of the returning bombers put down in the darkness of the runway at Lossie-mouth, that Group Captain Graham began to realise that the operation had been at best a failure, at worst a disaster. As the crews landed their aircraft, fuel tanks all but dry, and wearily told their stories to the briefing officers, the phrase '10/10ths cloud' told it all.

The aircraft captains had been told that, with the weather conditions as they were, they must cross the sea at a height of only 1,000 feet. With the cloud base 1,000 feet above them it had been easy enough for the navigators of 76 Squadron to make landfalls near Wick and at Sumburgh Head in the Shetlands. A break in the cloud had appeared briefly off the Norwegian coast, but, when the aircraft had climbed to 6,000 feet to make their approach, the mountains and fjords below them had become engulfed by sea-fog. As they circled the target area for as long as their fuel would allow them, little could be seen of the land below. About half the Squadron jettisoned their bombs, while several others dropped bombs that appeared to silence searchlights and the *Flak* defences. They then set out once more across the North Sea, heading for home.

The *Tirpitz* was linked to a telephone network on shore, which connected her Captain and his officers to German observation posts throughout the Trondheim area. News of enemy aircraft activity, both from radar contact and visual sighting, was thus instantly available to the battleship's officers.

Earlier that day, the 30th, in the middle of the afternoon, the officers on board the *Tirpitz* learned that a high-speed, twin-engined aircraft had been sighted 145 miles away to the southwest. Its progress was tracked and recorded as it flew along the coast before turning and flying towards Trondheim. This was in fact the PRU Mosquito (W4061) flown by Flight Lieutenant John Merifield. It had been fired on unsuccessfully by the anti-aircraft batteries in Trondheim and chased by five Messerschmitt 109s that took off to intercept him, but was fortunate enough to be able to shake off his pursuers and return undamaged to base, albeit without the photographs he had set out to take. His sortie was duly recorded in the battleship's log.

At about 22.30 hours the Port and Starboard Watches on board the *Tirpitz* were sent to their stations as the air-raid alarm was sounded in distant Trondheim. Half an hour later anti-aircraft fire was heard to the south of the ship and the ship's air-raid warning was sounded. There seemed to be aircraft above and around the ship in all directions and, when glimpses of them were seen through the cloud-cover, the gun-crews opened fire, although by the time the attack was over

De Havilland Mosquito PR Mark I. This aircraft, W4059, was flown by Flight Lieutenant John Merifield during the surveillance of the Tirpitz during March 1942. (via Author)

81

a total of only about 300 rounds of anti-aircraft shells had been expended. The only damage sustained by the *Tirpitz* was caused by an unignited flare, which fell from one of the attacking aircraft and superficially damaged the funnel. The attack came to an end at 23.32 hours, the all clear was sounded just after midnight and, as the last aircraft was heard disappearing to the southwest, the gun crews were stood down.

As peace descended once more over the fjord, brief reports received from the gunnery officers were entered in the ship's log, while a report from Trondheim gave the officers a little more information about the attack. The day's entries in the log concluded with the statement that between 25 and 30 aircraft, flying independantly of each other, and approaching from all directions except east, had flown over Trondheim in two waves. The observers there had been able to identify them as Halifaxes or (erroneously) Liberators. They reported that at least 25 bombs had been dropped, but no damage had been done. There had been no attempt made by German fighter aircraft based at airfields in the area to take off and intercept the bombers. However, three of the bombers were reported to have been shot down.

Nine aircraft returned safely to Tain and one, Halifax R9452:L, to Lossiemouth, as her pilot, Pilot Officer Michael Renaut, recalled in his book written some years after the war:

> "We set course for home and I began to work out with the flight engineer just how much petrol we had left. A quick calculation told us that we had about enough to make the coast of Scotland! I immediately throttled back and set the revs as low as I could so that we should use less fuel and we began a long haul back across the North Sea. We crossed the Scottish coast with all the petrol tanks showing zero and I put down at the first aerodrome I saw - Lossiemouth." [12]

Another aircraft, Halifax R9457:A, which had encountered heavy icing and had been running short of fuel was also unable to reach base. Luckily enough the pilot, Flight Lieutenant 'Hank' Iveson, was able to fly her into Wick:

> "After flying at 13,000 feet we descended into thick clouds, encountering severe icing at 8,000 feet. Full power was needed to get away from these conditions and in doing so it was obvious that our margin of petrol was

going to be critical.

"We managed to obtain a fix on Sumburgh, so we came out of the clouds, dropping down to 1,000 feet, only to discover that most of Sumburgh was fog-bound. My fuel state was such I knew we would not reach Tain and with my wireless operator (Flight Sergeant Craine) transmitting distress calls we set course for Wick. I had just told my crew to prepare for ditching when I saw the Wick beacon signalling. Landing lights on, we went straight in, cutting the inboard motors as we crossed the boundary hedge. Three quarters of the way down the flare-path I realised the brakes were not working, so not wishing to go through the fence and perhaps end up in the local churchyard (the nearby churchyard was below the level of the airfield), I swung the aircraft off to the right. The undercarriage held and after bouncing around the perimeter track we came to a halt." [13.]

Iveson's aircraft had only eighteen gallons of fuel left in her tanks.

The crews of 10 Squadron had similar experiences. Most of their bomb-aimers jettisoned their bomb-loads in the vicinity of the target, lightening their aircraft in order to make their fuel last longer. Eight aircraft returned safely to Lossiemouth. Few details are known of the 35 Squadron aircraft. Flight Sergeant Glenn Gardiner recalls that he and his crew did not get far before they had to turn back:

"Perhaps it was providence that my starboard outer engine packed up. The oil temperature went nearly 'off the clock'. We feathered the prop and carried on a few minutes. We could reach the target with three engines, but needed maximum power for nearly fifteen minutes in the target area. Upon re-starting the engine, it immediately overheated, so we dropped our containers of phosphorous into the sea and returned to Kinloss."

However, nine out of the twelve aircraft that took part managed to get back to Kinloss after their operation. Three of them failed to return. Two of them, R9496:L and W1015:P, were lost off the Norwegian coast and, of their fourteen crew, only two bodies were ever recovered from the bitter sea, washing ashore on the coast nearly three months later. Glenn Gardiner realised how lucky his crew had been in having to return early with an engine out of action, for:

"I think of providence because the visibility closed down and George Steinhauer (pilot of W1015:P) lies in a cemetery in Trondheim after hitting a mountain, and Bushby apparently forgot to adjust his Q.F.E. (barometric guage) from the target area and "scrubbed" one of the Shetland Islands."

The third aircraft of 35 Squadron to fail to return was R9438:H. Flying home, Flight Sergeant Bushby and his crew are believed by more than one member of the squadron to have crashed as a result of a simple error. The Kollsman number setting on the altimeter had to be adjusted as the barometric pressure altered during the flight and warnings to do so were broadcast when necessary. It is presumed that the crew omitted to make a crucial adjustment and ended up believing that they were flying higher above the surface than in fact they were. However, they may just have been unable, through lack of fuel or through damage, to maintain height at the crucial moment. In this way, as Grierson-Jackson writes:

"They had made landfall on Fitful Head, the great cliff at the south tip of the Shetland Islands. Most of one wing and an engine were on top of the cliff, the rest of the plane on the beach below. Obviously Bushby had banked sharply when Fitful Head loomed through the dawn haze, and he almost made it."

Of her crew of seven only two - Flight Sergeant Buckley and Sergeant Usher - were brought out of the water and now lie at rest in Lerwick Cemetery. On the headstone marking Usher's grave is inscribed: 'Here rests one, beloved by all, with brave heart, he saw his duty clear'. Of the fate of the remainder of the crew, despite exhaustive inquiries made by the father of one of the men, Sergeant Anthony Peach, nothing more was known for years. Only recently have recollections of members of the Shetland community come to light. In a letter to Ted Whittles, Anthony Peach's cousin, Averill Watt wrote:

"In March 1942 my late grandfather, Mr John Mainland, and a neighbour, both crofters at Brake, Quendale, were out driving their sheep on a hill called Fitful Head. Fitful, at 1,000 ft, is the third highest hill in Shetland and its west side is predominantly made up of precipitous cliffs. Among the rock faces there are grassy areas which provided grazing for sheep. My grandfather had to make his way down the cliff once or twice a year to round up his sheep. It was a dangerous task but he knew where it was relatively safe to walk. In March he and his neighbour were working in the cliff when, as he described, they were startled on going round a corner to see two men sitting. Both were wearing headsets and at first my grandfather thought they were alive. However, on approaching, he realized they were dead. A third airman was found nearby. It appeared that an aircraft had hit the cliff, which is under 1,000 feet at this point, and fallen into the sea taking the other crewmen with it. As far as I know no trace of the plane or the other crewmen was found. My grandfather and his friend left their work, returned home and telephoned the authorities at Sumburgh Airport which was an RAF base. Without waiting for details the RAF sent out fire

Sergeant Anthony Peach, RAFVR, who lost his life when his 35 Squadron Halifax crashed at Fitful Head, Shetlands, returning from the March raid. (Ted Whittles)

engines but soon realised this was not going to be a rescue operation. The main task was to try to recover the bodies. The precipitous nature of the cliff made this very difficult, but the bodies of the men found in a sitting position were taken up the cliff and buried in Lerwick cemetery."

John Eunson remembers the event vividly, for he believes that he is '... the only local man now alive after 50 years who had any part in seeking for and finding part of the crew of an aircraft here in our area.':

"I was not with the men who found the two bodies and brought them up, and had them taken to Lerwick. So I have no details about who they were. But the following day it was decided that a closer search of the area was necessary, and since I at that time was a young man of 26 years I was asked to come with the other men, so that we could be sure that no one was alive and suffering, for the area is very steep and in parts sheer rock. We therefore took cliff ropes and at considerable risk started a search of the cliff face, and eventually saw wreckage wedged in a crag in the cliff face. I, being the youngest man, was asked if I was willing to have this rope fastened on my body so that I could be lowered down to this wreckage to see it there was any of the crew there. I readily agreed and was duly lowered and when I got there I found one man's body which was lying among the wreckage. It was completely intact with only one head bash. His parachute was still in its original position and all his clothing was whole, which indicated that he had died instantaneously from the blow on the head. But with 150 feet of sheer rock face above, and some 300 feet of sheer rock face below, I was powerless to bring it to the top of the cliff. So since there was a crag in the cliff and some sheets of the plane there and some boulders, we decided that I should wrap it in the parachute and cover it with parts of the machine until such time as the military authorities decided what should be done about it.

"There was sufficient evidence in his clothing to tell us that his rank and name was Sergeant R. Meredith. And what's more, the remains were never brought up from the cliff face for only from the sea could it have been removed, and that was not advisable in this area in 1942 when U-boats were around our shores always."

85

Averill Watt continues the story:

"A service was conducted at the crash site for all those lost and was attended by an RAF padre, a serviceman and my grandfather. The padre would only go down roped to my grandfather, which gives some idea of the nature of the place. Ron Meredith's sister contacted my grandparents and corresponded with them for several years. She also paid for flowers to be placed regularly at the foot of a wooden cross which was erected as a memorial at the top of the cliff. The cross is apparently no longer standing."

John Eunson concludes his account of this tragedy:

"We found part of the aircraft scattered along the cliff face about 500 feet above sea level. This aircraft was believed to be trying to reach Sumburgh Airport, about 3/4 miles further on. Without doubt the other members of the crew never landed on Shetland soil, but rather landed in the sea below."

In March 1994 an account of this tragic accident, in which the fate of another member of the crew, Sergeant Peach, is recorded, was set down by Tom Warner, the RAF Padre at Sumburgh at the time.

"On the morning of the 31st March 1942 we could see a man dangling from a parachute about 200 feet over the water beneath Fitful Head. Group Captain Ian McMurtrie got in touch with the appropriate authority for instructions. Eventually Air Ministry forbade him to attempt a recovery on the grounds that you don't lose a life for a dead man. But the camp took a dim view. I volunteered to go down if I were roped and cut the cords but I was turned down, because they said the cliff slants inwards about that point. Meanwhile it was discovered that all the crew were senior NCOs and I overheard one airman say, 'If 'twere the Duke of Kent they'd recover him' which I knew in my heart was the truth. So, off I went to see John Mainland who told me he had gone down the Banks at the age of 16, but strongly advised against my attempting a rescue. 'If I get a long enough rope, John,' I asked, 'would you be prepared to stay at the top and make it secure?' He agreed; and I got an RAF van to take him and me and a friend of mine, Flight Lieutenant Taylor (who was killed shortly afterwards) to the area. The driver, LAC Finney from Birmingham, was all ears. 'You're not going down for that Bod, Sir, are you?' 'I'm going down,' I said. 'I'll go with you, Sir, it's bloody dangerous.' 'You will NOT go with me Finney.' 'I'm not going to let you go down alone Sir - I'm telling you now. Come! Follow me'!!! And Finney was over the top before you could say Jack Robinson! John Mainland followed us down a bit and threw the rope down to us, but we soon realised that a rope was useless because of the boulders that were lying about. So I shouted up to him to abandon the project, and Finney and I went down on our own. I remember thinking if only Finney weren't with me I'd be alright, especially when I heard a noise like something rolling down the cliff and thought it was Finney. Finney, however, had no intention of rolling down the cliff! After we had gone down about 800 feet (Fitful is 954 feet high, as you know) we came to where the cliff ceases to slope, and tends to slant in, if anything. I saw the body about 100 yards west of me, and we were able to climb along the face owing to a fissure that ran along 165 feet over the water. Now this is where Finney was a godsend to me, bless him. We were able to pull up the body into the fissure - something I could not do on my own. I cut the disc that identified him - he was Sergeant Peach - and found a letter from his mother in his battledress blouse, which I put in my pocket, noting the address. 'Now Finney,' I said, 'we'll push it down into the crack and I'll say a few prayers from the Burial Service', which I did. Then I handed my revolver to Finney and told him to fire three shots over 'the grave'. I took a revolver in my pocket because, quite frankly, I didn't think I'd ever come up alive. I am not a mountaineer! We put the parachute over the body and covered it over with stones from the fissure. About three-and-a-half hours later we appeared over the top. John Mainland and Taylor thought we were 'goners'. 'Drive Mr Mainland home, and then take me to the Station Commander', I said, wondering what fate awaited me for breaking an Air Ministry order. McMurtrie couldn't believe his ears, and apologised for having to ring up Air Ministry. I was sitting close to him and I could hear the reaction from some big shot in the Air Box. 'Good bloody Oh!' And I heard him say he will have to fly past the cliff, take a photo, and then take that, and the letter, down to his parents in North Harrow. That pleased me no end because it gave me a chance to spend a few days at home in Yorkshire - my wife and I had been married two months! So I delivered the letter and the photo of the grave to grateful parents."

One aircraft was lost from 76 Squadron, Halifax R9453:K, piloted by Squadron Leader Burdett. Her wireless operator was given a 'fix' from a ground tracking station at Inverness at 23.52 hours, nearly five-and-a-half hours since leaving base (at which time she was presumably just leaving the coast of Norway). Nearly four hours later, at 03.40 hours, she passed over the cliffs of Sumburgh Head and was believed to have ditched in the sea about eighteen miles from there. She had been flying for just over nine hours and, perhaps suffering damage to her engines or her structure, she had been unable to stay in the air. Nearly twenty aircraft took off to search for her, but, despite the assistance of two Royal Navy destroyers, no trace of aircraft or crew was ever found.

10 Squadron lost two Halifaxes, W1044:D and W1043:F, both of which were lost somewhere just off the Norwegian coast.

Charles Harrison of 10 Squadron (who did not take part in the attack since at the time he was not crewed up with a regular crew) has a strange tale to tell, concerning the wireless operator in Squadron Leader Webster's aircraft:

"Wireless operator Algy Hague was a great pal of mine and we shared a room in the Sergeants' Mess at Leeming. We had a habit of putting our hand in our trouser pocket, taking out a single ha'penny and telling the other to get a drink with it whilst away. On the day I left the room for an oxygen course at Farnborough, Algy lay on the bed waiting to go down to Flight later and then take off for Lossiemouth that day. I offered him the ha'penny as usual and instead of getting it thrown back at me, Algy said •ll keep this if you don't mind, I've a feeling I shan't see you again'. That was March 1942 and in the October I was taken PoW baling out over Bonn. I waited a further six months, making a year since Algy went missing (for security reasons) and then I approached the Germans requesting any information about Algy Hague who went missing in March 1942 at Trondheim. I wanted the information so I could inform his wife by letter if possible. I waited several weeks and then the German interpreter came to see me. He told me they had made a thorough search of their records etc, and could give me no information about anyone named Hague around that time."

Thus, 10 Squadron lost two aircraft, 35 Squadron lost three, while a sixth was lost from 76 Squadron. Little is known of the cause of the demise of the four aircraft that were lost off the Norwegian coast, although three were reported by the Germans as being shot down by defences around Trondheim Fjord. These included a 'big plane' reported by the Germans as having crashed into the sea on the east side of the island of Hitra, just southwest of the entrance to Trondheim Fjord, near a place called Laksåvika (probably Flight Sergeant Archibald's Halifax, R9496:L). Nothing is known of the fourth aircraft and no German fighters are reported as having taken off that night. The most likely explanation, then, is that they were shot down as they made their way either to or from the target. An alternative, or additional, explanation is that the surfaces of some of the aircraft became iced-up in the prevailing weather conditions and, losing height, they finally crashed or were forced to ditch in the icy seas.

The approaches to Trondheim Fjord and the sheltered harbour of Trondheim itself were heavily defended against possible sea and air attack. All the missing bombers appear to have crashed or ditched in the waters running between the offshore islands of Hitra and Smøla and the inshore islands and the mainland itself, for that is from where the bodies of the few crewmen who were found were recovered. The anti-aircraft defences, despite the poor weather conditions, appear to have

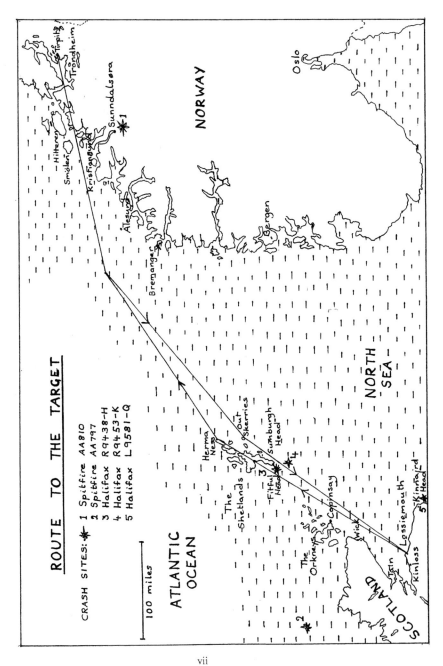

ROUTE TO THE TARGET

CRASH SITES:
1 Spitfire AA810
2 Spitfire AA797
3 Halifax R9438-H
4 Halifax R9453-K
5 Halifax L9581-Q

100 miles

ATLANTIC OCEAN

NORTH SEA

NORWAY

SCOTLAND

Oslo
Bergen
Bremanger
Ålesund
Kristiansund
Smølen
Hitteren
Trondheim
Tirpitz
Sunndalsøra

The Shetlands
Herma Ness
Out Skerries
Sumburgh Head
Fitful Head
The Orkneys
Copinsay
Wick
Lossiemouth
Kinnaird Head
Kinloss
Tain

been remarkably successful in either shooting down these aircraft or damaging them to such an extent that they had to ditch. In that mountainous terrain the only safe place to bring a damaged aircraft down in the dark would have been on the only visible flat surface available - the waters of a fjord or the sea - the crews hoping that they could then make their way ashore by dinghy. The belief held by several of the surviving aircrew that George Steinhauer's aircraft 'hit a mountain' is interesting, given that two of his crew were recovered from the water. This point of view merely emphasises the uncertainty of what actually happened. It also seems remarkable that four aircraft appear to have come down in the water in such close proximity to each other.

Of the forty-two airmen aboard these aircraft the bodies of only five were ever found, all in the water in the approaches to Trondheim Fjord. The body of Pilot Officer P.G. Brown, second pilot to Flight Sergeant Steinhauer of Halifax W1015:P (35 Squadron), was washed ashore on 20th June at Edo, while the tail gunner of this aircraft, Sergeant W. Cowan, was brought from the sea and now lies buried at Kristiansund. The body of Squadron Leader F.D. Webster, pilot of Halifax W1043:F (10 Squadron), was washed ashore at Terningen Lighthouse, 55 miles west of Trondheim, on 4th April, and was interred in Stavne Cemetery. The remainder of his crew, one of whom was Charles Harrison's friend Algy Hague, was never found, although a waterlogged flying helmet marked 'Stevens-Fox 60772' was found on the shoreline on 6th April. Pilot Officer G.C. Day and Sergeant R.G. Richards, both of Halifax W1044, are buried at Heim. [14.]

The photograph taken during the PRU sortie that took place the morning after the raid was of poor quality, but there was no evidence of damage of any kind. The raid had been costly in human life and still no damage had been inflicted on the target.

Despite unsuitable weather, by 4th April most of the aircraft had managed to return to their own bases, from where they continued their routine bombing assault on Germany. The eleven Halifaxes of 76 Squadron at Tain left for home on 5th April, but, encountering 10/10th cloud off Kinnairds Head, all but two returned to Tain. The following day, leaving behind two

Squadron Leader F.D. Webster, DFC of 10 Squadron. (via B. Aggas)

of their number with engine problems (glycol leaks), seven reached their home base. The ground crews of all the squadrons returned within the next couple of days, some by air, but the majority by rail.

At the beginning of April the sea and the enemy took its toll of PRU crews, when two aircraft were lost in quick succession, failing to return from Norway. On 2nd April Pilot Officer Hutcheson and his observer Pilot Officer Allen took off from Leuchars in Mosquito W4056, bound for the Trondheim area. It is certain that they reached the coast of Norway and may have managed to complete part or all of their mission. However, pursued and attacked by two German fighter aircraft, Pilot Officer Hutcheson was forced to make an emergency landing on a peninsular near the entrance to Trondheim Fjord - presumably while trying to evade his pursuers by flying out to sea. Hutcheson managed to bring his Mosquito down on the runway of the German-occupied airfield at Ørland, near Brekkstad, whereupon he and Allen immediately set fire to their aircraft to prevent it falling intact into German hands. They were both made prisoners of war. [15.]

On the following day, 3rd April, there occurred a sadder loss, as one pilot, homeward bound from his eleventh sortie over Norway, lost his way. Flying Officer Richard Cussons recalls:

"... many of the aircraft of 'C' Flight did not have radio, but our flight were given the latest (at that time) mark of PR IVs which had a VHF radio fitted - this had a range of some 200 miles at 30,000 ft., but much less at low level. Flight Sergeant Jones was plotted on radar flying between the Shetlands and Orkneys until he disappeared somewhere in the Atlantic and was not seen again - he had no radio."

By the end of the week, on 10th April, Flying Officer Peter Gimson became the last of the pilots flying reconnaissance flights over Norway between January and April, to fail to return. Tragically, this sortie in P.R.U. Spitfire AB307 was Gimson's first over the Trondheim area. It is not known whether or not he managed to obtain the photographs he had set out to take, but he was last seen flying a southerly course towards the *Tirpitz*, hotly pursued by two German aircraft. With no weapons with which to defend himself, and unable to evade the pursuit, he was shot down at 19.45 hours, some four-and-a-half miles from the battleship.

His fate was observed by a young Norwegian lad, Magnar Huseby. Born and raised in the Åsen area, Magnar was only a youngster at the time, but the events of that spring day made a strong impression on him:

"In 1942 I was 14 years old. We were busy playing that afternoon when we heard anti-aircraft fire and saw smokeballs in the sky. There was nothing strange in this, as there were *Flak* guns on almost every hill in the area, because of the *Tirpitz* lying in Fætten Fjord.

"The unusual thing this day was that when the anti-aircraft fire stopped, the drone of aircraft engines grew louder, and suddenly we could see a fight taking place between three aircraft. There were two against one, and the outcome was inevitable - the little British Spitfire was soon hit and on fire, and was spinning out of control. At first it looked as if it was going to crash among the houses by the railway station, but suddenly the aircraft turned and crashed into the still-frozen lake of Hammarvatnet, about 100 metres from Ytterøya, an island in the middle of the lake."

The German pilot who had managed to shoot down Gimson's aircraft was *Oberleutnant* Herbert Huppertz, the Commander of *9 Staffel Jagdgeschwader 5*, airborne from Lade aerodrome. Magnar continues:

"While the aircraft was still at a considerable height, we saw a trail of smoke falling from it. A fight in the sky and an aircraft crash were not daily experiences for boys in the Norwegian countryside in those days. We ran as best we could - the ice on the lake was just about safe - and we were among the first to arrive at the scene. Aircraft parts were scattered all over the place, but most of them had gone through the rotten ice.

"The two German fighters made several low passes over their fallen enemy.

"While the people were gathering on the ice, a rumour started, that the pilot had come down on the other side of the lake. There followed another 'sprint' across the island and the narrow sound to Faana-landet on the mainland. My friend and I arrived together with the first German soldiers. We were met by a terrible sight.

"The brutality and mercilessnes of war had put a sudden end to a strange

Flying Officer Peter Gimson.
(Jackie Gimson)

young pilot's life. His parachute had failed to open. The trail of smoke we had seen was from his burning parachute. A free fall of several hundred metres had taken its toll, although the fall had been somewhat cushioned by a tall pine tree.

"Helpless, we stood in a circle, everyone with his own thoughts. The German soldiers showed their fallen enemy their respect by standing at attention and saluting in a military way. It was a very moving moment, and it made an impression on a young boys' mind which has remained there ever since."

Peter Gimson's body was taken away and he was buried in Stavne War Cemetery, where there also lay the body of Squadron Leader Webster, the pilot of one of the Halifaxes that had failed to return after the ill-fated raid ten days earlier. Here, too, there were to be laid to rest more Allied airmen who were to lose their lives over the *Tirpitz* in the

A low-level oblique photograph of the pocket-battleship Admiral Scheer (nearest the camera) and the cruiser Prinz Eugen in Lofjord, taken by 1 P.R.U.

days to come. Peter Gimson had only just celebrated his 23rd birthday.

Herbert Huppertz was killed later in the war, but on May 10th, a month after his encounter with Gimson, he was successful in shooting down another reconnaissance aircraft sent to photograph the *Tirpitz*. His victim was Flying Officer Frederick Malcolm, veteran of more than a dozen sorties on *Operation Chamberlain*. P.R.U. Spitfire AB127 was found by chance on the high ground of Forbordfjellet, Skatval in Stjørdal, about three miles to the south of the *Tirpitz*, Flying Officer Malcolm still seated in the cockpit. A memorial stone now marks the site.

However, not all the emergencies that arose for the P.R.U. pilots had unhappy endings. Late on the evening of April 13th a Belgian Pilot Officer, André Cantillion, running out of fuel on his return from a successful sortie to Norway (during which he had managed to photograph the *Tirpitz*, the *Prinz Eugen,* the *Admiral Scheer* and the *Admiral Hipper*) had to put down at Sumburgh. A tyre burst on landing, but luckily neither he nor the aircraft were damaged. Cantillion was full of praise for the groundcrew who replaced the tyre within ten minutes, allowing him to be airborne a short while later, with sufficient fuel to get home to Wick.

Flying Officer Richard Cussons remarks that:

"Some things are remembered vividly when not normal routine; like the time my flight commander, Flight Lieutenant Ron Acott had a complete engine failure (a con-rod broke) one day on his way back from Norway and with the greatest luck managed to stretch his glide to land wheels-up on the tiny island of Copinsay. The lighthouse keeper radioed to the mainland and he was picked up (by a naval MTB I think) and taken to Sumburgh where I fetched him in the Anson. The remains of the Spitfire is, I believe, still on the island."

Cussons first took part in *Operation Chamberlain* in the middle of April, as he clearly recalls:

"On April 13th I took off from Wick on my first sortie to Trondheim. after topping up the fuel tanks at Sumburgh, I flew to Trondheim where I was able to photograph quite a large area showing the *Tirpitz, Prinz Eugen* (damaged), *von Scheer, Admiral Hipper*, the tanker *Altmark* and several destroyers. The weather was crystal clear and the photos were good and I still have a 'mosaic' of this sortie. I was airborne for five hours fifteen minutes total with another refuelling stop at Sumburgh on the way home.

Left: Hauptmann Herbert Huppertz. (via Author)
Right: Flying Officer Malcolm, having just landed after his first trip in a 1 P.R.U. Spitfire. He was shot down and killed by Hauptmann Huppertz over Forbordfjellet in May 1942. (via Author)

That sortie was the first of thirteen sorties which I made on *Operation Chamberlain* (four of which took place before the end of April), though only four were fully successful, the others being spoiled by cloud cover; there were many other sorties by other pilots."

NOTES

11. In a letter to the author:
12. From *Terror by Night* - Michael Renaut, DFC, 1982
13. From *To see the Dawn Breaking* - W.R. Chorley, 1981
14. See map page 201
15. See map page 201

Chapter Five

The April Raids - Plans
And Preparations

After the failure of the March operation against the *Tirpitz*, planning began on another attempt to be made at the next suitable moon-phase, the end of April. And so we come to the most complex raid of the series. Up until now, faced with such a tough nut to crack, Bomber Command had been tentatively trying out various ideas in the hope that one would cripple the *Tirpitz*. The first raid had been a hastily put together desperate measure: if aircraft could reach the target surely somehow the ship would be damaged.

The second raid, more considered than the first, introduced the idea of using mines in order to deliver the explosive punch required to really damage or even sink the battleship. The attack was planned to take place in two distinct phases, the first being an attempt to distract or silence the defences, while the second phase involved dropping the mines. Stirlings were discarded as being unable to carry the mines and bombs required and the Halifax force was increased by one squadron. Lancasters were tentatively introduced in a supporting role, although in fact they do not seem to have taken part. There had been no opportunity to judge the effectiveness of the modified mines and they were to be used again at the next available opportunity. The third effort, which took place on the night of 27/28th April, was to expand on the ideas used so far. Because almost the entire force managed to reach its objective, and attack the *Tirpitz* in the way planned, this attack deserves detailed coverage of both its intention and its execution. It is also the operation that involved Halifax W1048 'S-Sugar'. A considerable amount is known of this particular aircraft and her crew and, since W1048 'S-Sugar' now serves as a memorial to so many Halifax operations and Halifax crews, it is appropriate that her story, and the story or her crew, is told in some detail.

The full details of the plans for a third attempt to sink the *Tirpitz* were not sent to the squadrons of 4 and 5 Groups that were concerned until 11th April, but preparations had nevertheless already begun before that date.

It was not unusual for aircraft to be loaned by one squadron to another squadron or even to another Group, in order to meet changing demands. However, the advance preparations for the raid at the end of April were to require the unusual procedure of an exchange of aircraft between 35 and 102 Squadrons. At this time of the war aircraft were being delivered from the aircraft factories to the RAF stations, and from one station to another, by both regular squadron pilots and ferry pilots. Pilot Officer H.E. ('Batch') Batchelder DFM, a pilot with 102 Squadron at RAF Topcliffe, remembers being involved in this particular exchange operation because the aircraft he flew was none other than Halifax W1048 'S-Sugar'. He had just completed his conversion to Halifaxes by flying one solo for the first time on 7th April 1942, when, only two days later, he was ordered to take Halifax W1048 'S-Sugar' on the short delivery flight to Linton-on-Ouse:

"On 9th April I was ordered to go to Dishforth by transport, collect an aircraft which was 'DY-S' W1048 and deliver it to 35 Squadron at Linton. As so often in those days it was to be done in a hurry and I just had time to collect my flight engineer and wireless op and go to Dishforth. The flight was only 15 minutes duration and totally uneventful. At Linton I collected another Halifax, R9494, in which I flew to 102 Squadron's satellite base at Dalton, a trip of twenty minutes. The only thing I can recall of either flight was that the aircraft were quite lively because they were so lightly loaded, they only had three people and a small amount of fuel on board. I have a suspicion that R9494 may have been a rogue aircraft, it was almost immediately transferred from 102 to 1652 HCU at Marston Moor where, on 22nd June, it swung badly on landing and collapsed its undercarriage. That could have been the reason for its transfer from 35 Squadron!"

And so, W1048 'S-Sugar', a brand new aircraft, with only a few hours in the air, arrived at 35 Squadron. She had been delivered to 102 Squadron on 9th March, but as soon as she arrived at Linton-on-Ouse the newly painted 102 Squadron code, which W1048 had been given at Dishforth, was painted out and replaced with the Linton-on-Ouse code, TL, giving W1048 her final lettering, TL-S.

W1048 'S-Sugar' was one of six aircraft ferried by RAF pilots from No 102 Squadron on that day, being exchanged for six 35 Squadron Halifaxes having 'special modifications' on them. These 'special modifications' were the TR 1335 sets, the new, secret *GEE* navigational aid. Since the operation over Norway would be beyond the range of the *GEE* stations it had been decided either to remove the sets from these aircraft or exchange the aircraft themselves for others. In this way no unnecessary *GEE* sets would be in danger of being captured by the enemy if an aircraft came down on land. They could be put to use in the air over Germany instead. On 10th and 12th April a further three aircraft were ferried in to Linton in preparation for the raid, flown in, this time, by Air Transport Auxiliary pilots from the Ferry Pool.

The crew who were to fly W1048 'S-Sugar' to Norway had all had varying amounts of operational experience. But they had not all flown together as a complete crew before, although some of them had flown with each other on occasion. It was rare at this time for a crew to fly continuously together for very long, or indeed always to fly the same aircraft. There were only six in the crew, the usual seventh member, a second pilot, not being carried by any of the Halifaxes of 35 Squadron. Don MacIntyre, the pilot, explains:

"At about the time of the *Tirpitz* raids the second pilot was dropped on some raids (those where heavy losses were expected) A member of the crew sat in the right-hand seat on take-off and landing to assist. It was not always the flight engineer, usually it was a crew-member familiar with the aircraft and sometimes capable of flying. In our crew on the *Tirpitz* it was Dave Perry, the first wireless operator, as second pilot. He was the most experienced.

"To answer the question who would replace the pilot in case of injury - no one - we did not have such luxury. In early 1942 we were very short of Halifax pilots - our W/Op and our engineer were new and the rest of the crew except Perry unfamiliar with the Halifax flight deck - no one could have flown except the pilot."

Pilot Officer Don MacIntyre, pilot of Halifax W1048 'S-Sugar', shortly after his reurn to England after spending six weeks in Sweden. (D. MacIntyre)

The captain and pilot of the aircraft was Don MacIntyre, a bluff, decisive Canadian from New Brunswick, who had converted from Whitleys to the four-engined Halifax at Kinloss in October of the previous year and who had considerable operational experience. Ian Hewitt, a precise and practical man with a dry wit, brought up in the North of England, was the navigator. There were the usual two wireless operators who also manned the front and mid-upper gun turrets, first wireless operator/ air gunner being Dave Perry from Norfolk, a cheerful and energetic young man. The second wireless operator/air gunner was Pierre Blanchet from Montreal, Canada. Canadian-French was his mother tongue and he was still accustoming himself to the racy strain of English as spoken by young airmen. The flight engineer was Vic Stevens from Romford, London, a quiet-spoken man of considerable tolerance and perseverance and an easily roused sense of humour. His fellow Londoner, the easy-going tail-gunner Ron Wilson, had a cheerful, phlegmatic attitude towards the dangers of flying in the isolated rear-gun turret. The wartime RAF certainly did throw together people from widely varying backgrounds and cultures!

The aircraft allocated to MacIntyre, W1048 'S-Sugar', having been ferried into Linton-on-Ouse on 9th April, was not flown again until the 15th. Three days earlier Don MacIntyre and his crew had what Ian Hewitt called a 'dicey-do' on an operation in Halifax W1019, when several aircraft from the squadron took part in a raid on the city of Essen, in northwest Germany. On the outward journey, as they approached the Belgian coast between Ostend and Dunkirk, they realised that they were being shadowed by a Bf110 that approached to within 300 yards of the aircraft. They were then coned by searchlights and the resulting *Flak* from the ground defences began bursting all around them. In fact they were probably hit by it for one propeller went 'fully into fine' and the aircraft plummeted from 10,000 to 3,000 feet. They jettisoned their bomb load 'safe' over enemy territory and, with the port outer engine u/s (unserviceable), landed at RAF Manston, one of the emergency landing-grounds on the Kent coast.

When MacIntyre and his crew returned to Linton-on-Ouse on 12th April they were allocated their new aircraft, W1048 'S-Sugar'. Three days later, on 15th April, the men of 35 Squadron got wind of an unusual operation in the offing. Bill Grierson-Jackson, navigator in Halifax W1047:R of 35 Squadron remembers:

"The first clue of something unusual afoot was when the 'Tannoy' announced 'Night flying tests for all serviceable aircraft to be completed by noon. Briefing at 14.00 hours.' We were night bombers and a briefing at two in the afternoon was most unusual. We filed into the briefing room with apprehension, fully expecting to be briefed for a hasty, and murderous, daylight attack. Instead we were puzzled to see the usual battle map of Europe partially covered with a map of the local 4 Group flying area. A red ribbon outlined an irregular quadrangle that enclosed most of the Yorkshire moors. After Jimmy Marks had spoken briefly to the men, the Senior Intelligence Officer, a retired Indian Army Colonel, much admired by the men, read from a 'signals form'. It was from the Air Officer Commanding 4 Group and quite simply stated that the area circumscribed by the red ribbon was a 'designated low flying area'. It went on to say that, until further notice, low flying tactics would be practised as designated and such exercises were to be under the same close security rules as pertained with regard to actions against the enemy."

Grierson-Jackson recalls that the crews were then told that a series of routes were being planned by the Navigation Office, which were to be flown in one direction only. They were to practise jinking to port and starboard at low levels. The only way to do this with safety was to use flat turns and they were told to fly as close as possible to any steep hillsides and cliffs that were within the practice area.

As it happened, aircraft were only able to spend two days practising for the forthcoming operation and some aircraft were

Pilot Officer Don MacIntyre (on extreme left) with Pilot Officer Henry, Flight Lieutenant Pooles and three unidentified crewmen in front of a 35 Squadron Halifax. This was probably taken at Linton-on-Ouse in 1942. (D. MacIntyre)

only able to put in a very few hours in the air. Ian Hewitt's logbook gives details of W1048's flights at this time. At 1440 hours on 15th April W1048 'S-Sugar' took off for her first flight as a 35 Squadron aircraft, for an hour and twenty minutes, practising air-sea firing over Filey Bay. That evening they took off again in darkness, at 22.20 hours, this time to practise low-level bombing at the range at Strensall. This flight, again lasting one hour twenty minutes, added to the crew's curiosity about the nature of the operation being planned. As training for the forthcoming raid against the *Tirpitz*, lying as she was in such inaccessible terrain, however, it really was rudimentary and inadequate, as also was some of the equipment. Ian Hewitt, W1048's navigator, comments:

"It wasn't very well planned, if you compare it with the raid on the Dortmund-Ems canal, for instance. One of the reasons the *Tirpitz* operation was a failure of course was the lack of training. They didn't select a valley so we could dive down or anything like that. We went to the bombing range at Strensall on some low-level up and downers - that was all. Also we hadn't an effective bomb-sight at that time. The hope was that there would be enough of us for one of us to hit the target. We had what was called a CSBS (Course-Setting Bombsight) which unfortunately wasn't stabilised, so that when the nose of the aircraft shifted - you're squinting through the thing and you pick up a target, and it's there, you've got it in your graticule sight - when the nose went up you lost your image. With a 'Sperry' of course (a bomb-sight that came later) they were stabilised like a ship's compass, so whatever the aircraft did you had a stabilised base."

On 17th April MacIntyre and crew took off in another of the 'new' Halifaxes that had been flown in to Linton-on-Ouse from 102 Squadron on 9th April, her serial number, W1049, immediately following that of W1048 'S-Sugar'. This time they were to carry out a 'Consumption Test'. This flight test was always made with new aircraft in order to check that the fuel supply system was working as it should. Sometimes fuel tanks were connected incorrectly to their engines or a pipe was damaged. It took an extended test flight to discover any such defects in the system. The route for these flights was invariably the same and gave all members of the crew the opportunity to practise their various skills as they flew on a course over both land and sea. MacIntyre flew W1049 from Linton-on-Ouse, on a northwesterly course to cross the coast at Whitehaven, then northwards to the Port of Ayr, westwards out to Seagull Isle - a lonely island about 200 miles out into the Atlantic Ocean - and then home. The flight lasted three hours fifteen minutes and went without incident.

The following day the final crew combination that was to fly W1048 'S-Sugar' on the raid against the *Tirpitz* came together, when Sergeant Vic Stevens joined the crew as their new flight engineer, his predecessor having been posted elsewhere.

The way in which Sergeant Stevens became a member of the crew is typical of the 'ad hoc' but generally effective arrangement by which crews were selected:

"It was an accident I was with them. What had happened was that I'd been on the previous raid to Lorient and being my first, of course, I thought I had to be back to the squadron come midday or one o'clock. But no - they usually gave crews the day off. Anyway, I wandered back to the 'flights' and as I

Wing Commander 'Jimmy' Marks.
(via Author)

came round the corner to the front of the hangar I could see an officer talking to one of the senior flight engineers. I thought 'Hello, I can't turn round now, I wonder what he wants.' The officer came over towards me and he introduced himself, and said 'I need an engineer this afternoon, are you doing anything?' I said 'No, I'm not doing anything.' So he said 'Would you like to come on a consumption test?' I said 'Yes.' So he said 'Well alright, get your gear then'."

A short while later Stevens was on his way out to the aircraft, meeting the rest of the crew for the first time. They all levered themselves through the entry hatch on the port side of the rear of the aircraft and made their way to their work stations along the narrow fuselage.

Having carried out the normal pre-flight checks W1048 'S-Sugar' then took off on the consumption test. It was a largely uneventful flight, although in fact a minor problem did occur, for at one point Sergeant Stevens reported to the pilot a loss of oil pressure in the port outer engine. As they continued the flight he kept up a running commentary on the state of the relevant gauges, but the fault was not serious and they returned to base quite safely after three and-a-half hours.

Four days later, on Wednesday 22nd April, the newly formed crew took W1048 'S-Sugar', in the company of other squadron aircraft, for a second bout of low level practice at Strensall. Gordon Cranstone, who flew as second wireless/operator/air gunner in the mid-upper turret of Flight Lieutenant Petley's aircraft (W7656:P), recalls these practice flights with amusement and a plain admiration for the skill of his pilot, a skill shared, to varying degrees, by all the other pilots who took part in the low-level raids on the *Tirpitz*:

"We weren't told what the operation was about, but we were told that it was going to be a very important trip. We were to be taken off flying over the Ruhr, and trained on low-flying tactics, which we mainly did over the area of Yorkshire. Well, when we got down to those low levels it was very exhilarating and specially as I was sitting in that mid-upper turret. When you fly at height you don't really get the feeling of speed, but the lower you come and the lower you get to the deck - well then you know you're travelling, even in those days, and the animals used to scatter everywhere, and sometimes I used to think our pilot, good as he was, dear old Petley, used to overdo it, because quite honestly - mind you he was most likely being dedicated, he wasn't doing it just to play games - when Petley did anything it had to be right. But, God, I used to see things coming in this turret, used to see things coming up and I thought God, and they went up and over - it might be a row of trees on the edge of a field or whatever it was or a haystack. I mean it sounds daft, it sounds like a line-shoot, but it wasn't. You take that kite so low to the deck, and of course you saw telegraph poles coming up and wires - once or twice I thought 'My God we're going to take the lot!' But he always used to bring it up and over, no problem."

It was not long before the navigators had deduced where the operation was to take place, as Grierson-Jackson recalls:

"We were told nothing of what it was all about, but it is impossible to initiate such training without divulging clues to those who know enough to recognise them. One such clue was the selection of stars for astro practice. Only those planets and first magnitude stars in the far northern sky were considered. Clearly that indicated something to the far north. Intensive mining of the sea lanes between Orkney Islands and Norway was the most popular guess."

And so, five days after the start of low-level practice flights and, after only a very few hours of practice, the entire squadron was called together for a briefing. The crews were told that the operation was a most important one, which was to be flown not from Linton-on-Ouse, but from an advanced base in the North of Scotland. They were told no more. A paragraph in the 'Most Secret' operation order, which was for the eyes of senior officers only, stated as follows:

"Before they proceed to and while aircraft are at their advanced bases it is essential that secrecy should be preserved regarding the intended operation against the *Tirpitz*. The success of the attack will be prejudiced if the enemy obtain information from which obvious deductions can be made. The intention and the plan is therefore to be divulged to the least number of persons consistent with adequate preparation." [16.]

Pilot Officer Don MacIntyre (2nd from left) with an unidentified 35 Squadron crew in from of a 35 Squadron Halifax Mark II, probably in Linton-on-Ouse in 1942, before the April raids. (D. MacIntyre)

Everyone was ordered to prepare for the trip up north and, at 08.00 hours on Thursday 23rd April, W1048 'S-Sugar' and ten other Halifaxes and crews of 35 Squadron set off for the two-hour flight to Kinloss in Scotland, the advance base from where they were to launch their low-level operation against the *Tirpitz*. 115 men - officers, NCOs and ground crew - who had set out two days earlier had already arrived with all the necessary equipment. At about the same time groundcrew, aircrew and Halifaxes of 10 and 76 Squadrons, were proceeding to Lossiemouth and Tain respectively, while Lancasters of 44 and 97 Squadrons were making their way to their advance base at Lossiemouth.

The five squadrons involved had, of necessity, to base themselves at three different stations, although these were within a
short distance of each other. RAF Kinloss was to be the
temporary home of the detachment from 35 Squadron. Built just
before the war, RAF Kinloss overlooked the waters of the Moray
Firth in Morayshire. Along with nearby RAF Lossiemouth and
RAF Tain, where the remaining squadrons were making
preparations, it was no stranger to operations against enemy
shipping in Norwegian waters. Since the outbreak of war
bombers had flown from there to reinforce Coastal Command
attacks against enemy shipping in the North Sea and on a
number of Scandinavian ports. In the spring of 1942, when the
Halifaxes of No 35 Squadron arrived, Kinloss was the home of
No 45 Maintenance Unit where aircraft were stored and
repaired. As Pilot Officer MacIntyre recalls, it was being used as
an OTU (Operational Training Unit) for training night bomber
crews and that the Whitley ground crews stationed there were
agog to see the 'new' four-engined Halifax bombers come in to
land!

RAF Tain, named after the nearby town of that name, was a
Fighter Sector Station that had been developed from a pre-war
landing ground. From March to April 1942 the Fleet Air Arm
flew sorties in Sea Hurricanes from there, in anticipation of
enemy resistance to the Bomber Command attacks against the
Tirpitz. The arrival of bombers on the station was the most
exciting event to occur there at that time!

Lossiemouth, built at the same time as Kinloss in 1939, had a
dual role as a bomber training and maintenance base. Concrete
runways were laid as late as 1942 in preparation for possible 5
Group attacks against the *Tirpitz*. From the headquarters at
Lossiemouth Group Captain S. Graham (the Station Commander at Leeming, the home of 10 Squadron) was again to
command the operation. He travelled north to the advanced
base on April 24th, as a passenger in Halifax W1041:B, flown by
Wing Commander Bennett, an aircraft destined to be shot down
during the forthcoming raid.

Most of the groundcrews and their equipment travelled north
by train, but Corporal Reg Saunders and Leading Aircraftman
George Smith, both with 10 Squadron, were flown up north in

*A Halifax Flight
Engineer at his post.*
(via Author)

Halifaxes. Leading
Aircraftman Smith
recalls:

"Whilst stationed at
Leeming Bar, one of
the Halifaxes I was
in charge of at that
time was part of the
force sent to RAF
Lossiemouth. The
full ground crew
flew up in the kite, but the only name I can remember from the five of us
who went is Dave Richards[17]., Leading Aircraftman (Air Frame) and
because he played a part in the events that followed, I do not imagine I shall
ever forget the name. For reasons which I don't suppose I shall ever know, a
'sprog' (inexperienced) crew flew us up and our regular crew flew up in
another of 'B' Flight's machines. It was something I did not care for at all,
my beloved Merlins being thrashed by a Sergeant Pilot with about 20 hours
training on them.

"Because of the bombs we were carrying, our route was the coastline
about two miles out, in the event, I suppose, of anything going wrong,
crashing, etc. The crew purloined a helmet complete with mike and cord for
me to listen in and take part in their gab whilst flying. We had been
airborne approximately one hour when one of the crew yelled out words to
the effect that there was a convoy below us and how about going down and
having a closer look at them. That was enough for me, I fingered the mike
switch to talk and endeavoured to get through and explain that one did not
do that to convoys and expect to live. We were sitting in the rest position
and there were several port holes on either side. I could not get through to
the crew and as I was making my way forward I glanced down and just as I
saw the convoy, I noticed two orange flashes and in a second I heard the
Flak hitting us like pebbles, rattling on the side and underneath. I got into
the cockpit, tapped the flight engineer on the shoulder, and shouted 'Get
back up, you silly _____!', and pointed upstairs. They hadn't the sense to fire
the Verey pistol which had in it the colours of the day. I then heard a
commotion from the area of the rest position and when I looked round there
was a parachute billowing around - opened! I shouted, 'What the bloody
hell's going on?' and one of the ground crew shouted back, 'Dave's pulled his
ripcord and now he's trying to open the hatch to bale out!' I nearly broke my
neck scrambling back and by the time I got to the hatch he had practically
got it open. The others were sat gawping - must have thought it was a joke.

There was no time for talk, I thumped him good and proper, dragged him away and managed to secure the hatch again. When I asked the others why they hadn't tried to restrain him, I learnt that they had not noticed the *Flak* hitting the machine. Dave had, and one piece had penetrated the fuselage bottom and popped up between his feet. He had an idea what it was and thought 'to hell with this, I'm getting out!' If he had not pulled the ripcord by mistake he would no doubt have baled out before I got to him. He smoked twenty fags in ten minutes, and said, 'They'll never get me up here again!'

"The end result was that the port inner engine coolant tank was punctured, the engine shut off and propeller feathered, and upon arrival at Lossiemouth we were ordered from the watch tower to get rid of our fuel by flying around out to sea and back again for around two hours. They would not let us jettison it in case of danger to the Air Sea Rescue launches stationed there. On landing we counted approximately 60 holes in the fuselage and that gave Dave something to take his mind off his parachute incident. I finished up with a prop change and two coolant radiators."

Flying alongside George Smith's aircraft, in 'D-Dog', was Corporal Saunders, standing in the flight engineer's position. When he realised what was happening he fired the colours of the day from the Verey pistol above his position, to alert the convoy down below. As it turned out, neither of these two aircraft took part in the raid. Apart from this occurrence, echoing as it does the attack by a coastal convoy on the aircraft flying north to take part in the raid the previous month, all the aircraft reached their advanced bases without incident.

NOTES

16. Headquarters No 4 Group Operation Order No 11.
17. Pseudonym used to preserve anonymity and avoid unnecessary embarrassment.

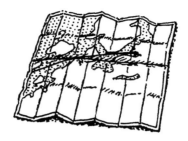

Chapter Six

The Final Briefing

On Saturday April 25th the crews at all three stations were ordered to their respective briefing rooms for the long-awaited full briefing for the raid. At last they would know where it was that they were to go. Pilot Officer MacIntyre recalls that there was considerable excitement when the crews of 35 Squadron at Kinloss heard what the target was to be.

The plan of attack had been drawn up by the Air Officer Commanding 4 Group, Air Vice-Marshal Carr. Forty-two heavy bombers of Nos 4 and 5 Groups were to attack the *Tirpitz* in Trondheim Fjord, Norway, either that night, or on the first suitable night thereafter. On the outward journey to Norway the aircraft were to fly under 5,000 feet in order to keep below the German R.D.F. (radar) cover for as long as possible. Their route was to take them directly past the Orkneys and over the islands of Shetland, changing course as they sighted Herma Ness, the northernmost tip of the Shetlands. As they flew a course that gradually converged on the Norwegian coast, the enemy would have little idea of their final destination even after the second change of course, which would

Air Vice-Marshal C.R. Carr, AOC 4 Group.

occur at 62°45'N 04°00'E, 80 miles from Aalesund. In fact they would then be on the direct route for Fætten Fjord. Their return route would take them back along the same course, although they would keep to the east of the Shetlands, making their first landfall at the Outer Skerries. Sea Rescue arrangements were made to cover the route the bombers were to fly: the Royal Navy had stationed three destroyers at points along the route to Norway to act as radio pinpoints and to rescue aircrew from the sea if the need arose. In addition, standing by to assist aircraft that ditched off the Scottish coast would be two seaplane tenders at Burghead near Kinloss and two High Speed launches at Buckie, a few miles from Lossiemouth. The offer by Coastal Command to station a submarine on the surface 300 miles out on the track of the bombers to act as a navigational aid, had been turned down by 4 Group.

Although not recorded in the official records of the briefing notes, Sergeant Stevens recalls that:

"In our briefing they said that fighters - Beaufighters and that sort of thing - would go off and shoot up the local fighter stations, just to keep them occupied and distract them."

Pilot Officer Hewitt adds:

"The navigation was, of course, the business of the navigators: Being land-trained crews and having now no radar equipment (our *GEE* sets were taken out for this particular raid as we were out of range of the station) the idea when routeing us, was to fly over as much land as possible. Our route lay first over the Orkneys and then over the Shetlands before turning for the Norwegian coast."

Having reached the Norwegian coast the aircraft were to fly directly up Trondheim Fjord and into Åsen Fjord, where the aircraft were to locate Salt Island, about one-and-a-half miles from where the *Tirpitz* lay at her moorings. This would give them a landmark from which to make their final run-in to the attack. Having dropped their mines or bombs the aircraft were then to turn to port and make their way out of the area by retracing their outward course.

The attack itself would be in two phases, with the first phase squadrons dropping bombs from a height, followed by a low-level attack by the second phase squadrons carrying the specially adapted type of mine carried on the earlier raid in March. The aircraft would spend over an hour over the target -

A PRU low-level oblique photograph of Tirpitz in Fætten Fjord, taken from the southeast. The bombers were to attack from left to right, pulling up sharply to avoid rising ground at the end of the fjord.

(via Author)

a typical length of time that was only reduced later in the war by the use of Pathfinding techniques.

Trondheim lay near the limit of flight endurance, weighed down as each of the 10 and 35 Squadron aircraft would be by the four massive three-foot diameter mines slung awkwardly between the only half shut bomb-bay doors. Shortage of fuel in the previous attacks in both January and March had been a serious problem; now any Halifax not equipped with a number 6 tank, thus giving it a capacity of 1,872 gallons, had been fitted with two extra Hampden tanks, bringing its total capacity to 1,792 gallons. The *Tirpitz* was going to be a very difficult target to hit. Camouflaged and tucked in under the lee of the northwestern bank of Fætten Fjord, her bows were held close into the staging on the shore and, although her stern projected about 30 feet into the fjord, she would be very difficult to see even in moonlight. Cliffs reached up steeply from her moorings to a height of 400 feet, which photographs taken by the PRU revealed to be largely tree-covered and pitted with cracks and crevices. The fjord itself was only 980 feet wide at this point and, although there was a strip of level ground on the southeastern side, this soon rose steeply to 700 feet. For the bombers of 35 and 10 Squadron, which would be flying in at very low level, there would be little margin for error. The planned exit from between the rapidly narrowing cliffs of the fjord would be by a steep climbing turn to port. The only other way out was to fly straight on, up the valley leading from the fjord's end.

Apart from the difficulty of flying low in mountainous country, the bomber crews would be faced with anti-aircraft fire. The ship herself had a formidable armoury of *Flak* weapons. They could expect to be fired at from the shore and from *Flak* ships as well. There were reported to be nine light guns on each of the northwestern and southeastern banks of the fjord alone, some of them mounted on platforms constructed on the uneven slopes of the hillside overlooking the battleship. Additionally, the Germans had mounted *Flak* guns in a variety of places surrounding Fætten Fjord and Åsen Fjord. It was also likely that the guns of the other two ships the *Admiral Scheer* and the *Prinz Eugen* would open up, particularly when the bombers turned from their run-in and began to make their way home, passing near the warships' berths in neighbouring Lofjord!

The chilling possibility that occurred to some of the crews of 10 and 35 Squadrons, that the Germans might have stretched wires across the fjord to catch low-flying aircraft as they approached the *Tirpitz*, was not without foundation. No Allied aircraft was brought down by such a device, although a wire was erected at the far end of Fætten Fjord some time during the war for just that purpose. Since the fjord ends in a very narrow, steep-sided valley, the Germans, mindful of the possibility of a surreptitious low-level attack from that direction, managed to stretch a cable between the hills. It is reported that the only aircraft to be caught by this 'web' was, ironically enough, a German one. Anxious that a clandestine radio was being operated in the locality by Norwegian patriots to transmit reports concerning German Navy vessels in the Åsen area, the Germans used specially equipped aircraft to pick up any such radio-signals and 'home-in' on their source. One such 'radio-homing plane' - a light, twin-engined aircraft (probably a FW 189) - flew into the cable. Its crew were killed in the resulting crash.

Units of the *Luftwaffe* were based at the airfields at Ørland, Lade and Værnes. The threat of aircraft from these units being put up to defend the target, or to attack the bombers on their way home, was countered in a more positive and comprehensive way than on the previous raid in March, although, rather surprisingly, there were few reports of sightings of enemy fighter aircraft during any of these raids. Nevertheless, aircraft of 18 Group Coastal Command were to stage a diversionary and supporting operation of some complexity, to prevent the bombers being harassed by enemy nightfighters. In order to distract the German R.D.F. units on the Norwegian coastline and at Aalesund, a dozen Hudsons and a Catalina flying boat were to patrol just off the coast for some time before and during the raid. And just before midnight four Beaufighters were to attack the airfields at Lade and Værnes where it was known that there were Messerschmitt Bf109s and '110s, Junkers 88s and Focke-Wulf 200 *Condors*. Of these, only the six Bf109s at Værnes actually constituted a threat to the bombers.

There were found to be difficulties in dealing with the unusual bomb-loads that 10 and 35 Squadrons were to carry. They were so large that the bomb-doors could not close properly, thus the aircraft would have to fly with the bomb-doors partially open. In order to release the mines, the navigator/bomb-aimer had to arm the mine electrically, prior to the run-up, then activate the release mechanism over the target. However, if a mine failed to leave the aircraft, remaining 'hung up' in the fuselage, and if it could not be released, then the crew had no option but to fly home with the live mine on board, with the possibility of it exploding as the aircraft landed. Let into the floor of the fuselage of the Halifax, in three different positions (beneath the after escape-hatch, between the two main wing-spars and near the door through to the flight engineer's compartment) were small, removable plates that provided access for the crew to reach the manual bomb releases beneath the floor. In at least one Halifax, W1048 'S-Sugar', the screws fastening two small round panels into the floor had been partly removed, leaving the flight engineer to remove the final couple of screws (as the aircraft neared the target area) and insert his hands to locate by feel two metal rings secured to the mine release cables. He was to pull on these 'toggles' as soon as the bomb-aimer had released the mines electrically, the intention being to ensure that the mines fell away properly.

The first phase of the attack involved ten Halifaxes of No 76 Squadron, carrying special light-case 4,000lb bombs, and twelve Lancasters of Nos 44 and 97 Squadrons, carrying RDX filled 4,000lb bombs. These would attempt to bomb the *Tirpitz* from 6,000 feet, using flares if necessary to identify the ship. The bombing of the ship herself was intended to cause chaos and to destroy any ship-board defences. The 4,000lb bombs (soon to be known throughout the RAF as 'Cookies'), which were to be dropped by 76 Squadron were shaped like dustbins, to slow down the speed of their descent. They were designed to explode on impact with the *Tirpitz's* deck and to produce the greatest possible blast effect in order to 'remove' the gun crews. Having released their main bombs the three bombing squadrons were then to drop their 500lb General Purpose bombs on any active *Flak* or searchlights in the neighbourhood in order to neutralise defensive anti-aircraft fire while phase two of the attack was under way. Finally they were to remain in the target area for as long as possible during the second phase to act as a diversion.

Once the higher-flying Halifaxes and Lancasters had completed their initial attacks, the second phase was to begin. Twenty Halifaxes of Nos 10 and 35 Squadrons, starting their run at 2,000 feet, were to descend to 200 feet by the time they reached the point where they were to release their mines. The bow of the *Tirpitz* was reported as facing east, towards the head of the fjord. The second phase aircraft were all to attack from west to east to minimise the possibility of collisions over the target. They were to attempt to drop their mines close to the stern and between the ship and the shore. As for the defences, it is unlikely that the Halifax crews attacking from very low level were particularly reassured by the following rather hopeful theory, which was presented to them at the briefing:

"The flak defences of the *Tirpitz* are formidable themselves, but after the shaking from those 4,000 pounders of 76, 44 and 97 Squadrons, the gun crews are quite liable to be still dizzy." [18.]

Careful timing was an essential element and had to be strictly adhered to. To avoid aircraft being hit by falling bombs the first

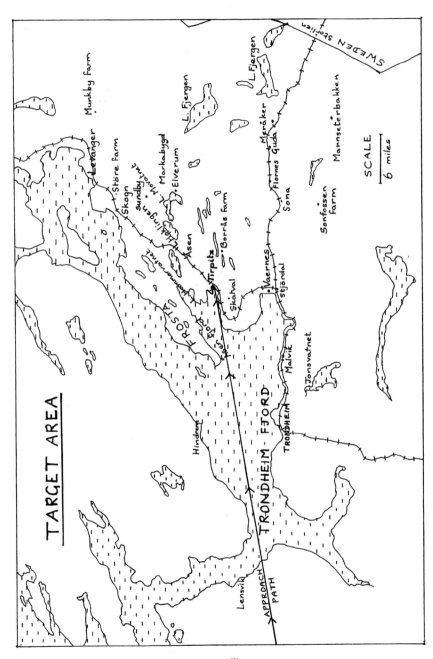

115

phase must have ceased before the second phase began. Any aircraft unable to attack the primary target, the *Tirpitz*, were ordered to attack the *Prinz Eugen* or the *Admiral Scheer*, lying one-and-a-half miles to the north of the *Tirpitz*, in neighbouring Lofjord.

One of the best defences available to the *Tirpitz* was a smokescreen, which could be used to fill the confines of the narrow fjord and prevent the bomber crews seeing her. The AOC 4 Group, Air Vice-Marshal Carr, ruled that if such a smokescreen was encountered they were to release their bombs using dead-reckoning. They were also told that if they were unable to see the target they were to aim to release their mines over the steep hillside that protected the *Tirpitz* rather than drop them on the other side of her into the water. It was assumed that mines that landed on the hillside would then roll down into the water and sink beneath her hull before exploding. It is strange that, despite photographic reconnaissance, it was not realised that the terrain of the hillside above the *Tirpitz's* berth would inevitably cause mines that were dropped there to be caught up long before they could roll down into the fjord. The effect of the hill's measured 1 in 2 slope was misleading if the nature of the ground was not taken into account.

There was no doubt about the importance attached to this operation by those of the highest authority. Pilot Officer MacIntyre recalls that, while at Kinloss, 35 Squadron was visited by Air Vice-Marshal Carr and a senior representative of the Navy. At the briefing messages from both the King and the Prime Minister, Winston Churchill, were read out to the crews: The message from the King was: *'Good Luck, we will be waiting up for your safe return.'* Churchill's message was: *'This mission you will be proud to tell to your grandchildren.'* [19.]

The Minister for Air, Sir Archibald Sinclair, attended the briefing given to 10 Squadron and Marshal of the Royal Air Force Lord Trenchard, accompanied by Winston Churchill, stressed the importance of the target to the crews of 76 Squadron at Tain.

The weather was a crucial factor in the success of the raid, for on the west coast of Norway in April winter has not yet released its grip on the land, despite the growing number of daylight

The King and Queen visit Leeming (home to 10 Squadron) in April 1942. On the right, Group Captain Graham watches the Royal couple, while Air Vice-Marshal Carr consults his watch. Don Bennett can be seen over Carr's right shoulder. (via B.Gibbons)

hours. Good visibility was essential for the bomber crews, but with warmer days and the cooling off of the land at night, there was always a chance of heavy fog in the coastal mountains and fjords. The general meteorological situation was that there was an anticyclone situated over Scandinavia and, apart from low cloud and sea-fog in patches over the sea, the conditions were clear. There were fresh southeasterly winds in the south and light variable winds in the east. However, to help the forecasting of weather conditions directly over the target area itself, a Norwegian meteorological expert had been called in. The conditions in general appeared perfect, but although the weather over the Moray Firth was bright, sunny and cold, the operation had to be called off on the first of the possible nights (Saturday the 25th) because fog in the Trondheim area was blanketing the target.

Corporal Reg Saunders of 10 Squadron recalls that while his Squadron was at Lossiemouth several of the aircraft took off for short flight tests over the Firth of Forth, carrying mines to practise their low-level technique while fully loaded. Since the bomb-bay doors could not fully close over the spherical mines the crews were told that to avoid damage to the doors by the use of the powerful hydraulic closing system they were to hand-crank them shut. Wing Commander Don Bennett warned everyone of dire consequences should the doors be damaged. After taking his own aircraft, W1041:B, out over the bay, Bennett was alarmed that he had forgotten to carry out his own order. He went up to Corporal Saunders and quietly asked him to repair the doors with wire. This Saunders did, the aircraft flying out to attack the *Tirpitz* in this condition! However, as Sergeant Ben Gibbons, second pilot in Halifax W1038:O, recalls, 'the results of these flight tests were to prove invaluable during the attacks'.

Pilot Officer Don MacIntyre, waiting with his squadron on the shores of the Moray Firth, has happy memories of this time:

"Some of the recollections of this stay at Kinloss will remain with me for some time. First, in a situation where food was always very scarce, we found on arriving at Kinloss that there was lots of good food. The meals lacked nothing, and I'll never forget the dear old lady who looked after the Mess Hall, cooking a great big turkey and stuffing it with goodies that we hadn't been accustomed to for many a month. Of course, the operation didn't come off as planned in that we stood down for two nights - and once having been stood down because of fog in the Fjord area we enjoyed ourselves to the full. One recollection that has stayed with me is that of having gone to bed, I awakened to find that my clothes had been completely washed and ironed by some very attentive WAAF who saw it as her contribution to make us as comfortable as possible under the adverse circumstances." [20.]

He made good use of the enforced postponement of the operation by very carefully studying maps and a model of the target area. This model had been prepared by the staff of the Model Making Section at RAF Medmenham, one of many models that were produced there to assist in the planning of raids and for the use of crews at operation briefings. These models were made with great care by the specialist modellers who reproduced in a three dimensional form what was interpreted from aerial photographs of target areas. With wood, a special modelling plastic and paint, the experts reproduced the target area in fine detail.

'The Highest Authority' at Leeming on 17th May, a fortnight after the raids. Foreground: Squadron Leader Seymour-Price, Wing Commander J.B. 'Willie' Tait (who was later to be involved in the sinking of the Tirpitz in 1944), Group Captain Graham, Air Vice-Marshal Carr (further back) and Winston Churchill. (via B.Gibbons)

"I can't forget the map, or a built-up papier-mache model of the area in which we were to bomb. Certainly I shall never forget in retrospect how useful it was because I knew exactly where each part of the country was in relation to the other part before I ever left northern Scotland - and how well it stood me in the knowledge that the lake in which we eventually put the aircraft was there as we expected it to be - and how that mock-up actually saved our lives." [21.]

Sergeant Stevens recalls that since aircrew on isolated stations like Kinloss had to make the best of their own resources when it came to entertainment, some of the men decided to walk up the road to the nearby village of Forres to spend that first evening in the nearest pub. They had a few drinks and at 'turning-out time' set off back to the airfield. Sergeant Stevens remembers an amusing incident that occurred as they made their way back to base:

"Now we'd been issued with whistles - this was because if you land in the drink a whistle would carry a long way across water, so all of us had been issued with these whistles - and anyway, being young and a bit merry we happily walked back through the village and suddenly somebody started blowing their whistle. Before long we were all blowing our whistles, until the local policeman came tearing out of his house. 'For God's sake,' he said, 'put those things away! That's our invasion signal! You'll have the whole countryside out!' A bit subdued we then went back to camp."

This time of waiting brought with it the chance for a bit of fun and, in quieter moments, the opportunity for some reflection of what lay ahead and the possible consequences. Pilot Officer Don MacIntyre:

"There is no doubt that on the two nights that we were stood down we did considerable partying - nor was there any doubt in any of our minds that this was an exercise from which we would not all return. However, I can truly say that I never met anybody in operations who ever thought that they would be the ones who were not going to return. It was always going to be somebody else, it was never going to be 'me'."

The weather forecast for the target area on the following night (Sunday 26th) was still unsuitable and, at 09.15 hours, Air Vice-Marshal Carr postponed the operation. Once again the men found their own way of entertaining themselves, for that night the squadron had what Stevens and Hewitt remember as 'one of the great mess-do's of all time' in the Station Mess. Sergeant Stevens had good reason to recall it:

"Everybody did his piece, either a song or a poem or jokes or anything you could think of - I sat in the corner, hid under the table; it wasn't that I didn't want to be seen, but the fact was I don't think I could have coped with balancing a pint of beer on my head. I think my stomach ached through laughing, and it was still aching next morning when I woke up. Absolutely tremendous!"

Notes

18. 4 Group Briefing Notes.
19. Pilot Officer Don MacIntyre.
20. Pilot Officer Don MacIntyre, in *FlyPast* October 1982.
21. *Ibid.*

Chapter Seven
Over The North Sea

The morning of 27th April dawned clear and cold over the Moray Firth and the hills of Northern Scotland. On the runways at RAF Stations Kinloss, Lossiemouth and Tain the Halifaxes and Lancasters of 4 and 5 Groups at their dispersal points were silhouetted by the early morning sun. Tarpaulins covered their engines to protect them from the damp. Equipment lay where it had been left the night before. It was 06.30 hours and the aircrew and groundcrew were only just getting up.

At 06.43 hours, sixty miles northeast of Kinloss across the Firth of Forth, a solitary Spitfire taxied to the end of the airfield at RAF Wick and took off in a northerly direction. Pilot Officer De Puysselyr, flying photographic reconnaissance Spitfire AA793, had orders to reconnoitre the areas of Trondheim, Værnes Aerodrome and Åsen Fjord.

The PRU sorties at this time were fraught with hazard. Of the thirty-four reconnaissance sorties that had taken place over the western coastal districts of Norway so far this month ten had not achieved successful results. In the course of these ten sorties, three aircraft had been lost, four had been adversely affected by bad weather or total cloud cover. On two occasions aircraft had returned prematurely with engine trouble and one sortie had been cancelled.

While the groundcrew at the advanced bases got to work that morning and carried out the usual daily inspections of their aircraft, De Puysselyr, wrapped up in his sidcot suit against the freezing temperature, climbed his aircraft to 30,000 feet and skilfully navigated his way by dead reckoning across the featureless sea far below to the coast of Norway. His flight went without incident and, just under five hours later, he came in to land at Wick. Within twenty minutes his report reached Operation Headquarters at Lossiemouth: the *Tirpitz* was in her usual position. Within forty minutes of his landing, this report had been expanded as a result of a brief interpretation of the photographs he had taken. All the shipping within the target area was in its usual position. Part of the full report produced by the photographic interpreters at RAF Medmenham at midnight on the 27th indicates the disposition of the enemy shipping and aircraft at 09.00 hours that morning. Although this detailed information was not available to Group Captain Graham at Lossiemouth until after the attack, it does report the true state of the target at that time. It read (in parts) as follows:

"(a) AASFJORD: *Tirpitz* present at her berth with boom closed and 'A' turret still to starboard. She is emitting smoke but most of the camouflage arranged round her stern and bow.

(b) LOFJORD: *Hipper* has returned to her previous moorings and *Scheer*, and *Eugen* remain in usual positions.

(e) VAERNES AERODROME: 13 F/W 200, 3 large aircraft, 4 JU 52, 1 large, 12 medium and 7 small aircraft visible."

Although she was emitting smoke, which could be a prelude to leaving her moorings, the fact that the anti-submarine boom around the *Tirpitz* was in place was a good indication that she would not be moving that day and would still be in the same position for an attack against her that night.

It was a question now of waiting for the most up-to-date weather forecast before Group Captain Graham could decide whether or not the operation would indeed take place that night.

Details of the planned raid were altered even as late as mid-afternoon, when Group Captain Graham decided that the aircraft of 35 Squadron should each carry an additional bomb-load of two 250lb bombs in their underwing bomb-racks. These were not for attacking the *Tirpitz*, but for dropping on *Flak* positions. By mid-afternoon the latest Coastal Command meteorological flight confirmed that the weather and visibility

Top: Although Halifax L9530 was lost over Berlin in 1941, this photograph gives an impression of the work required of ground crew in preparation for an operation. (via Author)
Bottom: This view of a 76 Squadron Halifax being 'bombed-up' gives an appreciation of the massive size of the aircraft and its bomb-load.
(R. Williams)

over the target area had improved. Conditions should be clear that night. At 16.50 hours the operation was 'definitely laid on'.

During the day the ground crews had been hard at work. Each airman had responsibility for several different aircraft. Fitters and riggers had tested the engines and the airframe, while radio engineers had checked that the radios were functioning correctly. The armourers had wheeled the bombs and mines on their trolleys out to the aircraft and had winched them yet again into the bomb-bays. On each occasion that the raid had been postponed the armourers had had to lower the bombs and mines onto their trolleys for fear that their weight would distort the airframes if left in place for too long. Four spherical Mark XIX mines had been loaded into each aircraft of 10 and 35 Squadrons. Although the size and shape of the mines made it impossible for the bomb-doors to be fully closed, giving the aircraft an unwieldy, overloaded appearance, this was not to affect their flying ability unduly, merely the fore and aft trim of the aircraft, despite the fact that they were also carrying a full fuel-load of 1,872 gallons. At Lossiemouth the Lancasters of Nos. 44 and 97 Squadrons were carrying 4,000lb RDX filled bombs, their load being made up to the full potential with 500lb G.P. (General Purpose) bombs. At Tain the Halifaxes of No 76 Squadron were carrying a single 4,000lb and four 500lb G.P. bombs each. Pilot Officer W.R. Waite of 76 Squadron recalls in his memoirs that:

> "The 4,000lb blast bomb, looking like a huge dustbin, was so large it could not be contained inside the bomb-bay with the doors closed - these had to be pumped up by hand until they rested on the belly of the bomb. The armourers had a difficult, sweaty job, winching these monsters on board, and one described the Halifax's appearance as that of a pregnant mayfly!"
> 22.

Many miles to the north of the advanced bases, where the final preparations were being carried out by the bomber ground crews, *Operation Bluebeard* had already begun. This operation was being mounted by Coastal Command to divert German attention from the main raiding force and to attempt to prevent German nightfighters from attacking the bombers of this main force.

At about 18.00 hours the crew of a Coastal Command Catalina was ferried by service launch out to their aircraft, where it lay idly pulling at its mooring-rope in the sheltered bay at Sumburgh in the Shetlands. This was Catalina AH535:J of 210 Squadron. The pilot, Flight Lieutenant Eadie with his second pilot and the remainder of the crew, climbed aboard. Although unaware of the purpose of this operation, Pilot Officer

A Catalina crew boarding their aircraft at Oban, preparatory to setting out on a sortie. (E. Schofield)

John G. Walker, the second pilot, had already flown on four sorties to the Norwegian coast and flew on two more after this one:

"As second pilot I did not attend the pre-flight briefings and so did not have a detailed knowledge of the purpose of the flights. Normally these were flown at 50/100 feet in order to keep under the German Radar, as we had no desire to attract unfriendly attentions from the German fighters. The sortie on April 27/28th lasted eleven and-a-half hours of which six were at night. I did not realise that we were part of an effort to swamp the German Radar (perhaps as well for my peace of mind). I have only two recollections of these patrols over Norway. The first was a magnificent view of the Norwegian mountains as we approached the coast. The second was a patrol in bad weather. We were flying at 50 feet, with a full load of petrol, when one of the engines started to give trouble. I looked out at the raging sea underneath and wondered what our chances were. Fortunately the trouble cleared itself. The Catalina was not a comfortable aircraft. It was draughty and it was difficult to keep warm however many clothes you had on. The patrols were long and it was difficult to keep alert especially as you probably had had only an hour or two asleep before take off."

They cast off from the mooring, taxied downwind, turned and finally took off in a flurry of spray at 18.30 hours. The crew settled down for the long, tedious hours of the flight.

Catalina 'J' reached the Norwegian coast at Halten Light and proceeded to patrol along the coastline changing course at various points. The crew reported that from 00.01 hours onwards they observed flashes of light from Trondheim. They flew back to base and touched down on the water at 05.30 hours, thus safely concluding one of their shorter patrols.

Two other aircraft were despatched with the same objective - the saturation of the enemy R.D.F. These were two Hudsons, 'W' from 608 Squadron and 'Y' from 48 Squadron. They met no other aircraft, although 'W' observed considerable activity - explosions and *Flak* - in the region of Trondheim that night. The crews of these three aircraft had witnessed, albeit at great distance, the attack taking place against the *Tirpitz*.

As the light began to fade from the sky on the evening of the 27th the bomber crews prepared for take-off. They nervously climbed aboard the crew truck where they joined the crews of other Halifaxes sharing the same dispersal area, all relieved that at last the period of waiting was over. Just before an operation most aircrew suffered, understandably, from nervousness of what lay ahead, as Sergeant Gordon Cranstone of 35 Squadron (who was to survive a ditching in Trondheim Fjord during the raid of 28th/29th April) remarks:

"I'll say one thing, I can honestly say I never flew without being frightened, I was always frightened. You see, I think you've got to be honest. Whenever I got into an aircraft I was always apprehensive and frightened, because, you know, things can happen. I won't say I knew something would happen that night, but I was always frightened of what might happen. But then it's a thing you have to conquer."

Once on board the aircraft most of the crews were too busy to think about anything else but their job; it was easier not to be apprehensive once the waiting was over. At Tain, where 76 Squadron crews were preparing for take-off, Pilot Officer W.R. (Ronnie) Waite remembers that:

The 'Boys of Coastal'

Top Left: Pilot Officer John Walker (back row far left), skipper of his own crew at Sullom Voe in 1942. (W. Balderson)
Top Right: Pilot Officer Richard Fairley, Navigator on Catalina AH535:J during 'Operation Bluebeard'. (J. Walker)
Below: Wing Commander W.H. Hutton, Commanding Officer of 210 Squadron (centre front) with Pilot Officer Fairley (left front). Both flew Catalina AH535:J during 'Operation Bluebeard'.

(via W. Balderson)

"The atmosphere inside our aircraft was expectant rather than tense. I felt - we probably all did - an inward excitement at the sound of the Merlin engines as they opened up to full power."

As the crew of W1048 'S-Sugar' prepared to climb aboard Sergeant Stevens remembers that the ground staff, including 'Chiefy', the Flight Sergeant in charge, gathered round to shake hands with them. He also recalls having a strange premonition that he would not be returning that night, but he dismissed this thought as soon as it occurred and got down to work.

Stevens recalls that he and his pilot, Don MacIntyre, carried out a brief inspection around the outside of the aircraft before climbing aboard to check that all the instruments were reading satisfactorily. Around them the other members of the crew were busy at their work.

Pilot Officer Ian Hewitt, navigator, sat at his table on the port side, near the nose of the aircraft. He spread out his chart and fastened it down with pins. Nearby he had his 'Nav. bag' with a good supply of sharp pencils and several india-rubbers. At his feet was the escape hatch and nearby was the padded couch on which he would lie when the time came to drop the mines. He checked the route he had pencilled in with great care after the briefing two days earlier, for it was affected by one unusual factor; they would be flying without the assistance of radar, by using dead reckoning only. He looked at his chart. They were to fly at 4,000 feet over the Orkneys and then the Shetlands before heading out to sea to make for the coast of central Norway. The aircraft were to carry out the usual procedure of making their own way to the target, arriving at their own individually pre-determined time. Navigation was thus the main responsibility of the navigator in each aircraft, although the wise pilot kept a general check on the route at the same time, thus ensuring that if something happened to the navigator the pilot would have a good chance of finding his way home.

Behind the bulkhead to the left of where he sat, Hewitt could hear the wireless operator, Dave Perry, seated directly below the pilot, preparing the equipment in front of him for the flight. As well as being the first wireless operator, Sergeant Perry would assist during take-off by sitting in the second pilot's seat.

Wilson in the rear gun turret and Blanchet in the mid-upper turret, rotated their turrets once or twice to ensure they were

A Halifax Mark II (via Author)

functioning properly, then sat listening to the sounds of the remainder of the crew getting ready. As gunners they would have little to do until they could test their guns over the sea.

MacIntyre and Stevens prepared to start the engines. By now the ground crew had plugged their external trolley-acc (accumulator) into the side of the aircraft and the power from its two massive batteries was turned on. Stevens switched the fuel cocks to numbers 1 and 3 tanks. First the port inner and then the remaining engines, roared into life. Then they checked that all the instruments were reading satisfactorily, before MacIntyre finally eased off the brakes. W1048 'S-Sugar' slowly taxied around the circuit towards the end of the runway. Although the light was beginning to fade from the early evening sky, the crew could clearly see the other aircraft as they ponderously jolted into position for take off.

The squadron was being led on this operation by Wing Commander Jimmy Marks and, at 20.20 hours, his Halifax, W7657:L, sped down the runway. Four minutes later his was followed by Squadron Leader Peter Cribb's aircraft, W1047:R and, at 20.30 hours, W1048 'S-Sugar's' engines roared up to full throttle as her brakes were released and she slowly picked up speed down the concrete runway to become airborne. She climbed after take-off and headed in a northerly direction while the crew settled down for the three and-a-half hour flight.

Flying Officer Hewitt comments:

"Our aircraft took off one after the other, but navigation as usual was to be left to each single aircraft, therefore from the moment of take off we were an aircraft on our own and under orders to sink a battleship (although none of us at that time would ever have thought of it in anything like so dramatic a way)." [23]

At about the same time the Lancasters and Halifaxes at nearby Tain and Lossiemouth were also getting airborne. Acting Flight Lieutenant Miller, pilot of Halifax W1037 'U-Uncle', recalls that 10 Squadron's leader, Wing Commander Bennett, renowned for his pre-war navigational skills, and soon to become the leader of the Pathfinder squadrons, took the unusual step of marking the way for the aircraft of his squadron to follow:

"We flew low all the way to Norway led by Wing Commander Bennett who dropped flame floats all the way and as the night was calm, the sea dead flat, they were easy to follow."

Flying Officer Jack Watts, observer in 10 Squadron's W1038 'O-Orange', remembers the long hours of the flight over the featureless sea:

"Though night flying was normal for our bombers, we were operating from a strange field and in a different sector of the sky. The flight over those cold, dark waters seemed longer and lonelier than before. It would be about four hours before we made landfall, with nothing positive to confirm our navigation along the way. Search and rescue facilities were just about non-existent, and the water temperature would make death quick and certain for any who were so unfortunate as to have to ditch or bail out. Despite the absence of enemy defences, the flight out was not particularly comforting." [24]

Not all of the aircraft, however, were to get as far as the target area. Warrant Officer Osborne and his crew must have watched with anxious anticipation as the Lancasters of 44 Squadron took off from Lossiemouth, for their aircraft, R5492 'M-Mother', was on standby. Would they be needed? Sure enough, within minutes of the last aircraft lumbering into the air, L7545 'K-King' was sighted, returning to land. Her rear-gunner had discovered almost as soon as the aircraft was airborne, that his turret was unserviceable. His skipper, Warrant Officer Wright, decided that he could not hazard his crew on this operation without the protection of the rear guns. As soon as they had landed and it was realised that the rear-turret could not be repaired in time to return to the operation, Warrant Officer

Osborne and crew took off in R5492 'M-Mother'. Lancaster L7581, also of No 44 Squadron, failed to fly more than a few miles before her port outer engine overheated. Her pilot, Flight Sergeant Jones, had noticed liquid leaking from this engine on take-off and, when this emission turned to steam, it became obvious that the engine was unserviceable. Flames were seen coming from her exhaust as the pilot ordered the bomb-aimer to jettison his bomb-load 'safe' in the waters of the bay before returning to base where they landed within thirty minutes of take-off. The engine was completely seized up and would have to be changed. Flight Sergeant Jones and his crew never did make it to the *Tirpitz*.

Wing Commander Young, leading the Halifaxes of 76 Squadron, was also unable to complete the operation. Two hours into the flight the starboard inner engine of R9447 'R-Robert' failed. Young feathered the engine's propeller but, when he realised that with the weight of bombs on board he still could not maintain height, he had no other option but to jettison his bombs 'safe' over the sea, which he did at 22.22 hours. Then they returned to Tain.

It took an hour and a quarter, from 20.01 to 21.15 hours, for the entire Main Force to become airborne from the three bases. Forty-two bombers from five squadrons were now on course for Norway.

———

All the aircraft of 35 Squadron successfully made the journey. As soon as W1048 'S-Sugar' was airborne Stevens operated the cocks in the fuel pipes to switch the fuel supply from the inboard tanks to the outer ones. This was to reduce the weight of fuel in the outer wings as soon as possible. He then reported the state of the fuel supply to the pilot, then regularly kept him informed in this way throughout the flight. Their target lay at the maximum range and the level of fuel in the tanks was thus of vital importance.

Flying in an early Halifax was a cold business. It had a ducted hot-air heating system that worked off the engine exhausts, but it was somewhat primitive and most aircrew wore 'long-johns', two pairs of socks, boots, helmet and two pairs of gloves with gauntlets on top. Don MacIntyre comments that 'In relation to footwear some aircrew had flying boots of leather that fitted inside the trousers - others, especially gunners - wore heavy wool-lined boots that fitted over normal footwear.' Despite all their gear some of the crew felt cold. Within an hour of take-off Hewitt, seated in the nose of the aircraft, was numb with cold. He took off his parachute harness and wrapped it around his chilled feet where they rested near the forward emergency escape hatch. He recalls:

"Early after take off, I made the first of a number of mistakes that might well have cost me my life. I had decided (quite wrongly as subsequently proved by other airmen) that attacking at mast height would give us no chance to bale out. I therefore removed my parachute harness which I wrapped round my feet, as one could feel the cold in those early Halifaxes."[24.]

Hewitt was not the only crew member to disregard his parachute. As Wilson had squeezed himself into his rear gun turret before they had taken off he had, as usual, put his parachute into the rack just inside the fuselage behind his turret-door; but he had not bothered to put on his harness - he felt it was just an encumbrance in the cramped turret.

Positioned where he was in the aircraft - either standing at his instrument panel just behind the cockpit, or sitting on the small seat nearby that pulled down from the starboard side of the fuselage (making calculations and entering his records on a pad on his knee) - Stevens felt extremely warm, so warm, in fact, that he almost wished the heating could be turned off! He was fortunate enough to be right next to one of the heating ducts.

Ian Hewitt continues:

"By the time we had passed Herma Ness at the northern-most tip of the Shetlands we were approaching nearly half way to Trondheim. It was thus a matter of steering something like 040 degrees for four to five hundred miles - or about three hours flying. We did not have anything much to go on over the sea, but the forecast winds with which we had been provided to calculate our courses must have been fairly accurate. Anyway, we hit the Norwegian coast more or less on time." [25.]

At that time of year in those latitudes it was still light enough to see the land below them and, having made their course change, they left the land behind, a darkening smudge on the wide horizon.

In the rear gun-turret Wilson stared out at the receding coastlines of the Shetland Islands and the steel-grey of the twilit sea. He had fired a few rounds of his guns into the sea shortly after take-off and now occasionally rotated his turret as he looked around just in case there was anything hostile in the dim evening sky. No one was expecting to see enemy nightfighters, but it was just as well to keep alert and watchful.

Hewitt tried to take a star-sight through the astro-dome, but the stars in the late evening sky were not easy to see and, flying at only 4,000 feet, the aircraft was bucking about in the air turbulence so much that it proved impossible. Nevertheless, his navigation by dead reckoning, taking account of the forecast winds, was to prove most accurate.

As he went about his work before his faintly glowing dials Stevens caught, through the side windows, occasional glimpses of other aircraft droning through the air in loose formation, gently rising and falling in the night air, their tell-tale exhausts glowing a dull red against the evening sky.

Apart from the occasional course-change, the flight out to Norway went without incident. Pilot Officer Waite, in Halifax R9486:Q, remembers seeing the coast as it loomed out of the distance, a beautiful and dramatic scene of 'snow-capped mountains that rose sheer from the fjords':

> "The Norwegians in their isolated farms and hamlets, hearing the sound of our engines, were aware that British bombers were overhead. Now and again lights appeared from windows; several times we saw curtains being drawn and withdrawn. These brave people were sending us the famous 'V for Victory' signal. I wished we could let them know what terrific encouragement it gave us." [26.]

Already, over the mountains and fjords of Norway, aircraft of Coastal Command were preparing the way for the bombers. The diversionary force dispatched by 18 Group Coastal Command in support of the main attacking force of bombers was small, amounting to only twenty-one aircraft in all. Their task was to prevent the bomber force being attacked during the raid and on its return, as well as diverting attention from the area around the *Tirpitz*.

Four Beaufighters were to attack Værnes and Lade aerodromes, another four were to attack Herdla aerodrome, with the intention of neutralising any enemy fighters that might harass the main force's bombers on their route home. Ten Hudsons were to attack shipping at Aalesund. Catalina AH535:J of 210 Squadron was already patrolling the coast of Norway in an attempt to saturate the enemy's RDF station situated on the off-shore island of Stokken. Further south, two long-range Hudsons were to carry out their reconnaissance patrol, also just off the coast, in order to preoccupy the RDF station at Kristiansund North.

Beaufighters 'T' and 'W' of 235 Squadron took off at about 21.20 hours and flew together over the North Sea on a direct course for Norway. They flew over the maze of islands that heralded the approach of the Norwegian coastline at 22.48 hours, after an uneventful ninety-minute flight, then turned onto a northeasterly heading flying at about 500 feet overland for some miles. Map-reading at low level over the Norwegian landscape flashing past beneath them was not easy for the crews, for it was difficult for them to distinguish the snow-lined valleys from the numerous lakes that dotted the desolate landscape. Just over an hour later they made another course change to fly directly north for Værnes, now only a few miles away.

Flying at low level over the mountainous regions of Norway is dangerous in daylight, more so at night. Many of the fjords are narrow, steep-sided and twisting, often ending abruptly and unexpectedly in a steep cliff face. An aircraft flying at low level along such a fjord could suddenly find itself rapidly approaching a rock wall with no room to turn round, the only exit being a steep climb over the summit ahead, where down-drafts of air spilling over into the fjord added to the risks. There is no doubt that the crews of the Beaufighters that flew low and fast over this territory had to fly with great skill, for a brief lapse of concentration could so suddenly bring disaster.

Squadron Leader Cook, flying 'T' on its new course, suddenly glimpsed a red light only 300 yards away to port. His immediate thought was 'Nightfighter!' and he reacted instantly by putting his Beaufighter into a diving turn to starboard, losing touch

The Bristol Beaufighter was fast and heavily armed. It formed the backbone of the Coastal Command strike wings. The lack of dihedral on the tailplanes shows this to be an early Mark I model. (via Author)

with 'W' as he did so. About five miles to the north Squadron Leader Cook also saw white flashes over the position of the *Tirpitz* and realised that the attack on the battleship had begun. It was now past midnight and, since his orders were to attack Værnes no later than midnight, he realised he had arrived too late. He turned for the coast, passing the city of Trondheim to starboard and finally leaving the friendly lights of many scattered Norwegian communities behind him as he set course for home.

Pilot Officer Crow in Beaufighter 'W', now separated from 'T' and flying at 1,500 feet, saw white and orange flashes bursting in the sky over the *Tirpitz* only five miles to the north and circled, turning south, looking for Værnes. He picked up the Stjørdalselva, the river that ran westwards towards the aerodrome and followed this, diving down to 100 feet to make his attack. However, the lights he took to be the target turned out to be those of a village and, since it was now past midnight, he too abandoned the idea of carrying out his attack. At 00.08 hours, making a speed turn to port Pilot Officer Crow suddenly identified the southern edge of the blacked-out aerodrome, surrounded by lighted houses. He could clearly see the runways lit up by the moonlight and was relieved that no *Flak* came arching after him from the darkness below. But it was too late to attack, so he flew southwards. An hour later, having curved round to the south of Trondheim on his way to the coast, Pilot

Officer Crow and his observer Squadron Leader Wigmore were startled by a huge white flash from the Trondheim area that, even at a range of several miles, lit up the inside of the aircraft. As they made their way down the rocky coast of Norway they saw numerous small vessels carrying lights. In fact they saw many lights along the shore and gained the impression that these lights came on only as they came abreast of them. Both 'T' and 'W' arrived back at base within minutes of each other, about four and-a-half hours after leaving. From a distance they had witnessed the main bomber force's attack, but had been too late to aid them by attacking the aerodrome at Værnes.

Squadron Leader Cartridge and Sergeant Osbourne in Beau-fighter 'A' and Acting Wing Commander E.L. Hyde and Flight Sergeant J. Paget in 'X', both of 248 Squadron, took off a few minutes later than 'T' and 'W'. They made their landfall a little to the south, nearer Aalesund. Flying at between 200 and 500 feet above the ground between the mountains, they flew inland up Langfjord, heading directly for Trondheim. Four minutes before midnight they recognised Jons Lake, which lay only a few miles to the west of Trondheim. 'A', continuing to formate on 'X', now flying at only 50 feet from the ground, turned to port and headed for the city.

Heavy *Flak* opened up dead ahead and Squadron Leader Cartridge watched as 'X' crossed the brow of a hill to his starboard and vanished from view. Immediately, the *Flak*, which had been bursting as red balls high in the air over the town, intensified. Pale blue, yellow, green and red tracer filled the sky from all directions as 'A' roared over the city. Squadron Leader Cartridge was unable to take action to evade the *Flak* for fear of colliding with buildings or the neighbouring hills. Suddenly, *Flak* struck the perspex in front and to the starboard of where Cartridge sat, shattering it and smashing the compass light. Splinters of *Flak* and perspex wounded him in the right arm. Despite this he managed to guide his aircraft out over the submarine base in the harbour, where they were attacked with accuracy by *Flak* batteries and armed merchant ships outside the submarine base. He swung his aircraft to starboard and headed for Lade Aerodrome, a short distance away, but was immediately picked up by a mauve-coloured searchlight beam as he prepared for his run-in on the target. Although partially blinded by the beam Cartridge caught a glimpse of the runway and, skimming the ground at 20 feet, he opened fire with a three-second burst with his cannon and machine-guns. Neither he nor Osbourne observed any hits, but they flew over a hill and sped on south towards Jons Lake. As they did so they were picked up by another mauve searchlight, which blinded Osbourne. As they topped the crest of the hill Cartridge put the Beaufighter into a contour-hugging dive and soon they had left behind the intense *Flak* and the searchlight beams. To the north they noticed heavy and intense *Flak* and observed three very large white bursts that they took to be bomb-bursts. From Jons Lake they retraced their outward track and gradually left behind the *Flak* that still lit up the sky in the Åsen region. Of 'X' there was no sign. The last the crew of Beaufighter 'A' had known of her was seeing her cannon and machine-gun fire, although they had been unable to see the aircraft itself. Presumably damaged by *Flak*, Beaufighter 'X' had crashed into the waters of Trondheim Fjord, a short distance from the city itself. Both members of her crew, Wing Commander E. L. Hyde and Flight Sergeant J. E. Paget, were recovered by the Germans from the wreckage. Flight Sergeant Paget was dead and Wing Commander Hyde died shortly afterwards. They were the only men to lose their lives during *Operation Bluebeard*.

The SIS agent Bjørn Rørholt vividly recalls this aspect of the raid, which he witnessed from a vantage point in Trondheim that night:

"On the evening of the 27th of April 1942 I observed the attack by the British Air Force which was quite a lively performance - they also attacked Trondheim - but the main target of course was the *Tirpitz*.

"I was standing on the hill right in front of the building of the Technical University with a good view of the town. It was not terribly high up, the hill was much higher behind me, but I had a good view of the entire bowl of lower Trondheim town, and I could see the harbour, the railway, it was a fairly good observation point. I had walked up there because it was my last evening in Trondheim, and I walked up there to take a look over the town and to get some fresh air - I had been coding some messages and I was feeling rather tight and I was just relaxing. And then all of a sudden this thing happened.

"It was getting dark and I observed one plane that came from the easterly direction, and I saw it turn around the fortress of Kristiansten and come towards me, and then turn again, low over the town so that the ack-ack actually went downward. The ack-ack was on the heights around Trondheim - you could see the tracers, they were going down on the plane. And then the plane turned and went over the harbour (the harbour that was used for float-planes) and then it went round what is known as Bynesset, a piece of high ground in the area, where it could hide behind and still go over the fjord.

"Now the Germans thought that that plane had fallen into the sea, and they made all kinds of searches for it, but they never found it, and my conclusion is that this was an aircraft that saved itself by going behind that protrusion (the high ground) and then had gone out over the fjord and hopefully back home. It was an inferno of ack-ack fire, but it was so close, you know, difficult to follow, very close, and whether or not it dropped any bombs I can't tell.

"I stood there for at least an hour, and the noise wasn't over when I left."

The aircraft Rørholt saw must have been either Beaufighter 'A' or 'X', the former making it safely home, the latter crashing in Trondheim Harbour, killing its crew.

Four other Beaufighters from 248 Squadron were detailed to attack Herdla Aerodrome, 200 miles to the south of Trondheim. Beaufighters 'G', 'D' and 'T' flew in formation with 'Q' leading the way, having taken off at 23.38 hours. Half an hour later 'G' lost contact with the formation and thereafter continued on her way alone. After an hour and a quarter, at 00.55 hours, the remaining three aircraft, still flying in formation, spotted the Norwegian coast about 30 miles ahead. They approached the coast and flew up it at a height of only 300 feet before turning inland, diving down to 50 feet over the town of Toft and then flying up Hjelte Fjord at 400 feet. At this height, beneath the bright moon shining in a cloudless sky on their port quarter, a slight sea mist had reduced the visibility to about one mile.

Two miles south of the target both 'D' and 'Q' were caught in the glare of two blue searchlights. Taking evasive action, 'D' turned and dived to 100 feet. Under fire, she was unable to attack the dispersal points on Herdla aerodrome. Instead the crew strafed the gun positions that flanked the main runway. One minute later she set course for home.

'Q', caught in the beam of one of the searchlights, was immediately fired upon by batteries on nearby islands and from the aerodrome itself. Red, green, yellow and blue *Flak* spangled the night sky. She ran over the main runway at 200 feet, firing her cannon and machine-guns and, as she left the aerodrome behind, she fired at a *Flak* post on a nearby island, before setting course for base.

When 'Q' and 'D' broke formation 'T' continued directly towards the target. A *Flak* battery opened up on her with heavy shell fire as she came in over the target at 200 feet. She was surrounded by green, white and red tracer, and also rockets that left a fierce trail of green smoke. 'T' dived to water level to escape the worst of the gunfire, then climbed to 300 feet to avoid hitting a balloon that fortunately had just been lit up by the white beam of a searchlight. The pilot decided that the *Flak* was too intense to carry out his attack and, abandoning it, he set course to the west, diving to sea level as he left the coast.

'G', which had lost touch with the others half way across the North Sea, arrived over the area of Herdla aerodrome at about the same time as the others and was fired upon. However, her crew was unable to locate the target with any certainty, despite sighting a fire in the middle of one of the islands. They flew around for about half an hour, carrying out a search for Herdla aerodrome, but finally, reluctantly, they had to give up the search and, at 01.30 hours, set course for base, landing at Sumburgh just before 03.00 hours.

Ten Hudson aircraft were despatched that night to Aalesund, an area some way to the south of the *Tirpitz's* anchorage. Their primary target was the shipping in the harbour there, although on arrival only one aircraft actually found any shipping to attack. That was a lone small motor vessel one-and-a-half miles from Aalesund, which one crew raked with gunfire from the forward guns while the pilot released four 250lbs G. P. bombs, one of which definitely struck the vessel.

Upon finding no shipping in the harbour several of the Hudsons dive-bombed oil tanks, their secondary targets, setting some of these on fire. One Hudson reported seeing two Halifaxes en route to Trondheim, while another spotted a Ju88 at a range of 1,000 yards. Fortunately it did not attack.

Another Hudson, encountering intense light and heavy *Flak* aimed at previous aircraft, decided to attack the secondary target instead. But despite cruising around for 65 minutes this crew was unable to find any oil tanks to bomb and finally set course for base.

Notes

22. From the draft manuscript of *Death or Decoration*. Newton, 1991
23. From *FlyPast* October 1982
24. *Ibid*
25. *Ibid*
26. From the draft manuscript of *Death or Decoration*. Newton, 1991

Chapter Eight
The Main Attack

For the inhabitants of Åsen there had been a feeling of spring in the air that day. Although the snow still clung to the forests and hills all around, the weather had been mild. The moon rose that night to add its light to the slowly fading twilight. But around midnight the calm was suddenly shattered by a spectacle never to be forgotten by those who witnessed it, as the few people who

Taken in 1973, this photograph shows the approach to Fætten Fjord, with Saltøya (Salt Island) on the left. Fætten Fjord is in the centre middle distance, the wooded southeastern slopes coming down to the water opposite where Tirpitz lay in 1942. (S. Usher)

were still awake in their houses in the Åsen area heard the unaccustomed roar of distant aircraft approaching. They realised that a major attack on the enemy ships in the fjord was about to begin.

The first of these aircraft flew up Trondheim Fjord, then on into Åsen Fjord. Suddenly, large areas of countryside were bathed in a strange bright light as parachute-flares, dropped by the attacking bombers, shed their eerie orange glow over Fætten Fjord and the battleship lying there. The *Flak* guns by the shores of the fjord began to fire, one after another in a chain-like sequence as the heavy four-engined bombers roared overhead. The brightly-coloured tracer spat into the air, while the searchlights stabbed their bright fingers into the sky. The attack on the *Tirpitz* had commenced shortly after midnight and, by the time W1048 'S-Sugar' and the second wave of aircraft were circling off the coast, the first phase had been in progress for some time. All crews that night found that there was excellent visibility with no cloud cover at all. In fact the nearly-full moon and the still-twilit northern skies made map reading possible right up to the target.

Details in the records imply that Lancaster R5515:A of No 44 Squadron was the first aircraft to attack. She had made her landfall at the offshore island of Smola, about 70 miles to the west of Trondheim. Then she had flown inland, climbing all the time, to pinpoint her position above the junction of the Orkedal and Gaulosen Fjords to the west of the city. Leaving Trondheim on her starboard side she then made her approach to the *Tirpitz* up the Strind Fjord at a height of 12,000 feet. Over Værnes Aerodrome she was attacked by what her pilot, Warrant Officer Stott, called 'intense accurate predicted heavy *Flak*', but was not hit. Making her run-up to the target she went into a dive, pulled out at 7,500 feet and, at 00.06 hours, released her 4,000lb bomb over the *Tirpitz*. She then flew out of the worst of the *Flak* concentration surrounding the battleship and dropped her stick of 500lb bombs on a *Flak* battery on a peninsular in Åsen Fjord. Cruising about the area, she observed other aircraft attacking the ship until, at 00.40 hours and thirty-four minutes after dropping her first bomb, she set course for home.

THE GERMAN DEFENCES FROM 1942 ONWARDS

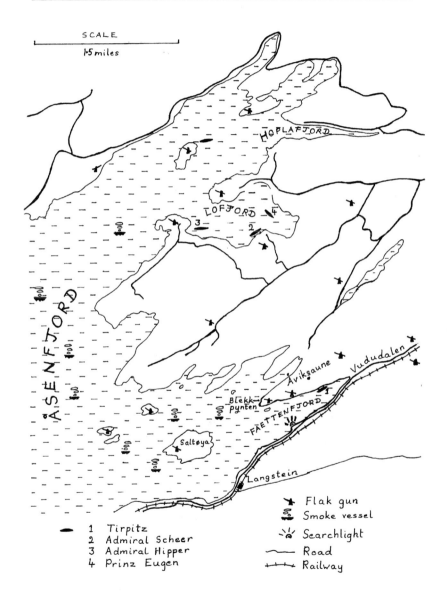

SCALE

1·5 miles

HOPLAFJORD

LOFJORD

3

2

4

ÅSENFJORD

Aviksaune

Vududalen

Blekk-pynten

FÆTTENFJORD

Saltøya

Langstein

1   Tirpitz
2   Admiral Scheer
3   Admiral Hipper
4   Prinz Eugen

Flak gun
Smoke vessel
Searchlight
Road
Railway

143

One after another now, the bombers came into the attack. As they approached the *Tirpitz* from the east they came under intense defensive fire. Tracer from *Flak* positions in the area soared up into the sky on all sides, vividly reflecting in the water of the fjords, as explosions rocked the aircraft, flooding the cockpits with brief flashes of brilliant light. The roar of the Merlin engines competed with the percussion of explosions, as the bomb-aimers, ignoring the bombardment around them as best they could, concentrated on keeping the *Tirpitz* in their sights before pressing the bomb-release button. As the words 'Bombs gone' were announced into the intercom, each aircraft pulled up out of the attack and left the fiercest *Flak* behind as it swung round to find a *Flak* position or a searchlight on which to release its smaller bombs. More than one pilot found the *Flak* so fierce that, when his aircraft lightened and surged upwards as the bombs fell away, he had to take such violent evasive action that none of the crew were able to see whether or not their bomb had hit the target. A number of crews saw a flash over the ship, or very close to it, as their bomb fell. Some believed that they had scored a very near miss, the bomb either throwing up fountains of spray within 100 yards of the stern of the ship, or striking the water between the cliff side and the ship's hull.

It was twelve minutes past midnight, six minutes after the attack had begun, when the crew of Lancaster R5494 'O-Orange' noted that a smoke screen was just beginning at the mouth of Fætten Fjord. From then on smoke hindered most of the crews to a greater or lesser extent. There were six different *Flak* batteries on the hillsides around Fætten Fjord alone, with others elsewhere. The attack went on for well over an hour and-a-half and, during that time, the electrically operated 'smoke pots', manned by full time crews and located at various points on the shores and islands of the fjords in the area, had to be ignited and then replaced once they had discharged their smoke. The situation was confused further by smoke from the intense light and heavy *Flak* barrage put up by the shore and ship-based defenders and by the great fountains of spray thrown up by bombs and mines hitting the water.

The height from which the Lancasters and Halifaxes dropped their 4,000lb bombs varied from between 8,000 and 6,000 feet.

It was a matter of luck, though, whether any given aircraft was able to see the target - some had to release their bomb on a position computed by dead reckoning, while others bombed the smoke directly over the battleship without actually seeing her at all, or at most only seeing her indistinctly through the smoke. Several of the attacking aircraft had the battleship in their bomb-sights when the bombs were released, but had no idea whether or not they had hit her. Sergeant E. Morrell, flight engineer in Squadron Leader 'Hank' Iveson's Halifax (W1013 'E-Easy' of 76 Squadron) remembers their aircraft being caught in a searchlight-beam as they flew over the *Tirpitz*:

Flight Sergeant Kenny Clack, who was awarded the DFM for his part in the April raids.
(R. Williams)

"We were coned by the searchlights just after our bombs were dropped. Hank put the plane into a dive and twisted and turned out of the beam. He said, 'I'm sorry lads, I've got to pull out - I'm down to 2,000 feet'. On pulling out we found ourselves flying at a low altitude parallel to the coast of the fjord just off Trondheim. Light *Flak* was coming up at us - tracers seemed to be coming between the mid-upper turret and the tail-plane. Hank ordered the gunners to fire, and with the smell of cordite in our nostrils we climbed out of the fjord and got back to base without further incident."

One Halifax of 76 Squadron, R9486 'Q-Queenie', arrived too late to attack the *Tirpitz* at all and so, at 00.45 hours, attacked the alternative targets, the heavy cruiser *Prinz Eugen* and the pocket battleship *Admiral Scheer*, where they lay at anchor in Lofjord, a little to the north of the *Tirpitz*. Pilot Officer Ronnie Waite was flying in 'Q-Queenie' as second pilot, 'more for the operational experience, than the simple duties I had to perform', alongside the nineteen year old pilot, Flight Sergeant Kenny Clack. It was Clack's twentieth operation, but Ronnie's first and he remembers it vividly:

"A few miles ahead, the sky was filled with the flashes of exploding *Flak*. Our spot in the sky seemed unnaturally quiet when, with frightening suddenness, searchlights started appearing from nowhere - flashing across the sky, searching for us, lighting the cockpit with a split second's brilliance."

They released their four 500lb bombs successfully, but the single 4,000 pounder hung-up as they flew over the target. They realised that they would have to make a second run, for, as their captain Flight Sergeant Kenny Clack observed, 'We haven't come this far to drop it in the sea'. This time, as they flew over the two ships below, 'Tubby' Lawes the flight engineer pulled on the manual releases when the navigator pressed the release switches near his bomb-sight. And this time the bomb fell away and the pilot pulled the aircraft out of the attack-run. Ronnie Waite continues:

"For the second time, our pilot took a steep turn away from the target, then straightened up, climbing to clear the mountain. As we did so, a large black fjord appeared below. All Hell was suddenly let loose. The sporadic *Flak* became a barrage - we were flying over the *Tirpitz*! The rest of the squadrons were almost certainly on their way home and, because we were late, we were now a lone target for the Nazis' fury. It was like putting a foot in a hornet's nest. Venomous red jets were flashing from the *Tirpitz's* guns; shells were exploding all round us. Kenny threw the Halifax all over the place, but there was no evading all the gunfire. He was banking so steeply I thought I would fall on top of him. At times we were flying so low that searchlights appeared to be pointing down on us! Several shells exploded so close that we could hear the pieces of shrapnel puncturing the fuselage."[27]

It was then that they discovered they had suffered considerable damage and wondered anxiously whether or not the aircraft would make it home.

Many of the crews reported seeing little heavy *Flak* and only a few crews reported seeing searchlights in operation. Flight Lieutenant Coton, the pilot of Lancaster L7577 'T-Tommy', saw neither the primary nor the secondary targets, obscured as they were by smoke. He dropped his bombs on Værnes aerodrome, some way to the south of the *Tirpitz*.

Only one aircraft of this first phase of the attack was shot down. Local people watched in horror as high above Langstein, the bay overlooking Salt Island, Lancaster L7572:L, totally engulfed in flames, spiralled downwards to crash in the mountains near Kaldadammen, killing all her crew.

As the first phase of the attack came to an end and the sound of the bombers lessened as they orbited the area, some of the

Ronnie Waite and his crew.
Flight Sergeant Kenny Clack, pilot (back row, second from left); Flight Sergeant Tommy Thompson (third from left); Pilot Officer Ronnie Waite, second pilot (extreme right); Sergeant 'Tubby' Lawes (front row left). (R.Waite)

local people presumed that the raid had come to an end. However, within a few minutes the roar of aero-engines approaching could be heard again as, with the target well marked with flares, a second wave of bombers roared up the fjord at full speed, diving down low over the water, the moonlight glinting dully on their metal surfaces. These were the mine-carrying Halifaxes of 35 Squadron.

About 50 minutes after the two Lancaster Squadrons and 76 Halifax Squadron had begun their attack, the remaining two Halifax squadrons, 35 and 10, began the second phase of the operation. 35 Squadron was due to make its attack between 00.40 hours and 01.00 hours, followed immediately by 10 Squadron. One after another these aircraft, their mines protruding ominously from their open bomb-bays, lost height and dived downwards to level out at sometimes as low as 250 feet above the surface of Trondheim Fjord. They swept up the fjord at low level, leaving the city of Trondheim well to starboard, the roar of their engines echoing between the mountains. Many crew members saw no other aircraft from this point onwards and they flew on with the impression that theirs was the only aircraft attacking a target that they could see was well and truly alerted and heavily defended. However, for nearly forty minutes now the German defences had been firing against Lancasters and Halifaxes flying above 6,000 feet. It must have come as some surprise for the gunners manning the *Flak* batteries to see the black shadows of a second gaggle of bombers bearing in on them from so low down, almost skimming the waters of the fjord - perhaps this even gave the first aircraft of 35 Squadron some slight element of surprise. The fact that many of the aircraft of this second phase seemed to be releasing their loads onto the sides of the cliffs next to the *Tirpitz* certainly surprised the defenders, although only momentarily, for these low-flying Halifaxes were the ones to suffer most from the *Flak* defences.

For each Halifax going in to its bombing run, the *Tirpitz* seemed to be lying at the end of an avenue of *Flak* that increased in intensity as the aircraft neared the target. The defences on both sides of the fjord were projecting a storm of cross-fire into the skies around the battleship.

Salt Island, two miles from the target, was used by the crews to pinpoint their position in the final run-up, thus enabling them to release their mines over the target by dead reckoning if necessary. Of the many crews that failed to see the battleship at all, several definitely saw the outcrop of rock that was known to be sheltering her and thus had an excellent aiming-point. Of 35 Squadron's eleven aircraft, seven dropped their mines on or near the target, although it was obscured by smoke. All but one of these, W1048 'S-Sugar', managed to climb out of the attack relatively unscathed.

Flight Sergeant Gardiner, at the controls of Halifax W1050 'F-Freddie', recalls the way in which he flew the aircraft out of danger after dropping his mines:

> "We were able to get out on a sharp left climbing turn only to play 'upsy-downsy' from *Flak* along the fjord all the way out to the harbour of Trondheim, where a gun boat greeted us with a single barrage that shook the controls like they had been disconnected. Having a course into the moon,

The only known photograph of a bomber that took part in the April raids. Standing (l to r) Flying Officer Jack Watts (observer), Pilot Officer Tom Godfrey (pilot), Flight Sergeant Jones (wireless operator), Sgt Gibbons (2nd pilot), Flight Sergeant Falkoski (air gunner). The ground crew are perched on the fuselage and an unidentified airman crouches between the aircrew.

(J. Watts)

I was able to fly very close to the water until *Flak* followed us there, and we simply hopped up and then down until we cleared the target area. We were told that the Royal Navy had rescue ships strung out across the North Sea to base, but we never saw any on either night."

The remaining four aircraft of 35 Squadron, however, failed to reach the *Tirpitz* at all. Halifax W1051 'C-Charlie' was hit by *Flak* as she approached Trondheim and, since the aircraft was losing height, the crew had to jettison her mines just west of the city, in order to maintain height, before having to return home.

The crew of Halifax W7656 'F-Freddie' failed to locate Fætten Fjord and so dropped their mines on an unidentified ship in Trondheim Fjord.

Squadron Leader Wilding, pilot of Halifax W7658 'H-Harry', found the *Flak* at the entrance to Fætten Fjord so intense that he had to jettison his mines there and abandon his attack. W1020 'K-King' was shot down, before her crew could release her mines over the target.

Following on behind the Halifaxes of 35 Squadron, almost all those of 10 Squadron succeeded in attacking the primary target from about 01.00 hours. Despite the number of bombers approaching the target, many of the crews felt entirely alone and saw no other aircraft during their attack. Flying Officer Jack Watts, the observer in W1038 'O-Orange', reflects on the scene and the feelings it evoked in him:

"The scene was awe-inspiring, with snowy mountains, steep cliffs rising out of dark waters, and the bright moonlight emphasising the stark black and white contrasts. Everything seemed so still and quiet beneath us as we flew into the Fjord. It was almost as if we were flying into a massive cathedral. We flew down that majestic fjord at our planned height of 4,000 feet, no sign of life to be seen, though we knew that the town of Trondheim lay quiet and invisible on the starboard as we penetrated more deeply into the Fjord. There had to be Germans down there, we knew; just as there had to be a *Tirpitz* lying ahead of us, like a stick of dynamite ready to explode in our faces." [28]

W1038 'O-Orange' was in fact among the first of the aircraft from 10 Squadron to attack, releasing her mines from 900 feet at 01.10. Flying Officer Jack Watts continues his account:

"We began our shallow dive and passed into the Åsen Fjord at the required speed of 225 knots. As we passed the sharp leading edge of the smaller Fætten Fjord, I punched my stopwatch and picked up the small hand-held bomb-sight with which we had been equipped for this operation. At that very moment, we flew into a smoke screen so dense it seemed to be solid. It was like flying in cotton wool. There was no sense of motion, no spatial relativity. We knew that we were thundering alongside a solid, rocky, cliff wall, practically brushing it with our wing tips and speeding towards an even higher and equally solid cliff wall not far ahead - all sight unseen. There was also a mighty battleship somewhere just beneath us in this ghastly smoke screen. The smoke persisted, not thinning in the slightest. We had reached the end of our timed run. The *Tirpitz* must be dead ahead of us, almost underneath us now. I pressed the bomb release, and we pulled up at full throttle, hoping against hope that we had not miscalculated, perhaps not so much at that very moment for the accuracy of our attack, but for the safe clearance of that bloody great cliff, in fact a steep hillside, ahead of us. No one would have wished to end their life like a fly squashed on the wall.

"As the extra power surged into the Merlins and the revs picked up, the angle of the Halifax turned upwards and the propellers bit more aggressively into that mat of thick, grey smoke, which seemed on the verge of suffocating us. There was nothing to be seen, above or below, and we hung on for what seemed like eternity before breaking clear of that smoky quicksand into a crystal clear winter wonderland again. Beneath us, and behind us now, the Åsen Fjord was covered in a thick, impenetrable layer of smoke. We flew out of the fjord with considerable relief at having made our attack and survived without casualty or damage." [29]

Halifax W1039 'C-Charlie', dropped her mines from 350 feet through the smoke over the *Tirpitz* at 01.06 hours. Her aileron

Above: Another shot of Flying Officer Watts' crew. (l to r) Sergeant Gibbons, Flight Sergeant Falkoski, Flying Officer Jack Watts, Pilot Officer Tom Godfrey, unknown and Sergeant O'Connor. Those named all flew on the raids.

(B. Gibbons)

Inset: Pilot Officer Tom Godfrey, pilot of W1038:O (B. Gibbons)

controls were shot away and her starboard flap controls damaged, but she managed to fly back to base successfully. Of the two aircraft that attacked in the next six minutes (one of which was W1038 'O-Orange') both met very intense *Flak* and one failed to drop one of her mines; it remained hung-up until she returned to base. In fact the crews of several aircraft found that one or more of their mines had hung-up. The next 10 Squadron aircraft to attack was Halifax W1052 'K-King', at 01.15 hours. Two of her mines hung up during the bombing run and were eventually jettisoned over Trondheim Fjord. The final aircraft of 10 Squadron, W1054 'H-Harry', also failed to release one of her mines when she attacked at 01.19 hours, but was able to jettison it after the attack.

The remainder of 10 Squadron successfully released their mines over the target, although no aircraft of either low-level squadron was able to observe the results of their attack, so effectively was the *Tirpitz* obscured by smoke.

Flight Sergeant Phil Ellison, a Canadian, was the tail gunner in Halifax W1055 'Z-Zebra' of 10 Squadron. He recalls:

"I personally got great satisfaction from the raid, as I felt we were at last at real grips with the enemy. We entered the fjord at about 6,000 ft. and dived to 600 ft., banked and dropped our load. I expended about 2,000 rounds firing at gun posts in the cliff sides. I claimed a 20 mm. *Flak* position as it ceased firing at us. The skipper pulled back on the stick and we stood on the tail, climbed over the mountain, turned and headed for home. It seemed as if all the guns were firing at us, all the time. All I know is, we were sure glad to get out of there."

During the attack there was frantic activity around and above the *Tirpitz*. The waters of the fjord erupted in fountains of spray, while the guns on both banks of the fjord and aboard the ship flashed their shells upwards to explode amongst the roaring bombers as they jinked their way through the *Flak*, their own guns spitting tracer and explosives, trying to hold a level course. Local people, watching in amazement as each bomber entered the ferocious cross-fire over the battleship, felt deeply for the crews struggling for their lives as one after another stricken bomber climbed out of the attack - many damaged by *Flak* but still flying, some falling in flames over the neighbouring hills and mountains.

For those families living within a short distance of the *Tirpitz*, this attack was a terrifying experience. Birger Hernes (whose brother Karl had taken photographs of the battleship), was eight years old at the time and living on the family small-holding within 500 yards of the battleship. He recalls vividly the events of this night when he and the remainder of his family took shelter in the cellar of their home:

"We knew that something special was going to happen. The German smoke-pots spewed out their thick horrible 'porridge'. Lots of noise came from the battleship and hectic activity broke out. The noise woke the whole family, the children as well, who suddenly had to experience the hell of war close at hand. First we heard a heavy droning and the intense roaring of the planes' engines. We knew what was about to happen: an air raid against the *Tirpitz*. The sound of the detonation of the bombs came gradually nearer - the earth shook. We fled down to the cellar. An oil lamp threw a weak shaft

Tail gunner Sergeant Phil Ellison with his 10 Squadron crew at Leeming in 1941. (l to r) Sergeant 'Woody' Wood (flight engineer); Sergeant Peter Siebert (observer); Pilot Officer Allen (2nd pilot); Sergeant Mike Gribben (pilot); Jock ?; Sergeant Dennis Windle (wireless operator); Flight Sergeant Phil Ellison on extreme right. All but Allen, Gribben and the unidentified 'Jock' took part in the April raids. (P. Ellison)

of light on frightened faces, and we had to hold the lamp to stop it falling on the floor.

"The noise was far worse than anything we had ever heard before. From the cellar we heard a loud droning noise that drowned out everything else. The whole house shook. The window-panes broke from the shock waves. One of the planes dropped a series of big bombs, perhaps 1,000 kg. The first bomb exploded on the top of Saltøya. The next hit the hill at Blekpynten. A third one frightened the life out of us - a terrible bang, frighteningly close, came from Aaviksaune Farm, not many hundreds of metres from our home. We children also felt the fear rising in us. We feared that the worse would happen, and that a bomb would hit the house and send us to heaven."

However, the Hernes family were fortunate; they all survived the attack, even though afterwards, when they searched around they found a number of unexploded mines. Many of these had 'bored themselves down into the earth' and they discovered that one mine had struck the earth only 50 or 60 yards from their house. Another family living near the *Tirpitz's* anchorage, for whom a huge tree on their farm was the obvious and natural place to take shelter, decided to take refuge on this occasion in the cellar. Bullets and parts of shells went right through the farmhouse itself and a bomb hit the area near the tree; fortunately no-one was hurt. Yet another family was saved by the 'roof' of their cellar. The explosion of a bomb, falling in a marshy area of Åsen, sprayed their farmhouse with mud and a large stone fell through the farmhouse roof.

A bomb falling on a farm-road near Lofjord threatened the lives of several people. A German soldier was killed outright, while a part of this bomb went right through six wooden beams in the ceiling of the living-room in a house nearby, finally coming to rest in the wall.

However, despite these 'near misses', no Norwegians are known to have died during the attacks.

Not so the airmen. Several aircraft of this second phase were mortally damaged and many of their crewmen were killed. The stricken Halifax W1020 'K-King' of 35 Squadron, piloted by Flight Lieutenant Pooles, having flown between two areas of high ground in the direction of Sweden, plunged into a hillside about seven miles from the *Tirpitz*, just above a farm at Borås in Skjelstadmark. With the bombs and mines aboard, she exploded with great violence on impact with the ground. For some reason her mines had not been released over the target and Flight Lieutenant Pooles and his entire crew perished.

Less than one-and-a-half miles away, not far from the edge of Ausetvatnet Lake, Lancaster L7572:L of 97 Squadron, piloted by Flight Lieutenant Mackid, had also lost height and, exploding just before impact with the earth, had flown into the ground, killing the entire crew instantaneously.

Solveig Skjeldstad, who as a young girl of seven years of age was staying in a farm at Borås, vividly recalls the impression the attacks made on her young mind. Fortunately, memories of death in the countryside of her childhood are tempered by many happier recollections, from the long days of the enemy occupation, of German soldiers coming to the farm for eggs and vegetables and of how well these young men treated Solveig and her sister. However, it was just chance that led her to become

Birger Hernes points to the cellar in which he and his family sheltered during the April attacks. (B. Hernes)

personally involved in the *Tirpitz* attacks at all. She and her mother and sister had come to stay with Solveig's grandfather, for:

"Now it was the end of school term, and time for visiting Grandfather again, so we went on a train, my mother, sister Aas and I. We were just at the point of getting off at Langstein Station when Mother bent down and pointed and whispered 'Look there, there's *Tirpitz!*' But we didn't ask any more questions because the Germans on the train had already looked at our papers and there was a little bit of a frightening atmosphere in the train. But we understood. So we got off the train.

"There wasn't a road, for in 1942 the road from Langstein to Borås was just for a horse and cart and, in springtime, the track was too bad for such a vehicle, so we had to walk. So we took the luggage and walked half the way. Well, we walked on and past Skei, up to a farm there and at this farm Mother and my sister and I put on the skis and started for the last trip through the forest, to Borås. It was brilliant moonlight, but it was a bit frightening through the forest because the spruce looked like Germans on duty letting us pass by. Nobody talked, but we had the same thoughts: Germans! And we were just finished with the forest, coming to the end of the forest down to Borås, when all of a sudden the sky was lit up and there was bombing and shooting and we skiied and cried, and skiied and cried -

you see we got up speed and we fell and we cried and fell. And then at last
we went into Grandfather's house. And I remember Mother, or someone
else, played the organ to stop the sounds from the aircraft."

As the sounds of the attack continued unabated the family
decided to take refuge in the cellar beneath the farmhouse,
where they could feel a little safer, albeit with little comfort:

"Everybody went down into the basement. And they put blankets on top of
the potatoes so we children could have a little sleep. And I remember we
were chatting down in the basement, but even then we could hear the sound
of the aircraft through the thick stone walls. The night went on to one
o'clock, two o'clock, and all of a sudden the whole building shook, and we
could hear the animals roaring and they spoke about someone having to go
up to calm the animals down. And when they got out into the fresh air they
saw all the window-panes were broken. And Grandfather stayed in his bed
and his bed was lifted and thrown into another room, and the farm-hand
went down to the barn and calmed the animals down, and then they saw the
burning Halifax, crashed into the ground, and another one (the Lancaster)
further west. Well I think it must have been five o'clock, six o'clock in the
morning. Everybody had to get up from the basement, the shooting had
ended, and everybody in the neighbourhood went up to the Halifax to have a
look, and my sister and I ran through rotten snow up to the Halifax. And I
can remember Germans standing there, and they bent down, a little bit
ashamed for what they had done to the English soldiers. And then my sister
and I stood in a bed of white flowers and looked at one of the men in the
aircraft and we were wondering why he didn't turn his head to look at us.
But then I realised he had passed away.

"No one had survived.

"All the bodies, just a hand in a tree, a foot in another tree - oh, it was
terrible - but it was picked down and put up into a lorry and driven away to
Trondheim. Some days later the bodies from the Lancaster were brought
down into my Grandfather's laundry (an outhouse). The Lancaster had
crashed in a rather rough area, so we couldn't use a horse and a cart, we
just carried them. And then, you see, we were just in the middle of all this
and I remember - it was the whole day through - they made boxes, wooden
boxes to serve as coffins, and they put, yes, they put the soldiers in the
laundry. And still today when I go into this room I can smell the oil - blood -
coagulated blood - and burning clothes - still the same smell.

"Well, we were running around, my sister and I, six years and seven
years, looking at everything, and the Germans standing in the middle of the
yard keeping a watch. And they were all carried to Stavne Churchyard.

"And the next day we went out and picked up splinters of metal,
shrapnel, and some of the splinters, I remember, hit Mother's cabin, and we
picked them up, and we still have this box at Borås.

"Five days later they found Raymond Day's body (the mid-upper gunner
from the Lancaster), and then you see we had a lot of time for the burial, for
there were no Germans present.

156

Above: Raymond Day, tail gunner of Lancaster L-7572 (third from left) with unidentified crew and Lancaster.
(Arthur Day)

Inset: Sergeant Raymond Day.
(Arthur Day)

"So we made a very big, nice coffin, and I went into the garden, and Mother said, 'Please, girls, run and fetch some branches from the spruce by the dolls-house - we had a dolls-house there - and I think she said this so to put us away from the terrible things. We had had a week of sorrow and maybe it's too hard for little girls, so run away! And we were soon back again and we put the branches in Raymond's coffin. And I remember Mother tried to tie his swollen fingers together before we put the lid on. And then he was taken to Stavne as well."

Most of the crews of the other three aircraft that crashed or crash-landed that night were more fortunate. Halifax W1037 'U-Uncle' came down in the waters of Trondheim Fjord, somewhere in the vicinity of Malvik, two of her crew dead. Her

Australian pilot, Acting Flight Lieutenant George Miller, was surprised, after the first phase attack on the enemy defences, at how fierce the defences still were:

"When I arrived at the mouth of the outer Trondheim harbour all was quiet, so I thought the Lancasters had done their job, and although the whole area was covered in snow and the fjords filled with white smoke, I saw the stern of the *Tirpitz* clearly and went in low, and got the most amazing hammering. I pulled up out of the fjord the *Tirpitz* was in, then dropped into the next fjord to make my getaway, but dropped right on top of the *Prinz Eugen*, which I didn't know was there, and again got a hammering, but made it out into the clear with the four engines sounding good and feeling good.

"A quick look at the instruments showed all seemed to be well so I started to set the throttles and pitch controls for economical cruising for the trip back to Lossiemouth, and was just reaching for my coffee flask when a voice came on the intercom. 'Tail gunner to pilot, we're trailing about 300 feet of flame. The whole starboard wing is alight, wing tip to root.' I had a look at the wing by half-rising in my seat and what I saw sent a cold chill down my spine, for I knew immediately that we had a very limited time before that wing would explode (when the tanks were empty) and the wing would probably come off. I pulled back the throttles and said, 'We'll have to ditch!' I assumed the intercom was connected to all other points of the plane and that all would hear and move to the crash position in the fuselage on the built-in bed on the starboard side just aft of the flight deck near the engineer's cabin. As the airspeed indicator showed about 160 mph as I flattened out (much too fast to put it down) I held it back, watching the airspeed fall off to stalling point when I lifted the nose so as it would not dive straight down (as I had heard a Halifax would do, if it landed on water nose down, because of the nose shape). Just as I was wondering where the surface of the water was - it was all glassy calm and still - I remembered the landing lights and put them on, and a splash in front, from a shell lobbed at us from the shore, enabled me to see the broken water. Just as the aircraft was skimming the water (I could feel and hear it) and as I eased the control column back, there was a flash from the starboard side as apparently an empty tank exploded. The explosion must have tipped the aircraft to port for the tip of the port wing dug into the water and we jerked around to a sudden stop.

"I put the lights on, bringing a fresh hail of cannon fire from the shoreline and walked down the aircraft, amazed at the damage. Everything was a mess in there and the water was rising and I was distressed to find two dead bodies, very mutilated from gunfire. Annable was still in his cabin behind the pilot's seat, he was half on and half off the floor, it was hard to see much, his cabin too was a mess.

"Then I returned to my seat to try to find my coffee flask and sandwiches. I couldn't find them in the usual place beside the right side of my seat, so I climbed out of the top, expecting to find the dinghy inflated, but only found

Flight Lieutenant George 'Dusty' Miller of 10 Squadron, captain of Halifax W1037:U. He spent the latter part of the night of 27th April aboard Prinz Eugen as a guest of the crew. (G.Miller)

a large hole and a mess of torn rubber while strands of mutilated rubber trailed from the edges of the hole. Petrol blazing on the water made a 'beaut' fire and in the bright moonlight I saw the Nav (navigator) and W/Op (wireless operator) in the water, and worried where the tail gunner had got to as his turret was empty when I looked into it.

"It was quite good moonlight, and the landing lights still on helped illuminate. I walked out on the wing, which was at an angle of about 30 degrees to the water, pointing upwards, and sat on the tip. I looked down and saw the navigator and the W/Op in the water and wondered how they got out, for normally they would climb out of the cabin (below the pilot), up past the second pilot's seat, and I would have seen them. Maybe they did, and I didn't see them, as I looked in the fuselage. I wanted to ask them, but never did, for the wing just then gave a jolt and moved upwards 'til I was looking 50 feet straight down into flames, and the fuselage was sinking, so I jumped off out towards the two in the water. I seemed to go down a helluva long way, and stopped in total darkness, not knowing which was up or down and my lungs were burning and near bursting it seemed. I let go a little air to relieve my lungs which was good, and panicking a bit at not being able to rise (I was very heavy with 'para' harness and heavy Canadian fur-lined over-shoes, which I then let go). Just as I thought I'd had it, I recalled the toggle of the air-bottle on my Mae West life-jacket and pulled it and immediately shot to the surface and gulped in the cold night air, looked around and found myself on my own. I looked for the shore and decided it was too far to attempt to swim as the water was freezing cold and decided even if I let go my shoes I could not make it (I am a good swimmer) and anyway if I got to shore with no shoes and wet clothes in a countryside not only hostile with Goons but freezing feet deep in snow, it would be useless. I looked again for the others, but couldn't see them, and decided there must be a drift or current and in the short time I'd been under water they had been moved away. Actually all this

159

is a bit of a blur for I can't remember clearly after so long and no doubt I was already being affected by the intense cold of the water. I felt quite numb - *not cold at all*, as I recall, only numb and sleepy and I realised that I was becoming unconscious. So I lay back in my Mae West and adjusted the inflated collar behind my head, lay my head on it, and must have passed out then and there."

Halifax W1041 'B-Baker', flown by Wing Commander Don Bennett, 10 Squadron's leader, was another of the night's casualties. As Bennett flew her into the target area he was taken by surprise by the whitish smoke screen that he ran into at about 400 feet. Flight Lieutenant Mick How, the rear-gunner, remembers hearing Don Bennett say:

"Look, there's a smoke haze! We can't see the thing (target)." By this time we had actually flown over it, and from the rear gun turret I could actually see the mast of the ship sticking up above this mist patch. By this time all hell broke loose, and we were being shot at from the ship itself, from the squadron of ships around the *Tirpitz*, and from the hills and downwards onto us as well. In no time at all the right-hand wing was well and truly blazing. I could see this well from the turret, by swinging the turret round, of course, and I was shit-scared. At this time also we had an almost direct hit on the turret which blew all the perspex out and gave me a nasty cut on the face and a bit of shock. I immediately told the Captain that I had been hit, and he said "Okay, keep quiet", which I did.'

As they roared along the fjord, Bennett, seeing the flashes of the anti-aircraft guns from within the smoke immediately below him, realised that they had just passed over the target and that it was too late now to release the mines. He pulled his aircraft up and clear of the smoke, climbing up to 1,200 feet, in order to make a second circuit to come in again from the west to release his mines. However, as Bennett realised later, it would have been better had he continued flying low inland, up the valley for a while, before climbing and turning west. As it was, his immediate climb out of the smoke presented the aircraft as, in his own words, 'a sitting bird' to the *Flak* batteries on the hills to the north and south of the fjord. The aircraft was hit, then the already intense *Flak* bombardment seemed to increase and the aircraft was hit again, the incendiaries this time starting a fire behind the starboard inner engine. His rear-gunner reported that he had been hit, but told Bennett that he was alright. Nothing that the crew could do succeeded in extinguishing the fire in the wing, so Bennett ordered them to prepare to abandon the aircraft. The aircraft continued to climb on the three good engines as they turned west and released their mines from about 3,000 feet, estimating that they had fallen about half a mile to the east of the *Tirpitz*. (In fact they fell not far from Almo in Skjelstadmark). They then turned east to make for Sweden but, when after two minutes the fire behind the engine died down, they turned once more to head for the Shetlands. A couple of minutes later the fire flared up again and once more Bennett turned the aircraft for Sweden. Then the starboard inner engine, which operated the hydraulics controlling the undercarriage, cut out and the starboard wheel fell down into the landing position. 'This meant that the aircraft was unstable,' recalls Sergeant Harry Walmsley, the second pilot:

"There were only three live engines, the other one was on fire and the fire was getting nearer and nearer to the petrol tank. And so, having attempted to climb to a reasonable height above the fjord we did succeed in reaching 700 feet.

"We then looked around for a suitable place to crash-land the 'plane, but unfortunately we were flying over forested ground with fairly thick snow, apparently. At this stage Wing Commander Bennett decided to give the order to prepare to bale out. We then each put on the clip parachutes to the front of our harnesses and also the rear-gunner at that stage said that he had been wounded by shrapnel. The flight engineer went to the rear turret to examine the rear-gunner and see if he was in a position to bale out from the aircraft. The rear-gunner, Mr How, decided he could make it and so Wing Commander Bennett said, 'Bale out now!' At this stage the flight engineer obtained Wing Commander Bennett's parachute from its socket in the 'plane, and clipped it on for him and the rest of us took our places near the exits and baled out."

Sergeant Phil Eyles, the navigator, lifted the forward escape hatch and was the first to leave, quickly followed by the second pilot, Sergeant Walmsley, who continues:

"I baled out from the front also, but the height above the ground was critical. Fortunately, we realised that there was probably thick snow and this would break the fall when we landed. For a moment as I left the aircraft I thought I was hitting the tail-plane but it was merely the tightening of the harness in the groin and under the armpits. So at last I opened my eyes to see where I was and I was floating down and probably hit the ground within a few seconds."

The two wireless operators jumped next. The flight engineer, John Colgan, brought Bennett his parachute from its stowage position in the fuselage, much to Bennett's relief, before going aft to help the injured tail-gunner to the escape hatch, as Mick How recalls:

> "At this time I heard Bennett tell Sergeant Colgan the flight engineer to come back and help me out of the turret. He managed to get the doors open at the back and I crawled out and slapped my 'chute on, it clipped on the front of me, of course, and in so doing the rip-cord got caught on a part of the tail unit and snapped the 'chute open. Immediately I grasped it from the front, trying to hold the thing together, and at the same time crawl up the fuselage. You can well imagine the panic I was in at this time, and God only knows how, but when I got to the jettison hole to jump out I managed to get my feet through, but the slip-stream took my boots off, and on jumping, of course, the 'chute exploded and I felt the straps break my ribs; and I came to a few moments later, hanging in a fir tree - for we were frightfully low at this time - swinging backwards and forwards, thinking 'Oh Christ, what am I doing here?!'

Colgan followed How immediately. Bennett, alone in his stricken aircraft, prepared to leave, but was suddenly surprised by a large explosion in the starboard wing. This was probably a fuel tank blowing up. Bennett believed that a large part of the starboard wing collapsed as a result. He attempted to reach the escape hatch while the aircraft was at about 600 feet, but his parachute became caught up twice before he made it and he only managed to jump as the aircraft reached about 200 feet. His parachute deployed sufficiently to allow him to reach the ground safely, as the aircraft crashed and exploded, burning furiously about a half-mile away, just south of the Flornes railway station in Stjørdal.

NOTES

27. From the draft manuscript of *Death or Decoration*, Newton 1991
28. From Jack Watt's unpublished account.
29. Ibid

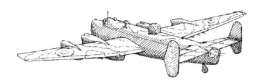

Chapter Nine
'S-Sugar' Under Fire

Halifax W1048 'S-Sugar' had cruised across the North Sea at about 175 mph. At eighty miles out from the Norwegian coast, at position 62°45'N by 04°00'E, Pilot Officer Hewitt called for the second change of course to take them in towards their landfall near the island of Smola. Sergeant Stevens remembers being surprised at how quickly the time had passed. It was now just after midnight and they were approaching the Norwegian coast, whose offshore islands pierced the water below, clearly visible in the bright moonlight. Hewitt was pleased with the accuracy of his landfall:

> "We hit the Norwegian coast more or less on time. I do not think that I had any particular sense of foreboding, but the rocks sticking out of the water reminded me of so many dead men's skulls. Finding the actual entrance to Trondheim Fjord cannot have caused me much concern, certainly not enough to remember and, as I recall matters, it was then bright moonlight. We arrived some minutes before we were due to attack and as our time was synchronised to fit in with other aircraft from our squadron and also particularly those aircraft dropping the four thousand pounders (which would have blown us up also), we had to orbit round at the Fjord entrance waiting our proper time to attack." [30.]

W1048 'S-Sugar' had flown over the Norwegian coastline about midway between Kristiansund North and Smola Island, as planned, for Hewitt's navigation had been excellent. The darkening landscape of striated rocks separating pencil-thin leads of water could be seen below, reflected in the moonlight, as they flew over Snill Fjord at 4,000 feet. Beneath them the long, thin fjord pointed the way over a network of lakes and marsh towards Trondheim Fjord. Hewitt, peering through the flat perspex bomb-aimer's window in the nose of the aircraft, pinpointed their position as they flew over Lensvik, a small community in the lee of the mountain guarding the western bank of the arm of Trondheim Fjord that led from the sea into the mountains. However, at this point they were five minutes ahead of their designated 'Time Over Target' and, in order to delay their attack until the correct moment, they crossed the waters of the fjord and flew on in a north-easterly direction over the land to the north of Trondheim, towards the large lake of Storvatnet. Several minutes later Pilot Officer MacIntyre turned W1048 'S-Sugar' to starboard and set course for the centre of the main branch of Trondheim Fjord. They left the mountains and lakes behind them and emerged over the waters of the fjord at Hindrem, where the only piece of low, flat land for miles curved out briefly into the fjord. Still flying at 4,000 feet, they came under fire from a light *Flak* battery sited at Hindrem, but no damage was done. To port now, Hewitt could make out several small islands dotting the steel-grey water, while ahead lay the dark land mass of the peninsular of Frosta. Moments later, over the centre of the Fjord, MacIntyre carried out a complete right-hand circuit, the land tilting steadily as they flew round, Hewitt identifying fjords and landmarks below him as they did so. The high ground of Forbordfjell, the waters of Stjørdalsfjord and Strindfjord, the city of Trondheim itself, the mountains they had recently crossed, all rotated steadily before his eyes while he checked his position on the map. As Frosta and the entrance to Åsen Fjord came once more into view in the distance, MacIntyre straightened up out of the circuit. He pointed the aircraft's nose to the northeast and began to increase speed in a shallow dive. As they descended Hewitt could make out more details of the land lit up by the bright moonlight. To port lay the low farmlands of Frosta, to starboard the high land that overlooked the approach to the target area. As they veered to starboard to leave the main branch of Åsen Fjord and continued towards Fætten Fjord, small rocky islands loomed out of the water to port - they were less than a minute from the target now. The *Flak* was intense, as Hewitt remembers:

FLIGHTPATH OF **HALIFAX W1048 'S-SUGAR'** APRIL 27th 1942

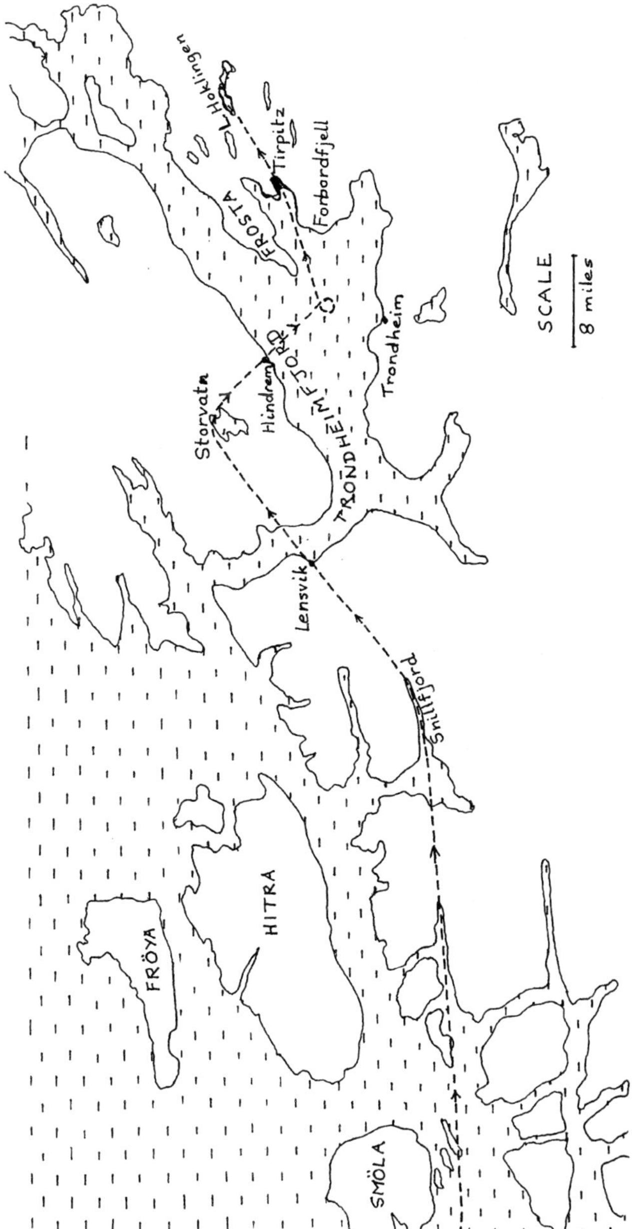

SCALE

8 miles

L. Hoklingen

Tirpitz

FROSTA

Forbordfjell

Storvatn

Hindrem

TRONDHEIM FJORD

Trondheim

Lensvik

Snillfjord

HITRA

FRÖYA

SMÖLA

"We must have been attacking towards the end of those from our squadron, as shortly after arrival we had a very good view of the light *Flak* hose-piping up and then down as the aircraft came in from 2,000 feet to mast height. The Germans were using their standard method of tracer sighting, which, if the lethal moment could have been ignored, would have been quite pretty to watch.

"It was the heaviest concentration of light *Flak* that I had ever seen and to us in waiting, it was hard to see how an aircraft could live through it. However, it was soon enough our turn to chance our luck and therefore off we went."

Stevens recalls that as they approached Salt Island and the target 'The pilot said 'Engineer! Approaching the target. To the crash position!'" He immediately unplugged his intercom and made his way back down the fuselage a few steps, before plugging in again, reporting his arrival, and lying down. He was now spread-eagled on the floor of the fuselage between the rear and forward wing spar, a space of about five or six feet, ready to manually release the mines. He lay there, his hands clasping the toggles of the release cables, waiting for the bomb-aimer to report 'Mines away!'.

The trees and rocks of Salt Island suddenly loomed up beneath the aircraft as the rising sides of the approaching fjord narrowed and concentrated Hewitt's view ahead. They had no more than 20 seconds to the target now. MacIntyre levelled out at 300 feet as they flew over Salt Island and at 260 mph they roared into the storm of *Flak* erupting from both banks at the entrance to the Fjord.

'S-Sugar' flew at full speed towards the *Tirpitz*, through the brilliant display of *Flak* that dipped and rose to meet her. Lying prone in the nose in his bomb-aimer's position Hewitt watched the tracer rising from the defending guns. He had already adjusted the settings on his bombsight; he was now watching the target area rapidly growing in size and detail in the sighting graticule.

W1048 'S-Sugar' was now flying close to the waters of the fjord, the cliffs looming above her. To the rear-gunner, Sergeant Wilson, it seemed as if they were almost skimming the moonlit waves:

"I can remember guns firing down at us, I could see them on the side. By this time I had my turret right the way round, facing the land, the side of the fjord, and I was firing at boats and cliffs as we went by. I can remember firing at the *Tirpitz* as we went."

They were being fired at from ships in the fjord and from guns mounted on the shore and the surrounding hills; many of the batteries had survived the earlier attack by the bomb-dropping squadrons. It was a most unpleasant experience for the whole crew as the aircraft bucked her way through the heavy barrage. The thunderous roar of the guns all around them filled their ears, while the exploding *Flak* flashed in their eyes. As MacIntyre reported later (in a de-briefing on June 22nd, shortly after his return from internment in Sweden), the *Flak* 'increased in intensity as the target was approached, and some appeared to come from double and quadruple barrelled guns.' Hewitt was lying on his couch in the nose, peering through the flat bomb-aimer's window, giving final course-corrections to the pilot. He remembers the terrific noise and the clouds of smoke that filled the gulf at the narrowing end of the fjord towards which they were heading. Suddenly the aircraft entered a patch of smoke, preventing him, to his surprise, from seeing a thing. Hewitt:

"We had a target map of the Åsen Fjord area, but the main thing in a situation such as this was to point the aircraft towards where the *Tirpitz* was supposed to be and get the thing down to 250 feet just as quickly as possible. It seemed as though we had scarcely begun when we found we were flying in thick smoke. As a form of protection the Germans had fired smoke pots. We had been warned of this hazard, but meeting it on a target run was a somewhat different experience. We were flying below the tops of the sides of the fjord and the whole thing was very unpleasant. Blinded as we were by the smoke there was nothing for it but to release our mines, hoping perhaps that very good fortune would intervene at a time when any skill we possessed was availing us nothing."

Wilson had opened fire with all his guns as soon as he had seen the first tracer reach out from *Flak* ships and shore batteries as if to claw them out of the sky. MacIntyre recalled that 'Two searchlights from the southern slope of the fjord picked up the aircraft, but both were dowsed after the rear gunner had given them some attention.' The fuselage vibrated to the rattle of Wilson's guns, the spent cartridge cases clattering out of the breeches into the empties bags as the tracer from his guns curved downwards. From the cockpit, MacIntyre had heard the Brownings open up:

"One very pleasant recollection of the attack on the *Tirpitz* was the noise from the tail turret of the aircraft. The tail gunner, throughout the attack, never stopped operating his guns. I'll never know exactly what he was shooting at, and maybe he won't know either, but it was certainly a pleasant feeling to know that he was there and he was shooting at something. There is some satisfaction in knowing that you are shooting back when you are being shot at."

A few hundred yards short of the *Tirpitz's* position, guaging her position from the relationship of the surrounding hills, Hewitt pressed the bomb-release button and reported 'Bombs gone!'. As the aircraft surged up the smoke-filled fjord, Wilson, his thumb squeezing the firing button of his guns all the time, sprayed the target with bullets. Further forward along the fuselage Stevens immediately pulled sharply on the toggles.

"The minute I pulled the toggles and said, 'Engineer - bombs gone!' there was a terrific thump! It seemed as if something was near on blasting the aircraft out of the sky. I was practically pinned to the floor."

As soon as he knew that the mines had been released MacIntyre pulled back on the control column and put the aircraft into a steep climb, turning to port. Despite, 'the terrific shaking to the aircraft, and several light *Flak* hits', he managed to coax 'S-Sugar' up and over the cliff at the end of the fjord.

In their debriefing six weeks later, MacIntyre and Hewitt stated:

"A fraction of a second after releasing the bombs (sic) the aircraft was violently shaken by an extremely heavy explosion, which must have been caused by a heavy calibre bomb from another aircraft. The alternative explanation of this was that it was some explosion of the *Tirpitz* herself."

Hewitt later expressed a different possibility:

"The *Prinz Eugen*, the *Hipper* and the *Admiral Scheer* were supposed to be in neighbouring berths in Trondheim Fjord, and I thought that we had been hit by one of them, but the *Flak* could have come from anywhere and mostly seemed to come from everywhere."

It seems most likely, in fact, that the aircraft had been hit by *Flak* from a gun battery on the southern side of the fjord, and that the 'extremely heavy explosion' was caused by one of the starboard fuel tanks exploding.

The smoke screen hiding the *Tirpitz* and extending up the hills on both sides of the fjord to a height of 200-400 feet must have been fitful and patchy that night. MacIntyre saw the *Tirpitz* throughout W1048's pass over her. So did Wilson who was firing at her continuously. Hewitt, stationed below the pilot in the nose of the aircraft, does not recall seeing the *Tirpitz* at all; he remembers only that, so shrouded in smoke was she, he had to release his mines blind. Stevens, too, recalls catching a momentary glimpse of the *Tirpitz* at some point. As he struggled to his feet, wondering what had happened, he glanced through the small round fuselage window and saw that the aircraft had been hit. Flames were streaming from the starboard outer engine, the brilliant glare lighting up the interior of the aircraft.

"I got onto the intercom again to the pilot and said, 'Engineer here. The starboard engine's been hit, it's well on fire, I should come forward, is that okay?' So he said, 'Yes, come forward'."

MacIntyre, at the controls, now knew they were in serious trouble:

"Exactly what hit us and where we were hit - I'll never know, except that considerable smoke was experienced inside the cockpit and I immediately pulled off the top hatch to allow the cockpit to clear. There was much burning, smoke and flames in the starboard wing and outer engine."

By this time, MacIntyre had throttled back and switched off the stricken starboard engine, feathering its propeller to help to reduce the drag created by the fire. He had also activated the fire-extinguisher next to the engine, but it seemed to have little effect on the fire that was now beginning to blaze more fiercely, spreading to the wing's aileron and flap.

When a wing catches fire the aerodynamic lift on that side of the aircraft is reduced. It becomes difficult, if not impossible, to keep the aircraft in the air. Smoke had seeped into the cockpit through the interior of the starboard wing root from the blazing fuel tanks, making it impossible for MacIntyre to read his instruments, despite the fact that he had opened up the hood above his head to clear the air.

Wilson continued to spray .303 rounds at the target now rapidly disappearing behind him, while Stevens made his way forward, uphill against the aircraft's angle of climb, his nostrils filled with the stench of cordite from the bursting *Flak*. He wanted to check his instruments to see what could be done, for he was hoping that the standard procedure of closing the fuel cocks to isolate the blazing engine would enable the fire to burn itself out.

As Stevens began to check the dials on his instrument panel, MacIntyre, struggling to keep the aircraft airborne and in the centre of the tree-clad valley that led on from the end of the fjord, reported to the crew that he couldn't get the aircraft above 1,000 feet. Somehow he managed to haul 'S-Sugar' over a rise in the ground and, almost immediately, realised that, with the fire in the starboard wing increasing, and the fact that he was losing aileron control, there was no hope of keeping her in the air for more than a few more minutes. Since he could not gain height he would have to put the aircraft down. MacIntyre knew that, although they had been told at the briefing to make for the Swedish border only forty miles away in an emergency, if he did not land 'S-Sugar' very soon she might blow herself and all her crew out of the sky. 'Crash positions!' he ordered. The cockpit was still filled with smoke and MacIntyre was now flying blind along an unknown valley, with high ground on either side of him. Just forward and below him lay Hewitt, still lying in the bomb-aimer's position. Realising that MacIntyre could not see he started calling out instructions on the intercom for the pilot to avoid hitting the valley's mountainous side as the aircraft veered to starboard. He continued calling out flying instructions as MacIntyre struggled to keep the aircraft in the air, weaving an uncertain course up the Åsen valley.

Below them, in the farms and houses scattered along parts of the Åsen valley, the inhabitants were startled by this aircraft that roared over them, seemingly just above their heads. Asbjørn Fossum, fourteen years old at the time, recalls:

"We heard the roar from the aircraft from 2300 hours. I remember being in the sleeping room, an attic, together with my brother and my parents. My father was looking out of the window, staring at the 'chains of pearls' (anti-aircraft fire) creating a strange feeling of either Christmas or New years Eve. My father bent his head slightly away from the window as my mother calmly remarked that the situation was rather dangerous!"

Asbjørn's brother Ragnar, two years his junior, remembers that as 'S-Sugar' roared over their home:

"For a moment my father thought the approaching and burning aircraft would actually hit the house, but it gained some height in the last minute, passing just over the spruce-tops nearby (the trees were relatively low at the time) and landed on the ice. W1048 'S-Sugar' flew right over our house, and I remember the curtains blown onto the ceiling by the air pressure from the aircraft! The noise was terrible - I'll never forget it! The artillery nearby came into activity and the sound of shells, bullets and grenades was appalling."

When Asbjørn and his family went outside after daylight broke,

it seemed to them that parts of their farmyard were silver-
plated - aluminium parts had fallen from 'S-Sugar' as she had
flown over the farm and, as Asbjørn explains:

> "It was like a street of silver parts down towards the forest nearby, and an
> object from the rear part of the plane seemed to have been too much
> overheated, as it sparkled in all colours, standing upwards in the ground 7
> to 8 metres from our barn. If this object had hit the roof of the barn, (the
> roof was made of wood in the old way), the whole barn would have caught
> fire. Parts of shells were found everywhere, and parts of the plane (one part
> of the propellers) are still in our possession."

On board the aircraft, MacIntyre was able to feel some relief
that they had somehow managed to clear the high ground.
'S-Sugar' emerged from the valley and headed towards the lake.
He recalled:

> "At the time of the run over the ship Hewitt was lying in the nose operating
> the bomb-sight. It was his position, and his calmness in remaining in this
> position, that saved our lives. During the time when considerable smoke in
> the cockpit caused us to be actually flying blind, and I mean blind in that I
> couldn't see the instruments and I couldn't see outside, Ian Hewitt saved
> our lives by telling me to go left as we were headed for the mountains on the
> right hand side. Corrections were made and we didn't hit the mountain."

As they flew over the small town of Åsen they were subjected to
several bursts of light *Flak* from a gun battery there. The
aircraft banked to starboard, then to port, before straightening
up as Lake Hoklingen loomed up ahead. MacIntyre recognised it
from the model he had studied with such care at Kinloss. They
needed to land as soon as possible and this lake was their only
hope. MacIntyre had little choice:

> "The distance between the target and the lake, which was just beyond Åsen,
> was short and I reckon that we were only about three minutes in the air
> from the time we went over the ship until we ditched on the lake. There
> wasn't very much of a decision as to what one should do. I was unable to get
> the aircraft to climb so I had to get her down. I knew there was a lake
> straight ahead, so we went down. I knew the lake would be frozen, or would
> have spring ice on it - and, whether it had ice or didn't have ice, I also knew
> that I would be landing without wheels - which we did."

Crash-landing with undercarriage retracted was the standard
procedure since the aircraft would be much safer sliding along
on its belly than landing with wheels down on an unknown
surface. The crew prepared themselves in their own ways for
the crash-landing. Hewitt:

171

"Prior to the landing, I had come back from the nose in order to secure myself - perspex noses had a habit of being smashed in when water was hit. However, whilst I was making up my mind what to do, the aircraft hit the ice with just enough force to make me lose my balance."

Picking up the Verey pistol and its ammunition (for the flight engineer's standard procedure after a crash-landing was to fire flares into the aircraft's fuel tanks in order to destroy the aircraft once it had been evacuated), Stevens made his way back to his crash position. He hurriedly clambered over the two wing spars and sat down behind the rear one with his back to it, facing aft. As he braced himself for the crash-landing he suddenly realised that he had forgotten to do something:

"I hadn't done a specific job that was mine to do, and that was to release the upper escape hatch, and let it go, so in an emergency the crew could at least get out. Having realised this I jumped over the rear spar, and as my right foot went over the spar so I put my foot straight through the inspection hole in the floor, which he had earlier opened to gain access to the mine-release toggles. Thinking back it may have been a good thing, because at this vital moment we hit the ice. I doubled myself up into a ball as I hit the floor, and I suppose the aircraft just skidded unbelievably here and there. I was flung around, but when I finally came to my head was only about half an inch from the front spar. So, thinking back, my foot going through the floor could have saved my life."

As soon as he heard MacIntyre shout that they were going to crash-land onto the lake, Wilson, in the rear gun-turret, took action to avoid being trapped in an aircraft that might well sink, inside a turret whose doors might be jammed shut by the force of a crash-landing.

"Immediately I swung my turret round to face starboard, and I opened my doors to go out. We were going into the lake, don't forget."

And so, with remarkable gentleness, W1048 'S-Sugar' touched down on the snow-covered ice. The surface of the lake was still frozen to a sufficient depth to bear the weight of the aircraft and was covered with a layer of snow to a depth of about three feet. Hewitt waited with bated breath:

"Until running out of momentum, the aircraft skated across the ice at a seemingly enormous speed. For its sake as well as our own, it was very lucky that the lake was still frozen over."

Busy at the controls, MacIntyre still had time to glance around:

"Landing on the ice we went straight ahead for a good distance and on looking back it appeared as if there was a flare path of fire - which I

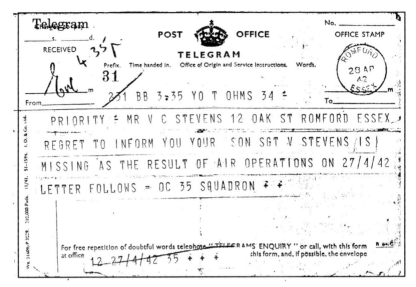

The telegram received by Vic Stevens' father, informing him that his son had been reported missing in action. (V. Stevens)

presume would be droppings from the aircraft, or oil or gasoline, or something of that nature. We appeared to go ahead for quite a long distance, and when we finally stopped, the left side of the aircraft was much lower than the right - and the right side continued to burn."

In careering along the icy surface of the lake at about 120 mph, Stevens was thrown about in the fuselage. MacIntyre, his hands grasping the control column, had the presence of mind not to try to use the flaps (which might well have caused the aircraft to turn, for the starboard flap had been destroyed by the fire). So the aircraft slid forward in a more or less straight line. The tips of the laminated wooden propellers were smashed off and disappeared in a whirl of splinters and flames as blazing fuel and oil fell to the ice in the wake of the sliding aircraft. She yawed wildly from side to side for what seemed an eternity to the crew and, when she finally shuddered to a halt, after sliding for nearly a half-mile, she was lying near the centre of the lake, tilted over onto her port side, the outer section of the starboard wing burning fiercely. Stevens lay where he had been thrown for maybe a minute and when he regained his senses he immediately sensed the strange quiet after the throbbing roar of the struggling engines had ceased. There was water seeping onto the fuselage floor. The remainder of the crew had gone.

NOTES

30. Unless otherwise indicated, quotes from Hewitt and MacIntyre are reproduced from *FlyPast* October 1982.

Chapter Ten

The German Defence
and the Aftermath

Before discovering what happened to those crews who found themselves in the water or on Norwegian soil, an account of other events needs to be given.

The experience of both this raid and the one that was to follow, was a very different one for the German sailors aboard the *Tirpitz*. The airmen's task was to reach the target, deliver their bombs as best they could, then fly home. The penalty for failure at any point was at best the threat of being taken prisoner of war. At worst, they risked serious injury or death. What really mattered to the airmen was to do their job and to survive. But they were in command of the situation. They had the initiative; they were the ones who were doing the attacking. For the sailors on board their steel-girt warship there was no way of knowing how long the attack would last, or when it would end. The chance of injury was smaller for them than for the aircrew flying above them and the chance of death even smaller, although at the height of the bombardment many must have wondered how long it would be before a bomb scored a direct hit. But, however long the attackers chose to bombard them, there was no escape from the aerial onslaught. They had, simply, to endure.

Just after 09.00 hours that morning of April 27th, the officer of the watch on board the *Tirpitz* was informed by telephone that a lone Spitfire was at that moment flying high (at 25,000 feet) directly over the peninsular of Frosta, only a few miles to the west of the battleship. The Spitfire, flown by Pilot Officer José de Puysellyr, had taken off from the north of Scotland at 06.43 hours that morning for a routine reconnaissance patrol over Trondheim. On board the *Tirpitz* the starboard 'aircraft warning post' was put on alert, as the Spitfire flew over the *Admiral Scheer*, a few miles to the north in her berth in Lofjord. It then made off to the southwest. The six fighter aircraft that took off to intercept the reconnaissance aircraft were unable to catch her.

The Germans were not to know that this was a prelude to the raid that was to materialise that night, for de Puysellyr was able to report that the battleships were still in their berths in the Åsen Fjord area.

After a routine day aboard the *Tirpitz*, the crew first became aware of the possibility of a full-scale attack when, at 23.08 hours, the steady approach of four-engined bombers flying way below the cloud-ceiling of 30,000 feet, was reported from Kristiansund, 100 miles away to the southwest. Then, just before 23.30 hours, the sailors of both port and starboard 'warning posts' were sent to their stations. The nearest aircraft was reported as being over the sea sixty miles to the southwest. The air-raid sounded a few minutes later and, just before midnight, the attack itself began. It was to last about 90 minutes. The action was fast and furious with little respite for anyone, either in the aircraft above or aboard the ship below.

Searchlights probed the twilit sky, two aircraft were spotted and the ship's artillery opened fire on them at 23.58 hours. Eight minutes later the smoke that had been billowing from the smoke-pots on shore and aboard the ship herself, laid their shroud over the entire vessel, successfully hiding her from the waves of bombers roaring overhead. Several flares burst overhead and floated down and, at 00.27 hours, a burning bomber crashed. This was probably shot down by the guns aboard the *Admiral Scheer*. It was, in all probability, Acting Flight Lieutenant George Miller's Halifax, W1037 'U-Uncle'. Then a few minutes later the *Tirpitz's* own artillery brought down a bomber, hitting it many times (probably Flight Lieutenant Mackid's Lancaster L7572 'L-Leather', all of whose

A PRU photograph of the Tirpitz in Fætten Fjord, taken by Flight Lieutenant John Merrifield on April 24th. (Air Photo Library)

crew perished). Suddenly, nearby, flying fast and low, a bomber roared past the ship and once again the artillery opened fire. First the bomber's starboard wing caught fire, then the port. Finally the aircraft curved away to crash in the mountains two minutes later. Flight Lieutenant Pooles and his crew aboard Halifax W1020 'K-King' perished instantly in the explosion.

The crew aboard the *Tirpitz* heard 'plane after 'plane weave its way up the fjord and they heard the crash and thump of bombs exploding in both the fjord and on the surrounding countryside. Another aircraft was hit (the *Tirpitz's* third) and

177

caught fire, disappearing quickly behind mountains. This was probably Halifax W1048 'S-Sugar'. Thirty-five minutes later, at 01.37 hours, the sound of the last aircraft was heard fading into the distance. Twenty minutes later, as the 'All-Clear' sounded, the northern lights flared suddenly in the sky. In the waters around their vessel the crew noticed the silvery sheen of the scales of the dead or senseless fish that had floated to the surface of the fjord, concussed by the exploding mines.

The Germans took careful stock of how they had fared during the attack. They recognised with some admiration that the attack had been 'very spirited' and carried out 'without regard for defence.' The *Enigma* message reporting on this raid, intercepted and deciphered by the British at the time, described the attack as 'most courageous', although, as it concluded, the ship had sustained no damage, protected as she was by the smoke-screen.

The artillery aboard the ship had expended over two thousand rounds of ammunition and the only damage they had sustained was a burst barrel in the muzzle of a four-barrelled gun. Thousands of rounds had of course been used by guns on other ships and on the shore. The crew had observed that the light artillery from shore-based batteries had provided a sweep of fire that, in general, lay behind the attacking bombers as they approached the ship. Flying as low as 200 feet from the surface of the waters of the fjord, the bombers had made a difficult target, particularly as the gun-crews had also to fire at the aircraft flying between 6,000 and 8,000 feet up in the sky. This was the first occasion that the crew had had to hide their vessel behind a smokescreen while in harbour. It was recognised that, despite the fact that it hampered the work of the defending gunners, it had provided the most effective protection from the bombers. However, since the upperworks of the vessel's superstructure, in particular the 'admiral's deck', was rarely well hidden by the smoke, they decided that the smoke canisters needed to be placed higher up the sides of the mountains, laid-out in a terrace formation. Also, their number needed to be increased to cover all outlets from Åsen Fjord.

But of greater concern was the unexpected use of what was identified as a new type of mine. Edmund Kuhnen was a

A view of the Tirpitz in Fætten Fjord with Salt Island in the background right. This is the route the bombers took up the fjord.
(via V. Stevens)

member of the crew at this time and, although recalling little of these raids because 'our crew suffered no casualties and there was no damage to the ship - such attacks do not stay in the memory as clearly as those which cause suffering to comrades', one aspect of the raids does stick out in his mind:

"What I do remember from that time is the weapons with which we were attacked. During the war I only experienced these in Fætten Fjord. We called them 'rolling mines'. The mines were supposed to roll down the cliffs and detonate under the ship. For defence against these, torpedo nets were spanned between the ship and the shore on top of the water to catch the 'rolling mines'. But I cannot remember that we ever caught a mine in this way."

Although there is no official record in the plans of the Bomber Command operation to suggest that aircrew should drop their mines on the cliffs in order for them to roll down under the ship, a number of aircrew who took part recall this being suggested at the briefing. It is evident that the German sailors also believed this was their intention. Nevertheless, as the Norwegian spy Bernhard Bergersen remarks:

"When you look at the landscape and the hills, it was a bad mistake using mines to be 'rolled down the hills' instead of regular bombs. Of course they didn't succeed, as the hills were covered by forests."

Eight unexploded mines were found, some in the water and were made safe by the *Sperrwaffenkommando* (the safety division on the ship) by detonating them just off the shore during the day. At least one of them was carefully secured onto a make-shift wooden frame, which was lifted clear of the water with the aid of several of the buoys used for suspending the anti-torpedo netting; the chief gunnery officer opened it up to find out how it worked, making a detailed sketch of it, before it was prepared for demolition and exploded.

All afternoon a thorough search was carried out by mine-sweepers and small vessels with mine-sweeping equipment, to establish that there were no more 'rolling mines' in the area and that there were no other types of mine that may have been dropped and now lay beneath the water, waiting to explode. Nothing was found and life aboard the battleship resumed its regular routine.

The *Flak* experienced by all the aircrews was of unusual intensity, as Glenn Gardiner who flew Halifax W1050 'F-Freddie' (35 Squadron) on both nights now recalls:

> "The *Flak* from the defence was the most intense that I had ever experienced, criss-crossing in front of us, the incendiaries were like red-hot beans thrown across our path."

The *Flak* gunners were able to track the direction of their shots by watching the tracer that accompanied them. Roy Williams of 76 Squadron comments:

> "The defences were using tracer ammunition and it was awesome to see the trace following your path and getting closer until what seemed only a few yards behind, it suddenly switched to another target."

All the bombers that survived the *Flak* over the Trondheim Fjord and from the *Tirpitz* also survived the journey home. They arrived at their advanced bases in the two and a half hours between 03.50 hours and 06.21 hours. Patrolling the skies over Lossiemouth, as the bombers returned, were Sea Hurricanes from the Fleet Air Arm's 883 Squadron. This was a precaution to cover the possibility of German retaliation against the returning bombers. The first aircraft to land back at its advanced base was Lancaster R5515 'A-Able' of 44 Squadron, which touched down at Lossiemouth at 03.50 hours. But for some crews it became a great struggle to fly their stricken aircraft home at all. Halifax R9486 'Q-Queenie', which had

Left: One of the unexploded mines recovered by the Germans.
(via Author)

Above: After careful preparation, the recovered mines were detonated at a safe distance. (via Author)

arrived too late to attack the *Tirpitz* and instead had attacked the warships in Lofjord, had been severely damaged by *Flak*. One of her mines had hung-up too. Sergeant W. 'Tubby' Lawes, her flight engineer, had to release it manually on a second run over the target:

"We suffered a lot of damage on this run - tanks holed, one engine out, hydraulics out and bomb-doors open and jammed, 90 holes in the aircraft."

After discussing whether to make for Sweden or chance the North Sea and fly home, her second pilot, Pilot Officer Ronnie Waite, writes in his memoirs:

"We all agreed and settled down to face the formidable journey back. Once Kenny had trimmed the Halifax for straight and level flight, his task was to remain awake and alert during the tedious four hours ahead. The flight engineer now had the most important task of watching his fuel gauges, working out the best use of the fuel and changing the tank cocks as required. The only thing I could do was to adjust the 'rev' levers to keep the three engines synchronised." [31.]

Sergeant Roy Williams, her wireless operator/air-gunner, remembers what happened as they staggered homeward:

"Homeward bound we continued to gradually lose height, so endeavoured to lighten the aircraft by jettisoning all 'surplus' equipment including flares and ammunition. In due time it became increasingly evident that it was almost inevitable that we would ditch before being able to make a landfall, so an SOS signal was sent and acknowledged."

Somehow, however, they managed to maintain height and the SOS signal, radioed when the aircraft was nearly three hours from base, was cancelled. However, it was to be 'touch and go'; Ronnie Waite completes the account of their journey home:

"The hours dragged on and fuel was getting dangerously low; we had to face the possibility of ditching in the sea. We were almost resigned to this, when 'Tubby', who had been peering out from the astrodome above his head, almost yelled, 'Good God, Kenny, I think I can see a light in the distance'."[32.]

It was Wick, but the captain pointed out that, with only three engines, it would be safer to land on the longer runway at their base at Tain. So they flew on in the grim hope that the fuel would last out. Ronnie Waite now waited to discover whether or not his first operation would also be his last:

"It had been nine hours since we took off from Tain, when we spotted the airfield again. No one spoke. We all felt the tension Kenny must have been experiencing as he concentrated on making the landing. There was no room for error - the first attempt had to be the only one. There could be no second chance. I watched tensely as Kenny held the aircraft straight 'till the final squeal of the tyres indicated that we were safely down. Almost everyone shouted 'Hooray!'

"Shortly after landing, all three engines cut - one after another - as the last petrol tank became drained. I am not sure whether I felt pride, satisfaction or relief at having completed my first operation.

"A few days later, we heard through the 'grapevine' that Kenny Clack had been recommended for an immediate Distinguished Flying Medal for this operation, for his 'outstanding courage and determination'."[33.]

The crew were unaware of the extent and severity of the damage to their aircraft, until the following day when, as Roy Williams recalls:

"Upon inspecting the aircraft next morning we realized just

Sergeant Roy Williams, who flew in Halifax R9486:Q in 1942.
(R.Williams)

182

(l to r) Sergeant Kenny Clack, Pilot Officer Ronnie Waite and Flight Sergeant Tommy Thompson, shortly after the April raids on Fætten Fjord. (R. Waite)

how lucky we had been. The fuselage was peppered with holes, the hydraulic system had been badly damaged - hence the open bomb-doors - and in addition to the No. 1 engine being completely u/s, Nos. 2 and 3 had both been damaged and the throttle control rods to engine No. 4 had been almost severed in two."

The ground crews and staff watched as bomber after bomber came in to land in the dim light of dawn, waiting until it became clear that no more were coming home. The thirty-sixth and final aircraft to return was Halifax W1056 'N-Nan' of 10 Squadron, which reached Lossiemouth at 06.21 hours after nine hours and seventeen minutes in the air. Five aircraft and their crews had failed to return.

At the debriefing, which began to take place as soon as the crews emerged wearily from their aircraft, the events of the night were gradually pieced together. Of the forty-one aircraft from five squadrons that had reached the coast of Norway, thirty-two had attacked the *Tirpitz*, three had attacked other targets only, while four had had to jettison their bombs or mines, thus failing to attack any target at all. Although bombs had been seen to burst over the target no one had seen any part

183

of the ship damaged. Aircraft of Nos. 44, 76 and 97 Squadrons had been ordered to take photographs (with the aid of photo-flashes) of the operation as it took place (although the use of photo-flashes during the second phase of the attack, had been strictly forbidden; they would only light up the aircraft for the benefit of the German *Flak* gunners). It was hoped that these night bombing photographs and the day's reconnaissance flights would reveal more promising information.

Certain facts were already established. The crew of 10 Squadron Halifax W1052 'K-King' had seen an aircraft being shot down in flames 'over the city of Trondheim'. Three members of the crew had been observed baling out. This was probably Halifax W1041 'B-Baker', piloted by Wing Commander Bennett.

Another crew from 10 Squadron, in Halifax W1055 'Z-Zebra', reported 'A small ship thought to be a tanker, observed burning off Trondheim.' Maybe Halifax W7656 'F-Freddie' had scored a hit with her mines. The crew of Halifax W1038 'O-Orange' reported that they had observed a fire on the west bank of the entrance to Trondheim Fjord.

While preparations for a possible second raid on the *Tirpitz* that night went ahead, the crews had a meal and went to bed. Their heads were ringing with the roar of aircraft engines and their minds relived their experiences in the *Flak*-filled fjord containing a battleship which, despite their great determination, it seemed that they had failed to hit.

The following day, PRU flights at 13.00 hours and 14.30 hours observed the effects of the raid. The photographs taken over the battleship revealed that the *Tirpitz* appeared not to have suffered any damage at all. There was no change in her position, although her 'A' gun turret was now trained forward and further camouflage rafts had been added to her stern. The *Altmark* tanker still lay in the same position in Åsen Fjord as on the previous day. It seemed that the raid had failed in its chief objective; the *Tirpitz* remained afloat and undamaged.

A page from Don MacIntyre's logbook, completed by himself on his return to England and signed by the Officer Commanding 'B' Flight, Squadron Leader Peter Cribb. (D. MacIntyre)

Squadron Leader Peter Cribb.
(via Author)

Bombs dropped by Lancaster L7577 'T-Tommy' had obviously hit Værnes Aerodrome, for the reconnaissance aircraft reported a bomb crater on the western edge of the north-south runway, the activity seen around it suggesting that repairs were in progress. It was learned later, that a barracks on the aerodrome 'received a direct hit, many Germans being killed'.

Of the forty-three aircraft (twelve Lancasters and thirty-one Halifaxes) that had taken off on this operation, thirty-eight had returned, including the two aircraft that had had to return early with engine trouble. But, entered in the Squadron Record Book against the serial number and crew list of five aircraft is the stark comment so often found in the pages of these books: 'This aircraft failed to return from this mission, no contact being made after it had left the advanced base.' It took time for news of what had happened to these aircraft to trickle back to England and the fate of some of them was not to be known until after the war.

However, one of the crew reports from the raid indicated a drama that was still being played out. After dropping his 4,000lb bomb, Squadron Leader Dugdale had cruised about the target area in Lancaster R5496 'U-Uncle', until 01.35 hours, dropping flares and 500lb bombs. In the report he made on his return he had this to say:

"On the other side of the fjord where the *Prinz Eugen* is situated, presumed to be aircraft on fire and crashed on frozen lake to the east of fjord."

Since only one aircraft is known to have 'crashed' on a frozen lake that night, the last few words of this report presumably refer to W1048 'S-Sugar'. This, however, was not the only information about W1048 'S-Sugar' to reach England with the returning aircraft: The Officer Commanding 'B' Flight, Squadron Leader Peter Cribb, pilot of 35 Squadron Halifax W1047 'R-Robert', had circled over W1048 'S-Sugar' as she lay blazing on the ice of Lake Hoklingen. Seeing no sign of any of her crew (as he told her pilot, Pilot Officer MacIntyre, some years later) he 'had given them up for goners'.

NOTES

31. From the draft manuscript of *Death or Decoration*. (Newton 1991)
32. *Ibid*
33. *Ibid*

Chapter Eleven
The Second April Raid

The aircrew were woken before noon of the 28th to learn that the *Tirpitz* was to be attacked again that night. Sergeant Ben Gibbons of 10 Squadron recalls that at the briefing, 'there was an ominous quiet compared to the previous day'.

This second operation was an exact repeat of the first raid, with one difference. The two squadrons of Lancasters took off 35 to 40 minutes later than they had the previous night. It had been realised that the gap between their operation to reduce the defences and the main force's attack, had been too great. This had been quite evident to some of the crews, for Sergeant Gibbons remembers that on the first night's raid:

> "As we neared the coast we could see *Flak* inland and as we crossed the coast our worst fears were confirmed: the diversion had bombed early and the aircraft were passing us on their way home."

The Lancasters of 44 and 97 Squadrons took off for the second night's raid under a full moon at about 21.00 hours, shortly after their crews had received a message of encouragement from Winston Churchill. Once again they flew the same course and once again they experienced the difficulties of bombing blind from 6,000 feet into a dense smoke-screen that quickly built up around the *Tirpitz*, although some reported seeing their bombs hitting the land and the water within 100 yards of the battleship. Several crews in 97 Squadron, whose rôle, once again, was to provided support for the low-flying, mine-dropping Halifaxes that followed them, commented that the *Flak* was even heavier and more accurate than on the previous night.

Some of the Lancasters flew over Lofjord and bombed the *Prinz Eugen* and the *Admiral Scheer* there. Only three out of the nine aircraft from 76 Squadron (the Halifax squadron carrying out the first phase attack with the Lancasters) actually saw the target and these crews saw some of their bombs drop close to the target. Ironically, Wing Commander Young's navigator realised after the attack that they might not have attacked the *Tirpitz* at all. The report in the Operations Record Book states that:

"The navigator believes that the bomb was dropped in error in Stranden Fjord as ground visibility was at this point obscured by smoke."

After their attack on the primary target, those aircraft of 76 Squadron that could, went on to attack light *Flak* concentrations, searchlights and aerodromes in the vicinity with some success. The crew of Lancaster R5492 'M-Mother' (the 44 Squadron standby crew of Warrant Officer Osbourne who had found themselves taking part in the previous night's raid at short notice), carrying one 4,000lb blast bomb and three 500lb general purposes bombs, released all their bombs in one stick as they ran over the target (although one GP bomb hung-up and had to be brought home). The navigator and rear-gunner saw a large burst close to the stern of the *Tirpitz* and they all felt their aircraft buck with the percussive effect of their bombs exploding fifty yards from the ship.

Warrant Officer Lamb, flying Lancaster R5494 'O-Orange', remarked afterwards that the light *Flak* had been lighter than on his previous night's raid, but they were attacked by light and heavy *Flak* from three warships, one of which was using a searchlight, on their approach up Trondheim Fjord.

After making a successful attack on the battleship, with little opposition from *Flak*, at 00.35 hours, the crew of Lancaster R5515 'A-Able' released their four GP bombs over a *Flak* ship near Fætten Fjord, scoring a direct hit, the ship eventually disappearing from sight.

Lancaster L7545 'K-King' successfully attacked *Tirpitz* at the same time, in what the pilot called 'perfect visibility', then flew on to attack the *Prinz Eugen* and the *Admiral Scheer* where they lay in Lofjord four minutes later. Warrant Officer Wright climbed his aircraft and circled to starboard as soon as his crew had seen their bomb burst 150 yards from the stern of the *Tirpitz*, then made a shallow dive over Lofjord. Two of their four bombs burst between the two cruisers anchored in the centre of the fjord.

8,000 feet above the fjord, the crew of Lancaster R5502 'M-Mother' watched as their bombs fell to explode close to the *Tirpitz*, three in the water, one on land. Their aircraft was then caught in a searchlight's beam that held them for several minutes before they were able to extricate themselves.

The crew of Lancaster R5496 'U-Uncle' reported experiencing heavier *Flak* than on the previous night and their four GP bombs burst on the landward side of the *Tirpitz*. Several of the Lancasters of 97 Squadron followed up their main attack by dropping bombs on *Flak* positions and one aircraft attacked Værnes aerodrome.

Once again aircraft from Coastal Command played their part. Four Beaufighters from 235 Squadron were despatched from Sumburgh to provide fighter cover for the main attacking force. Their job was to patrol for enemy fighters and if possible to divert the gunners around Trondheim Fjord, although they had little effect in this respect. Patrolling the area around the Fjord they were fired at intermittently and ineffectively, but saw little of interest other than observing the smoke and the bombs and mines bursting in Fætten Fjord in the distance. They also reported seeing Flight Sergeant Roe's Halifax, W1053 'G-George' (35 Squadron), on fire in the trees to the northeast of the *Tirpitz*.

This time, however, the nightfighters that had long been expected did make an appearance, although not in any force; Squadron Leader Dugdale's crew, in Lancaster R5496 'U-Uncle' of 97 Squadron got a shock when they saw two nightfighters flying on a reciprocal course (the same course, but in the opposite direction) as they ran over the target at 8,000 feet, but there was no exchange of fire. The rear-gunner of R9447 'R-Robert' (76 Squadron) spotted one in the target area, but his skipper was able to take successful evasive action and it was not seen again. These were the only two crews to report the presence of nightfighters during any of the raids. There is no evidence that these fighters attacked any of the bombers. In fact there were no enemy nightfighters stationed in the area; any fighters reported by the crews must have been Me 109s or FW 200s from the aerodromes at Værnes or Lade.

The Halifaxes of 10 and 35 Squadrons (and also 76 Squadron) had taken off about 45 minutes before the Lancasters, climbing up into a sky that was still lit by the last rays of the sun. Once again the navigators were able easily to map-read their way to the target.

Returning to attack the same target for a second night running gave the crews an unusual familiarity with the terrain, as Bill Grierson-Jackson, navigator in Halifax W1047 'R-Robert' of 35 Squadron, recalls:

> "And so we went back for more of the same, but this time prepared for the smoke and with all members of the crew briefed for the landmarks to look out for as soon as we entered the Fætten Fjord." [34.]

The crews also had a fuller appreciation of what would happen once they were approaching the target. Flying Officer Jack Watts was grateful that he had plenty to do:

> "The hours of flight over those dark, cold waters were a repeat of the previous night's experience. My thoughts and my activities were fully involved in the task of navigating us to the fjord. Once again, we made our landfall at the entrance to Trondheim Fjord, right on schedule. The air was clear and cold; visibility was excellent; the nearby mountains stood out in the same black and white relief in bright moonlight as they had on the previous night. The feeling this time was more foreboding than religious as we turned into the fjord at the planned 4,000 feet and began our run to the Åsen Fjord." [35.]

Jack Watts has a vivid recollection of the last few minutes of flying up Trondheim Fjord:

> "As we came alongside the town of Trondheim, we were surprised to see a searchlight reaching out across the fjord for us. We were caught in the beam, but at that relatively low altitude, we felt that we were probably out of the slant range of any anti-aircraft guns which might have been sited there. We didn't feel unduly concerned, therefore, since we weren't being shot at. Suddenly, the mid-upper gunner shouted on the intercom, 'Fighter! Fighter! In the beam on the starboard.' This came as a real shock, a totally unexpected turn of events. We hadn't been expecting any fighters. It was enough to raise the hairs on the back of your neck as you expected at any moment to hear those cannon shells hammering into the fuselage.
>
> "We were almost at the approach to the Åsen Fjord by this time, so I directed Tom (Pilot Officer Tom Godfrey, the pilot) to make his dive immediately while I guided him towards the entrance of the fjord. As we

entered the fjord, the need for guidance became minimal. Ahead of us was a cauldron of anti-aircraft fire. The small fjord had been ringed with light anti-aircraft guns which were firing continuously across and down into the fjord from the cliff walls. The tracers were laced across the fjord from side to side and the shells were striking the water surface as well. In the centre of this fury lay the *Tirpitz* firing all the guns of her anti-aircraft batteries into the sky over the top of the ship. The criss-crossing tracers from the shore guns and the fire from the ship's guns made the air space over the top of the *Tirpitz* a maw of molten metal which appeared to be absolutely impenetrable. Talk about your Charge of the Light Brigade. No one in his right mind would fly through that barrage. Certainly no German night-fighter. I took Tom through the barrage, over the *Tirpitz* and out again over the cliff wall at the end. The fighter broke off and made no attempt to follow us into the Åsen Fjord.

"However, I had not been able to make a satisfactory bombing run either. So, I made no attempt to drop our mines as we flew over the top of the *Tirpitz*. We would have to go round again, make a second diving approach for a more precise bombing run, this time, hopefully, with no fighter to distract us.

"As on the previous night, of the 27th, we must have been the first aircraft on target when we ran in to shake off that fighter. We had been able to see the *Tirpitz* clearly for its entire length, with dark canvases stretched on frames at the bow and stern to disguise her outline. As we climbed out from that first run and began our turn, it was obvious that other aircraft were making their bombing runs. We saw one Halifax rear up out of that hell-fire of *Flak* to escape the cliff wall. It was ablaze, and obviously crippled. This was either Flight Lieutenant Petley's Halifax which flew on to ditch in Trondheim Fjord, or Pilot Officer Roe's aircraft that crashed near Lake Movatn.

"Everything was happening too quickly now for cogent observation. When we made our second run through the fjord and the *Flak*, the picture had changed. We ran along the edge of the fjord, exactly at mast-height, and began the drop of our four mines in a short string aimed for the stern of the *Tirpitz*. As we pulled up, we could see the explosions of our weapons. One and two were clean spumes of water, three was dirty and four was slightly delayed, presumably as it rolled off the cliff wall or the deck of the ship. But it was dirty as well. The canvas camouflage at the stern of the ship was almost totally destroyed, the ship appeared to be clear at the bow, but awash at the stern. We were so excited at what we could see and the apparent success of our own attack that we paid little heed to the hail of fire through which we were flying and to the damage which we were absorbing. Our stomachs sank as we pulled up to clear the cliff and to escape the *Flak*. Only then did we begin to think about our chances of making it back. We realised that we had probably been first on the target when we made our initial run, and probably the last to attack when we made our second run.

"The damage which we had received seemed to have been superficial, and, miraculously, no one in the crew had been injured in either of our runs through that *Flak*. It looked as if we would be able to make it back to Lossiemouth, and we began to think about the report we would make. We were exuberant about the success of the attack and our escape with whole skins. Our joy was tempered, however, by the knowledge that others had not been so fortunate. And we wondered just how many had been lost." [36.]

Bill Grierson-Jackson, navigator in Halifax W1047-R (35 Squadron), recalls their attack:

"Peter (Squadron Leader Cribb, the pilot) went up Trondheim Fjord 'right down on the deck' where it would be hard for the *Flak* gunners to see us anyway, they were not used to shooting downwards! Entering the Fætten Fjord, he climbed to just above the top of the smoke screen. It was strange that there did not seem to be any enemy fighters around, but just as well as we would have been as visible to them as flies on a white plate. The gunners called directions trying to keep us aligned on the assigned landmarks as nearly as they could with Peter co-ordinating. We bombed 'by consensus' and it certainly seemed to me that we were in the very heart of the fountain of *Flak* that, presumably, came from the *Tirpitz*, though we could not see any masts. The smoke screen was just too deep. Peter did a split-arse turn to avoid the cliff and headed up the fjord towards Hoklingen. Immediately behind us there was a tremendous explosion from the general direction of the ship. We profoundly hoped that was *Tirpitz*, but no one could know for sure." 37.

Once again, the crews of the low-flying Halifaxes, following hard on the heels of the Lancasters of 44 and 97 Squadrons and the Halifaxes of 76 Squadron, were convinced that they had achieved some very near-misses indeed. While one crew reported seeing their mines burst 'beneath the stern of the ship', another crew saw, 'two of the mines undershoot, one burst very near the ship and two struck the bank.' The rear-gunner of W1039 'C-Charlie' (10 Squadron) saw 'bursts and rising bubbles similar to an underwater explosion', while the crew of W1057 'X-X-Ray' (10 Squadron) watched their mines actually fall between fjord side and the ship, a most accurate shot. However, they reported that, 'Result of attack nil, although two definite colours of water seen rising between side of target and edge of fjord'

Once again, it was these low-flying Halifaxes that took the brunt of the enemy fire. Climbing away from the target immediately after his attack, Flight Sergeant Glenn Gardiner, piloting Halifax W1050 'F-Freddie' (35 Squadron), was severely affected by the *Flak*, as he recalls with some amusement:

"It was so intense that I made a wider left climbing turn only to learn, to my chagrin, that we would pass over the cruisers (actually *Prinz Eugen*, *Admiral Hipper* and *Admiral Scheer*). We were so low on the tree tops that the mid-upper gunner reported that we had disturbed a bird from her nest to which the rear gunner added that there were four eggs in the nest! We didn't return for verification. Those cruisers were most unfriendly!"

Several of the Halifaxes of 10 Squadron suffered considerable damage during the final minutes of their bombing runs and some of the men on board were injured. W1039 'C-Charlie' (10 Squadron) was hit by *Flak* over the *Tirpitz* - a hole 18 inches square was blasted in her tail-plane and a smaller one in the tail fin. The bomb doors were damaged, a shell exploded in the starboard engine and the leads to some of the petrol cocks were shot away. Despite a severe shortage of petrol the crew managed to fly their aircraft to Sumburgh where they landed safely.

This was not the only aircraft that struggled on to land at Sumburgh. The first wireless operator aboard W1057 'X-X-Ray' (10 Squadron) was Flight Sergeant Chris Charlton, who remembers that after their bombing run:

"We climbed away at full power over the cliffs. We found out later on inspection that we had lost our main hydraulics which left 30 degree flaps on and bomb-doors open. Also, we had one football mine hung up, due to Lossiemouth sand in the switches. After all this was found out we decided to conserve what fuel we had and made for Sumburgh, Shetlands, which gave us an extra two hours fuel endurance."

They were only able to maintain a maximum of 110 mph. The captain, anxious that his aircraft might not make it back to base at all, ordered the crew to jettison as much equipment as they could. Into the gale that buffeted up into the forward hatchway the crew tossed the bomb-sight, ammunition boxes (perhaps the heaviest item of all), the sextant case, Verey cartridges, oxygen bottles and even tin hats - all instantly lost to sight, spinning down in their wake. Charlton continues his recollection:

"When daylight was with us we found we had four Beaufighters stationed above us, also from Sumburgh Coastal Command. They announced their presence above us to us and asked us if we could make it, which we said we could, heading to Sumburgh and breakfast and the aircraft to be checked over. They agreed to that and said they would hold off until we had got in and they would then follow. We got down quite well, landing down the hillside onto the runway and pulled up quite well long before we were near the beach at the other end."

Halifax W1052 'K-King' (10 Squadron), piloted by Flight Sergeant Rochford, flew into the attack without the assistance of the rear guns, which had become unserviceable during the outward flight. They were flying a different aircraft from the one in which they had carried out the previous night's raid (when the way in which Sergeant Rochford and his crew had pressed home the attack despite the 'very severe *Flak* encountered from both banks of the fjord' earned a DFM for the pilot). The decision to continue their attack, despite the lack of the defensive fire-power of the rear guns, is a measure of the determination of this crew. Their aircraft was hit by a shell from the banks of the fjord during the attack, the shell exploding in the wireless operator's compartment, severely wounding the wireless operator, Flight Sergeant Clear, and the second pilot, Pilot Officer Dempsey. Despite the damage to the aircraft and the injuries sustained by two of the crew members, Flight Sergeant Rochford was able to fly his aircraft back to base, where the two wounded men were quickly removed to hospital.

Warrant Officer Lloyd's Halifax, W1058 'L-Leather' (10 Squadron), having released her mines blind into the smoke-screen over the battleship below, was extensively holed in the fuselage, while the rear-gunner, Sergeant Gifford, received slight shrapnel wounds in his legs. This crew, too, managed to get their aircraft home. Pilot Officer Murray of Halifax W1055 'Z-Zebra' (10 Squadron), having delivered his attack at 800 feet amid, 'severe and accurate *Flak* from both sides of the fjord', had to return home with one of his mines hung-up in the bomb-bay and his port outer engine out of action. He managed to land without incident.

Two of 35 Squadron's Halifaxes that had taken off had barely lost sight of land before they both had to return with engine trouble. Squadron Leader Wilding, piloting W7658 'H-Harry' and Flying Officer Jones in W1049 'V-Victor' jettisoned their mines 'safe' in the sea before heading for base. Of the remaining five aircraft from the squadron, three dropped their mines through the smoke-screen, while two became the only casualties of that night.

After making her attack, W1053 'G-George', too badly damaged to continue flying for long, somehow made her way up the Åsen Valley in much the same way as W1048 'S-Sugar' had the previous night. It is probable that the pilot, Flight Sergeant Roe, intended to put down his aircraft on Movatn Lake, just to the northeast of Lake Hoklingen, but as he brought her down over the water it seems that he suddenly saw a small tree-covered peninsular looming up ahead. He pulled the aircraft up into a sudden climb in a desperate attempt to avoid hitting it. He succeeded, but had run out of landing space. Unable to keep his aircraft in the air any longer, he put her down on the far shore, where she ploughed through trees before coming to rest. A fierce fire broke out, intense oily black smoke boiling upwards, while intermittent magnesium flashes illuminated the aircraft as it blazed fiercely amongst the trees.

The second Halifax to be shot down was W7656 'P-Peter'. Although his aircraft was on fire, her pilot, Flight Lieutenant Petley, managed to ditch her in Åsen Fjord, about three miles off the shore at Røkke in Skatval. Sergeant Gordon Cranstone, her second wireless-operator, vividly recalls the events of that night. This was the third sortie he and his crew had made against the *Tirpitz*:

"The last flight was unfortunate. We had a cracking bloke, he was one of those who was killed, a fellow called Columbine - he was observer. He laid in the belly of the nose of the Halifax for the run-up to let the bomb-load go, and I don't know what happened, whether it was all the *Flak* coming up, but we did this one up (a first bomb-run) and came out of it, and thought that was it, when he said over the intercom to the skipper that he hadn't let the mines go. Our skipper, he was a marvellous bloke. He said 'It just means that we'll have to go back the other way.' Now, when we came down the second time that night we didn't go in the way we were supposed to. The pilot said, 'I'm going to drop over the mountains and go round at them'. And that's what he did. When we came in, God, there was stuff flying everywhere. Well, it had gone quiet, you see, and we'd got away the first time, and he circled. As we came in it was very, very quiet. I couldn't believe it, that they would let us get away with it. I should have known better! Anyhow, we got to a point where he was ready to drop in on it, he was coming in fast, and all of a sudden all hell broke loose. They were waiting for us, obviously they knew, and everything broke loose, everything. I mean quite honestly you couldn't have seen anything because there was so much *Flak* and every fifth one is a tracer, there was everything.

"Do you know, all I can remember seeing was lots of flashes, the odd thuds, smell of cordite, and then all of a sudden (mind you this is taking longer to tell it than it actually happened), all of a sudden the port wing went up. It was on fire, one minute it was okay, the next minute it had got a hit, I suppose. It just went up. We were lucky it didn't take the wing off, obviously. The engine must have had a hit, but it all went up in a tremendous burst of flame. I got out of the mid-upper turret and got down. Just forward of it there was a hatchway which you could jettison in case you had troubles and crashed, and you had to get out quick. I always remember that'd been jettisoned by the engineer, Price, our flight engineer. There was a wire ladder leading up to this hatchway, and when I got down I remember holding on to this wire ladder, because all hell was breaking loose. All I climbed up it - I'd got a fire extinguisher - I know it was absolutely daft to do it, in fact it was a waste of time - but I got up, and I remember sticking my head out, and all I could see was these colossal flames, and of course the blast from the engines was coming back, and there was me trying to stick an extinguisher out. It was ridiculous, it was just like spitting into the wind, but you don't think correctly at the time. All I felt was I'd got to do something and I grabbed a fire extinguisher and I got up there with it.

"It was a helluva struggle, but the moment I stuck my head out, it was ridiculous, and all I could see was flames on this side of the kite. I don't suppose I did a thing - it couldn't have done - if the fire had been behind me I'd have got it! You would say on analysis, 'The man must be stupid!' But you don't think at the time, you see. And then, the next thing ... I was lucky: I got down, and at that moment the skipper decided he'd got to put it in the drink, fast. And I always remember, I just got down, and I still had my hands on the wire - you know you'd think the wire would go through my hand like cheese, but it didn't - I'd just got my foot down in the fuselage, onto the floor level, and I was still holding the wires when we hit the drink. And all I did was sway backwards and forwards like that, but I'd still got hold of it, so I went straight back up the ladder again, because I knew by this time that we had hit the drink. I went straight up and I was the first man out."

The air-raid siren aboard *Tirpitz* had sounded at midnight and, with the moonlight providing excellent visibility despite a slightly overcast sky, the crew were under no illusions. This was a return of the bombers of the previous night.

As the dense, reeking smoke-screen began to fill the air around the ship, several waves of aircraft were reported approaching in the distance. Within twenty minutes the first bombs were beginning to rain down and, for the next 75 minutes, there was no let-up from the bombers. Every few minutes either bombs were dropping or aircraft were heard roaring overhead.

At one point stone chippings spattered the deck, the debris blown aboard by a bomb that struck the hillside overlooking the battleship. Then the ship's gunners suddenly saw a bright green star erupt from a passing aircraft. They held their fire. The recognition signal for the day was green; that was one of their own fighters, running the gauntlet over Fætten Fjord. It was the only fighter they saw and may have been the only one, for they learned later that the fighters had been unable to take off that night at all. The Allied attacks on the local airfields by aircraft of both Coastal Command and the support force, in particular the damage caused at the nearest aerodrome, Værnes, by a 4,000lb bomb, may well have had such results.

A red flare burst about 2,000 metres from the ship as more bombers flew overhead, then more bombs fell to the stern of the vessel. At 01.06 hours, just when the smoke-screen was ineffectually covering the vessel in patches, and the night sky was briefly visible to the gunners on board the vessel, a bomber flew into range. Shots were seen to hit the aircraft, but the results of this success were not observed (and it is not known which aircraft this was). Towards the end of the raid one bomb or mine struck the water only 66 yards from the starboard side of the battleship, but no damage was done. By 01.30 hours the crew heard the sound of the last bomber dying away in the distance, as it made its way home. Half an hour later the 'All-Clear' sounded and, once again, the crew took stock.

They had been attacked eleven times and had observed or felt the percussion of at least 25 bombs or mines. Although the smoke-screen was thicker than it had been on the previous night, the smoke canisters on the south-eastern side of the fjord did not appear to have been activated at all. However, the gun-crews measured the effectiveness of the smoke-screen's protection by the fact that they had only had to open fire once - when the screen had suddenly and briefly cleared, exposing their ship to the aircraft above them.

That evening, as darkness fell, fearful of a third attack, the *Tirpitz* left Fætten Fjord and sailed out into the main Trondheim Fjord. She sailed at slow speed along the east coast of Norviksundet and up Skansund, returning to Fætten Fjord with the daylight. She refuelled during the day, then made for a night-berth at Væna-Sund, making a point of not returning to Fætten Fjord until the early hours of May 1st, when the anti-torpedo net was again linked into place around her.

Although not damaged, it is clear that the Germans were anxious not to put their vessel at such risk again. The excellent smoke-screen had been their salvation, but luck had played a part and had favoured the Germans - so far.

In the Bomber Command Operations Record Book the following statement sums up the results of the second night's raid:

> "A photographic sortie on the 30th April, failed to reveal any signs of damage to the enemy vessels, or to the town and docks."

The crews of the PRU Spitfires and Mosquitos that had laboured for nearly four months now to keep track of the *Tirpitz*, had their own comment, part tongue-in-cheek, to make. Someone at RAF Benson with a sardonic sense of humour had produced a small poster. Above a photograph of a PRU Spitfire flying above the clouds this caption was printed:

RE - TRONDHJEM
NEVER, HAVE SO MANY
GONE SO FAR FOR SO LITTLE

But Arthur Harris recognised the toll these operations had taken on his crews. The telegram he sent to Group Captain Graham on May 3rd, and which was circulated amongst the crews that had returned from the raids, acknowledged this. [38.] A total of seven aircraft, five aircraft on the first night and two on the second, had failed to return. 58.2 tons of bombs (ie. explosives, whether they were bombs or mines) had been dropped by aircraft attacking the *Tirpitz* during the first night's raid and 58.8 tons on the second. It is surprising that, with such a weight of bombs raining down on the *Tirpitz*, from aircraft whose crews pressed home their attack with such courage and determination, the battleship was not hit or damaged at all. However, from the nineteen photographs taken during the attack it was deduced that the nearest bombs fell about 440 yards from their target (although *Tirpitz's* log-book records the nearest as falling seventy yards from the ship). The difficulty of flying up the narrow fjord against a considerable barrage from land-based *Flak* emplacements and through an extremely effective smoke screen, had prevented the airmen from achieving any better bomb-aiming than they had. The explosive force of the mines and bombs that narrowly missed the ship was insufficient to cause the damage expected of them. Given the crews' determination, to have achieved the accuracy they did was a considerable feat in itself. It is clear that results better than these were unlikely to occur without greater loss of men and aircraft.

Glenn Gardiner referring recently to his days on operations as 'flying scared', believes that, 'The early raids on the *Tirpitz* certainly were the most difficult and required a lot of extra flying training, both day and night'. Of the second night's raid, Ben Gibbons of 10 Squadron has remarked: 'although we did not lose any aircraft, damage and injuries were more severe'.

The determination of the crews in the face of appalling danger is well illustrated by the following extract from the book *Terror by Night*, written by Flight Lieutenant Michael Renaut of 76 Squadron, who piloted Halifax W1006 'K-King' in both the April raids. Of the ferocity of the *Flak* on one of the two raids, he wrote that as they approached the target, 'We then saw the most colossal barrage ahead from the *Tirpitz* and it seemed as if every gun in Norway had been moved to Åsen Fjord.' As they came in for their high-level bombing-run, they saw a Halifax below them catch fire and explode:

"We could see the *Tirpitz* faintly in the light from the blaze and Tim, the navigator/bomb-aimer, started to ask me to hold a steady course. It was not fear that prevented me, it was the sheer intensity of the *Flak* - I just couldn't hold the Halifax steady and listened to the *Flak* punching holes in us. The first bombing run was hopeless because the Hun had started a smokescreen, the *Tirpitz* had now disappeared under the smoke but we knew near enough where she lay and I attempted to hold the Halifax steady for a moment, imploring Tim to drop the bomb. Tim's temper was raised and he said, 'I haven't come all this bloody way to drop the bomb haphazard - you hold a steady course and I'll let go.'

"Round I went for a third bombing run, frightened to death and not at all anxious to be shot down over the snow-covered mountain. Tim said: 'Hold her steady at that,' but the *Flak* was murderous and I could hear chunks of

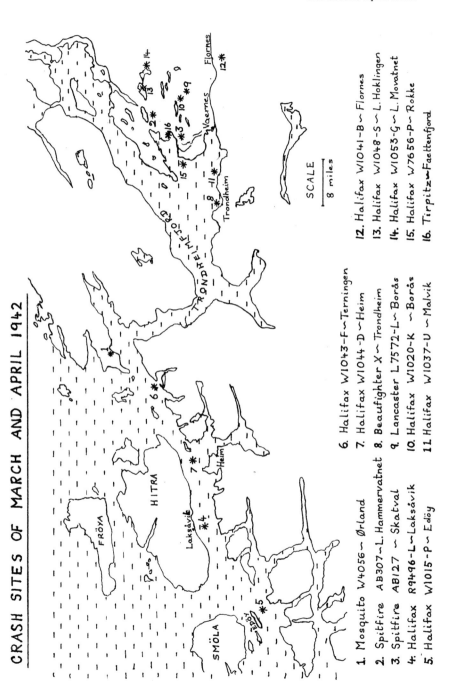

CRASH SITES OF MARCH AND APRIL 1942

SCALE
8 miles

1. Mosquito W4056 ~ Ørland
2. Spitfire AB307 ~ L. Hammervatnet
3. Spitfire AB127 ~ Skatval
4. Halifax R9496-L ~ Laksåvik
5. Halifax W1015-P ~ Edøy
6. Halifax W1043-F ~ Terningen
7. Halifax W1044-D ~ Heim
8. Beaufighter X ~ Trondheim
9. Lancaster L7572-L ~ Borås
10. Halifax W1020-K ~ Borås
11. Halifax W1037-U ~ Malvik
12. Halifax W1041-B ~ Flornes
13. Halifax W1048-S ~ L. Hoklingen
14. Halifax W1053-G ~ L. Movatnet
15. Halifax W7656-P ~ Rokke
16. Tirpitz ~ Faettenfjord

it hitting the Halifax again.

"Still I couldn't fly a steady course and again Tim refused to let the bomb go, so round I went for a fourth time. I tried to hold the Halifax steady but the *Flak* was just as severe as before and I knew I had to risk being shot out of the air to give Tim his chance. I did hold her steady for twenty seconds which seemed like twenty years and Tim seemed fairly confident that we dropped our bomb in the centre of the smoke screen but all I was concerned with was getting out of that bloody inferno, and quickly!

"Tim Collins seemed to me to be quite fearless, and the way he calmly bombed the *Tirpitz* with light *Flak* being pumped straight up at him from the ground was nothing short of cool-headedness and unconcern at danger."[39.]

With the moon-phase passing, and even lighter nights expected as summer shortened the northern night to a few hours of twilight, the planners at Bomber Command had to take stock of the situation from a fresh viewpoint. There could be no more night-attacks until the autumn, for there was no more 'night' available. A suggestion to mount a daylight raid by flying bombers up Fætten Fjord, towards the *Tirpitz* with the rays of the sun behind them to dazzle the defences, was made and seriously considered, but finally shelved indefinitely when the *Tirpitz* left Fætten Fjord on a short coastal voyage to Bogen Fjord near Narvik on 2nd July 1942.

Harry Walmsley adds his comments to the ending of these attacks at this time:

"The newly appointed C-in-C of Bomber Command, 'Butch Harris' won the argument with the Royal Navy 'top brass' that it was not Bomber Command's job to attack ships and, from May 1942 onwards, the onslaught on Germany continued. It appears that he was much more forceful than his predecessor."

It may also be that the Navy, disappointed at the lack of success of the raids, did not continue to insist on help from Bomber Command, particularly since they were already preparing an attack of their own (with a small force of 'human torpedoes' or 'chariots') to take place in the autumn.

It is difficult to judge the effectiveness of *Operation Bluebeard* in preventing enemy fighters taking off and intercepting the bombers of the main force, or of diverting attention away from what was going on in Fætten Fjord. Many of the Coastal

Command Beaufighters had either been unable to find their targets or had arrived too late to attack them, but they had contributed to the general confusion of the night's events by attacking a variety of targets over a wide area of the Norwegian coastline. It does seem surprising that only a small number of RAF aircrew reported seeing German fighters during *Operation Bluebeard* or the Main Attack.

Ample evidence that *Luftwaffe* aircraft were available is provided by the reports of photographic reconnaissance. Among the enemy aircraft dispersed around the aerodromes near Trondheim were Focke-Wulf 200s, Junkers 88s, Heinkel 111s and Messerschmitt 109s. Only the Messerschmitt 109s could have been be used to attack the bombers, but why were so few of them seen in action? There would have been an understandable reluctance among German pilots to fly their aircraft near the battleships in the fjords at the height of the attacks (although it seems that more than one did just that!). However, the most opportune moment for fighters to attack the bombers would have been either just before or just after their bombing run and when they were on their way home, but this did not occur. The activities of Coastal Command's aircraft and those Halifaxes and Lancasters of Bomber Command that bombed the *Tirpitz* and then went on to bomb *Flak* emplacements, *Flak* ships, a destroyer, searchlights and local aerodromes, may have had a greater effect on the *Luftwaffe* presence than would appear likely from the record of the bombing of the aerodromes. Værnes aerodrome was bombed successfully on both nights with a total of four tons of bombs and the runway was damaged. Bombs were also seen to burst on the aerodromes (but not the runways) at Rinnleiret on the first night and Orlandet on the second. Lade aerodrome on the outskirts of Trondheim was not attacked.

The loss of seven aircraft to *Flak* during the two nights' raids at the end of April was serious enough without the greater loss of aircraft that would undoubtedly have occurred had the *Luftwaffe* played a more prominent role. A total of eighteen Bomber Command aircrew and two Coastal Command aircrew died during these two raids.

Wing Commander Bennett of 10 Squadron, who was shot down during the first April raid, had a number of comments to make concerning the raids when he was interrogated on 29th May, shortly after his return to England, as the following extracts from the Intelligence Officer's report show:

"29. As regards the whole operation, he considers that the interval after the first wave of the attack before the low level attack was too great (this problem was addressed successfully for the second night's raid). He saw no shooting in the target area all the time he was approaching it over the Fjord, until just before he came in to attack, when another aircraft had evidently preceded him.

"30. At the briefing they were given full particulars of the target but only a vague, more or less general reference, that there might be a smoke screen. No definite information of a smoke screen was available at the Squadron.

"31. While in Sweden he heard from the Naval Attache that a signal had been sent from the Naval Attache, Stockholm, to London in February that smoke barrels surrounding all the ships in Trondheim were permanently manned, and considers that this information should have been available to the Squadron."

Bennett also remarked that he was told that the sound of the bombs exploding in Fætten Fjord had been heard as far away as Sweden.

On 29th April, at Tain, Kinloss and Lossiemouth, when the tired crews who had flown back from Norway earlier that morning awoke, they learned that the operation was over. Despite the evidence of the photographs taken by reconnaissance aircraft that no damage had been sustained by the *Tirpitz*, there was to be no further attack. The moon period was coming to an end, the crews had flown two very long operations for two nights running and seven aircraft had been lost. The aircraft were needed over the Ruhr. Arthur Harris had done what he could for the Navy, now he wanted his bombers back.

During the day preparations were made to return home, although one squadron spent much of this day in the air. The two aircraft lost that night had been from 35 Squadron and Wing Commander Marks and Flying Officer Lane, along with their crews and with other aircraft, in spite of the fact that they had already spent eight or nine hours in the air with little or no break, took off again. In the words of the Operations Record Book, they 'searched unceasingly for nine and a half hours but without avail' for the wreckage of the missing aircraft, or their crews adrift in dinghies.

Despite their lack of success, among the men that morning there was great relief that the operation was over. As Ben Gibbons (10 Squadron) recalls, there was an element of celebration:

"There was a lighter side. During debriefing there was a supply of rum available without restriction. A Warrant Officer, I think it was 'Taffy' Lloyd, had a very rough trip. His aircraft had been extensively holed and his rear-gunner injured and had been treated to a generous supply of the refreshment. Having completed the debrief he set off for our huts without a care in the world, quite oblivious that he was crossing the parade ground - winding his way in and out of the ranks of future aircrews marching-past during the Station Commander's Parade!"

The following morning, 30th April, the crews who had gone on the 'special operation for HQ Bomber Command', taking with them as many of the ground crew as possible packed into the narrow fuselages of their aircraft, made the three-hour flight home to their bases without incident, in fine weather. A Whitley of 77 Squadron carried the A.O.C. No. 4 Group, Air Vice Marshal Carr, from Lossiemouth to Leeming. The effort was over.

Jack Watts remembers meeting Air Vice-Marshal Carr the following day:

"Those of us who were serviceable flew back to Leeming to rejoin the squadron members we had left behind. The next morning, Tom Godfrey and I were walking down the flight line when a saloon car drove up behind us and stopped by our side. It was our Air Officer Commanding, A.V.M. Carr. He had driven from Group HQ looking for us so that he could de-brief us again, personally. It had been determined from all the crew reports that we had indeed been the last aircraft to attack and, therefore, the last to see the *Tirpitz* that night. He wanted to hear our report again and to clarify some of the points he had in mind to assist him in assessing the probability and the extent of the damage done to the *Tirpitz*. This assessment must have been a vital content of the decision which had to be made on what might still have to be done to keep the *Tirpitz* from escaping into the open sea.

"Shortly after our return to Leeming, Tom and I were both awarded the Distinguished Flying Cross for our attacks on the *Tirpitz*." [40.]

Jack Watts goes on to recall that shortly after the squadron returned to base a message of congratulations was received from A.M. Harris, the C-in-C of Bomber Command (reproduced on page 13). Jack remarks:

> "Had our success been more readily apparent, had those weapons we carried been capable of sinking that mighty battleship, who knows what would have followed." [41.]

Some of the crews took with them vivid memories of their extraordinary experiences over the *Tirpitz*, while for others the operation was to become no more than a part of their overall recollections of 'flying scared' over enemy targets throughout the remainder of the war. The crews of 44 and 97 Lancaster Squadrons returned to Waddington and Woodhall Spa, respectively, from where they flew once more over the industrial targets of Germany. The crews of 10 Squadron returned to Leeming and, two months later, a detachment of them flew their Halifaxes out to the Middle East to take part in operations from there. 35 Squadron crews flew home to Linton-on-Ouse and, in August 1942, became part of the new Pathfinder Force brought into being at that time. Crews of 76 Squadron returned to their bombing missions over Germany from their base at Middleton-St-George, a detachment of them flying out to Palestine in July. The Spitfires and Mosquitoes of No 1 PRU continued their surveillance of the *Tirpitz* and the other enemy shipping units in Norway, while the men of Coastal Command, who had supported their colleagues in Bomber Command, persevered in their unremitting reconnaissance over the North Sea and in their attacks on enemy bases and enemy shipping in occupied Norway.

In the 76 Squadron Operations Record Book, after recording that on April 30th the detachment returned to Middleton-St-George from Tain 'on the conclusion of Number 4 Group Operations from advanced base', the Commanding Officer added this somewhat unexpectedly cheerful postcript:

> "All crews returned in excellent spirits having thoroughly enjoyed two successful operations and also the opportunity for sport and recreation afforded by the Scottish Highlands."

For those men who had not returned, but were still alive, the struggle to reach safety was far from over.

NOTES

37. From the unpublished memoir *We Band of Brothers* by W. Grierson.
38. See page 13.
39. *Terror by Night* - M. Renaut (Wm Kimber, 1982)
40. Flying Officer Jack Watts, from his unpublished memoirs.
41. *Ibid*

Chapter Twelve
Survival

Most of the attacking aircraft taking part in the raids on both nights in April, having made their bombing run over the target, were able to turn for home. Within a very short time they were clear of the defending guns and safely winging their way over the sea. In some aircraft, as the crew's tension lessened and tiredness began to set in, a flask of coffee or a sandwich appeared, to ease the long journey ahead. There was now time for a more detailed assessment of the damage (often considerable) that had been caused to their aircraft. For these crews, all that lay between the present and their landing at base was a relatively safe three to four hour flight.

But seven aircraft failed to return from the two nights' raids. Within seconds of their aircraft being mortally hit the crews of five aircraft were flung from the well-ordered and disciplined world at their stations inside the aircraft, into the wintry terrain of German-occupied Norway. They were often cut off from the remainder of their crews and forced to fend for themselves. For the entire crew of two aircraft there was oblivion, mercifully swift. Five aircraft failed to return home after the first raid and two after the second. Of the 45 men whose aircraft were shot down during these two raids, eighteen were killed, eighteen became prisoners of war, while nine men from among the crews of two of the aircraft were able to evade captivity to return to England.

Many of those who did survive their aircraft's fate were extremely lucky to be alive. The determination and dogged tenacity of many of them to evade capture was remarkable. Similarly, great courage was displayed by a number of Norwegians who risked death for themselves and their families in attempting to help unknown British airmen reach the safety of Sweden. Neutral Sweden, whose border lay no more than forty miles to the east of Åsen Fjord, could only be reached on foot across moors and mountains where snow still lay to a depth of about three feet. But this was the goal of all the aircrew who were able to parachute, walk, swim or paddle away from their downed aircraft. They were faced with a totally unfamiliar and hostile terrain in winter conditions, with temperatures hovering around freezing. Crossing icy streams and rivers, whose waters were swollen by the melting snow, increased the danger of death from the exposure of skin through sodden clothing to the raw winds and blizzard conditions that some of the airmen met. Those men who made this journey did so with inadequate clothing, insufficient or non-existent equipment and very little food. For those who succeeded, the assistance of the local people was essential.

The inhabitants of this mountainous district of Norway are a hardy, outdoor people. They are self-sufficient, used to a tough, often solitary, life in the open expanse of the moorlands and fells in which their homes nestle. They are supremely qualified to assess the difficulties and dangers of winter travel across their land. The overall impression these people give, all these years after the events of 1942, is of enormous admiration for the young airmen who made their way across country to Sweden on foot.

However, despite courage, resolution and perseverance, some very nearly did not make it at all. Some, indeed, were not even able to set out on the trek.

Flight Lieutenant George ('Dusty') Miller's Halifax W1037 'U-Uncle' had ditched in Trondheim Fjord in the early hours of 28th April, having been attacked by the ships in Hopleelven Fjord. He remembered jumping deep into the water off the wing of his stricken aircraft. After struggling not to open his mouth to breathe until he reached the surface, he had floated in the numbing water, supported by his Mae West, until he lost consciousness.

"Next thing I knew I awakened on a table surrounded by German sailors, for on their caps I read *Kriegsmarine* and an officer was holding a white pannican to my lips full of rum as I found out as I swallowed, and immediately a sea of fire flowed through my body, and felt so good I said 'More, please!' and drained the pannican and felt real good in body. I tried to get off the table, but my feet felt puffy and I started to fall, but was helped up by the Officer who lay me back on the table and said 'Your feet are still frozen' in excellent English and said something in German to the sailor who pulled off my shoes and socks whilst another produced a bucket full of snow and started to massage my feet with it. I found later the decks were at least 6 inches deep in snow."

Dusty believes that he had been rescued from the water by German sailors on board a Norwegian trawler that had been commandeered by the Germans for patrolling the fjord:

"The next thing I recall is sitting in a large place on a large ship and the room was filled with tables and on each table was a German sailor and there was lots of blood about. I was wrapped in a blanket and sitting with the Navigator, P/O Peter Roberts, and the W/Op Sergeant Jack Ryder, and I wanted to say to them, I'm sorry about this, but never did. Don't know even if we did speak to each other. I just recall we just sat there, all a bit dazed no doubt. A Medical Orderly came and said 'I'm going to give you all some injections' - I think they were anti-tetanus, anti-typhoid and another. Then the Lieutenant Commander who had given me the rum on the trawler appeared and said 'Are you the Captain of the aircraft?', and when I said 'Yes' he said 'Would you like a rum?' and took me with him down some stairs to his cabin. He gave me a cigarette and a glass and handed me the rum bottle, and, still feeling a bit shaken, I gave myself a generous nip. We talked a bit, don't recall what about, when two sailors appeared with sub-machine guns and spoke to the Officer. He turned to me and said 'The Admiral wants to see you.'

"So I went with the two sailors along passages and up stairways to the top of the ship just behind the bridge, I think - all this is vague now. I went into a beautifully set up large cabin with, I recall quite clearly, a coal-fire burning in a fire-place, and a most distinguished-looking, gold-braided, grey haired fairly large gentleman sitting at a table with a bottle of Dewars Scotch Whisky on the table."

Dusty was told that he had been very foolish to attack the German battleship with his aircraft, that he would now be sent to Germany as a prisoner of war and, in answer to Dusty's own question, that the whiskey had come from the Naval Officers' stores at Narvik when the area had been taken by the Germans.

"Next I recall is being taken down into the lower parts of the ship, which I had found out to be the *Eugen*, and put into a cell with a hard wood bed. I was made to strip and fold my clothes (blanket) in which I had been draped since taken to the sick-bay. It's hard to feel any dignity stripped naked and wrapped in a blanket. In the cell it was nice and warm, with the sound of an engine running and a slight vibration in the ship, no doubt from the auxiliary power units supplying the power for lights, heat, and the pumps - I could hear a pump going 'dockety-dock' somewhere and to its sound I fell asleep, first looking around the area which was lined with cells, all apparently full of German sailors, judging by the folded clothes outside the doors. There were several sailor guards with rifles looking bored and fed up, pacing about.

"After a night on the *Prinz Eugen* - that is, what was left of the night after my aircraft was shot down at approx. 2 am - I spent the next night in the jail at Trondheim, and next morning was taken by a guard outside to a bus that was to take us to the railway station. I was back again with Ryder and Roberts and three guards all laden with large kit-bags filled with food they were taking back to Germany. The bus got promptly bogged in the snowy slush and we were ordered out with lots of shouting and I was given a shovel and ordered to dig. I refused promptly which started a lot more shouting and rifle waving and I loudly, very loudly, refused again saying 'No, we are Officers and do not work.' The guard in charge who spoke good English, much to my delight grabbed the shovel and handed it to one of his men. Eventually on the train we travelled all in one compartment to Oslo where we were taken up to the top of a large building (Rathaus) to a fairly large suite where we stayed some days. I recall a radio receiver there playing some music and when I looked at the set I noticed it had a SW band and so tuned to 31 metres and got the BBC and soon the BBC news. I expected to be abused but the guard ignored me but said 'That is *verboten*'. I said '*Verboten* for you', and continued to listen and he moved away to the doorway.

"Next we were flown to Germany by a Ju52."

So, Dusty Miller, Ryder and Roberts were all taken prisoner of war. Flight engineer Sergeant E. Annable and the mid-upper gunner Sergeant H. H. Stott had been killed either before, or as a result of, the ditching. The tail-gunner Paddy Curran, who had first given the alarm about the state of the aircraft, and the second pilot, the New Zealander Flight Sergeant Gregory, had been taken prisoner of war. As soon as their aircraft had ditched they had clambered into the inflated survival dinghy and had paddled and drifted ashore, landing near the old railway station at Malvik, where they had been found as day broke that morning. They both survived the war. The responsibility for what happened to his crew laid a heavy burden on Dusty for nearly 47 years and he was only too glad to learn in 1989 that only two of his crew had been killed.

Dusty has in his possession an unusual piece of evidence of his remarkable survival. This is a cutting he himself took from a

German newspaper. As a prisoner of war in *Stalag Luft III* some months later, he saw in a German newspaper a photograph of himself, Ryder and Roberts, taken while they were leaving the *Prinz Eugen* on 29th April 1942, surrounded by several German naval officers and crew. This photograph and another one (both rather indistinct), were reprinted in the magazine *The Aeroplane* in July 1942, with the caption:

> "OUT OF THE FIGHT - These photographs, taken from German papers, are said to be of RAF prisoners who were shot down during an attack on the *Prinz Eugen*, and were picked up and taken on board the cruiser."

The main photograph shows Pilot Officer P. Roberts beginning to descend the boarding ladder at the side of the *Prinz Eugen*, carrying what appears to be a coat. Behind him, just about to descend, is Miller himself, looking into the camera. Just emerging into the photograph to the left is Sergeant Jack Ryder, a chunky white pullover poking out below the waist of his battledress. The second photograph shows an airman who has not positively been identified, but who may be Jack Ryder, accompanied by a couple of helmeted guards. He may be just landing from a launch, for in the background can be seen what appear to be trees on a nearby shoreline. All three airmen look shocked and pre-occupied with their experience. The fact of both survival and capture was beginning to sink in, for they were, after all, en route for Trondheim and finally a prisoner-of-war camp in Germany.

The small and scattered population in the area around Åsen Fjord is concentrated in farms, small communities, villages and towns along the edges of the fjords and in isolated dwellings nestling among the valleys that wind up into the hills. Inland, towards the east, high mountains and desolate moorlands stretch all the way to the Swedish border and beyond. It is the occasional river valleys threading their way through the mountains, that provide the main natural routes to the east. And it was along the two valleys that cut their way through these mountains or across the high moorlands that lie between them, that the crews of aircraft that crash-landed in the area had to find their way.

'Out of the fight'. The photographs referred to on page 212.

(via Author

From Halifax W1048 'S-Sugar', which had come to a slithering
halt and lay blazing on the ice of Lake Hoklingen in the early

hours of 28th April, the first of her crew, the rear-gunner Sergeant Ron Wilson, struggled to reach the ground.

"When it stopped, I was the first one out. I was the first one up on top of the fuselage. I didn't even realise then, what with hitting the thing - water was on my mind, I suppose, I was thinking we were on the lake. And when we stopped I was out onto the fuselage, right to the front, and then the crew started coming out, and I could see then that the aircraft was stationary. We got along the wing to the end of it and jumped off. Then we noticed there was somebody missing, and I then went back for Stevens.

Inside the aircraft, Sergeant Vic Stevens was trying to evaluate what had happened:

"When I finally came to, everything was still. There was already water on the floor, coming through. I then struggled to my feet and got up and found the escape ladder and started to crawl out of the top, and that's when Ron Wilson helped me."

When Wilson asked Stevens if he was alright, he replied that he was, although it felt as if he had hurt his ankle. Together they slid down to the port wing, ran along it until they were between the two engines, then jumped off. Knowing there might be smashed ice or even water close to the aircraft Stevens jumped outwards as far as he could. He felt his ankle jar on hitting the ice and realised that it must have been injured in the crash-landing. Although not injured in the landing, Pilot Officer Ian Hewitt had an unfortunate mishap as he left the aircraft:

"When the aircraft came to rest, there was some sort of hurry to get out of her as aircraft on fire frequently blow up. I had selected escape by one of the top hatches. I duly made my exit and then ran along the port wing from which I jumped off to join the others. I fear however, I had not reckoned that ice which would bear the weight of chaps would not bear the weight of chaps augmented by a few feet of gravity. Anyway, I jumped clean through the ice and could only be fished out with difficulty, albeit not without some laughter on the part of the others.

"The ice had been broken by the weight of the port wing as it had tilted onto it, and dark water showed through the cracks in the ice on which the aircraft lay."

It was important that the crew put as much distance as they could between themselves and their burning aircraft as soon as possible in case she exploded. There was also the danger of her breaking through the ice at any moment and sinking into the lake, taking the crew with her. So:

"We immediately left the aircraft, which was in flames, and scattered to a safe distance on the lake. Realising that we were surrounded by enemy soldiers, by the shots that were fired at us as we ran from the aircraft, we thought of surrender but the firing continued and we decided to take our chances in escape. It was evident our lives were imperilled in standing still."[42.]

Stevens vividly recalls these events:

"We were all together then, and we all started to run towards the shoreline. We'd only got a few feet when Don MacIntyre stopped us and he said 'Who's got the rations?' Now, we always take a large box, half-filled with sandwiches and chocolate and a flask of tea or coffee, and this was left in the aircraft. (There was also a standard issue Emergency Pack of rations). Nobody had thought of the rations. So we ran back. Now just as we'd got about half the distance back, it was only a few yards anyway, the Germans then were firing at us from the other side of the lake on the aircraft's port side, and I can assure you that the bullets were ricocheting for real! So we all stopped again and Don said 'Leave everything! Get going!'"

They turned their backs on their aircraft once again and, with the soldiers in the anti-aircraft battery on the farther shore still firing at them, made for the edge of the lake a hundred and fifty yards away. Encumbered by their flying gear and clumsy boots, the six of them reached the muddy bank that marked the lake's margin, then clambered up breathlessly. Out on the ice lay W1048 'S-Sugar', the fire on her starboard wing flaring vividly, while the sky above reflected the glow of the snow on the tree-shrouded hillsides. The lake was about seven miles from the *Tirpitz* and the crew could hear a considerable amount of noise still coming from her direction. Hewitt remembers:

"One or two of our own aircraft were seen overhead turning for home. Perhaps more than anything else, this brought us sharply to the realisation that we had a bit to do before we would be getting home."

Hurriedly they made their way towards some trees that stood back from the lake-shore, where they stopped to recover from their dash across the ice. Sigmund Mossing, the farmer who lived in the farm overlooking this part of the lake, had come out to see what was going on. He recalled seeing the crew come ashore and stop for a few minutes to light up cigarettes. He, however, made no attempt to contact them. The crew realised that the aircraft was now out of sight and assumed that W1048 'S-Sugar' had now sunk through the ice, although she was in fact merely hidden by a small rise of ground by the lake-shore.

Mossing later recalled that it was not until 10 o'clock that morning that the aircraft sank beneath the ice, disappearing into the depths of the lake. Earlier that morning two local men, Nils Mossing and Birger Sonstad, went out on the ice on skis to have a look at the wreck, but they had to return because too many German soldiers were there. Indeed, before she sank, a few of these German soldiers climbed aboard the stricken bomber, but dared not climb inside her for fear she suddenly sink. Consequently most of her contents remained untouched and undisturbed, until she was recovered many years later. Vic Stevens continues:

> "Well, we clambered up the muddy side at the edge of the lake and onto a track. It seemed to be a track, as you would have through a forest. And we stopped there for a couple of minutes. Don said 'Who's got things that they shouldn't have?', so I said 'I've still got the Verey pistol.' (In pain, and in a hurry to leave an aircraft which it seemed was likely to explode at any minute, he had not carried out the usual procedure of shooting a flare into a petrol tank in order to prevent the aircraft falling into enemy hands.) 'Bury it!' he said and I think somebody else put some letters or notes or something in the ground, so we made a hole in the ground and buried it."

Then they had a hurried discussion to decide what to do. It was the duty of all crashed aircrew to attempt to evade capture, therefore the obvious course of action was to make for the Swedish border, about forty miles to the east. However, their way was barred by the trackless moors and mountains that rose to between between 2,000 and 3,000 feet above sea-level. To travel directly east would mean walking over a countryside blanketed in deep snow, through dense forests and across open moorland with few tracks. This was a daunting prospect. Searching for a way to the east they were drawn northwards, along the lower ground between the mountains and the main arm of Trondheim Fjord, towards the town of Levanger. There were good reasons for travelling northwards before turning to the east. The nearest natural route around the mountains was to the north of where they had come down and, since the Germans would expect escaping airmen to head immediately towards Sweden, they would be out searching to the east of Lake Hoklingen. A different route might put them off the track. MacIntyre, with his Canadian backwoods experience, would have known that the direct route was not necessarily the best

EVASION ROUTES TAKEN BY CREW OF HALIFAX W1048 'S-SUGAR'

route if it involved travelling over high, trackless ground through snow.

Within a few minutes they got to their feet and set out through the trees, leaving the lake behind them. They had been shot down a few minutes after 1.00 am. and it must have been about 1.20 am. when they set out, walking along what seemed in the darkness to be a rough track through the woods. Memories of the exact route taken have dimmed over the years and it is not easy now to trace their route on a map, as Stevens recalls:

"Then we set off walking. I suppose we walked for three hours, say. I remember coming to a T-junction and we turned right."

By the time they had covered about eight miles, which was quite a feat for Stevens with his injured foot encased in ill-supporting flying boots, it was beginning to grow light and was becoming rather dangerous for such a large group of men to be walking around the countryside. Their route had largely avoided roads and had been somewhat circuitous by design. But they were beginning to feel exhausted. It was now time to find a secure hiding place in which to lay up and regain some of their strength.

"By travelling all that night and hiding our direction by the use of swamps, woods and back tracking, a considerable distance was made before morning." [43].

They were approaching the little community of Støre, to the north-east of the village of Skogn. Crowning a slight rise in the ground to their right they could see a copse, so they climbed up into this small wooded area to find cover. Snow covered the ground but, under the trees in a small hand-shaped hollow, they could see bracken and fern peering through the wind-blown snow. By gathering some of it they were able to make rough beds to lie down on and rest for the first time since leaving Kinloss. Stevens continues:

"Then Don said 'Right: emergency rations.' So I put my hand in my pocket. I hadn't got mine on me, mine had gone. Well I suppose with all my rolling around during the crash-landing that was quite excusable. Then one or two others said 'Mine's gone as well.' So, we had three. We then decided to split the three up - half each."

This box of emergency rations was known as a 'Pandora'. The box was like a tobacco tin, containing a map of the operation area, some of the local currency and some concentrated food and chocolate tablets. It was enough to last a man two or three days, taking one every four hours or so. It was meagre fare, but put some life into their aching muscles.

They stayed there all morning and most of the afternoon. Wilson recalls that while they were lying there, they glimpsed the occasional German troop lorry passing along a distant road. Once or twice they caught the drone of a light aircraft overhead. It was evident that the Germans had 'spotter' planes out looking for both the crash-sites of aircraft that had come down during the raid and evading aircrew trying to escape to Sweden. Perhaps a search was being mounted for them and, whatever else happened, it was satisfying to know that they were diverting some of the German war effort. Stevens continues:

"During the afternoon a young lad ran across the field, into the wood, and suddenly saw us and sheered off again. We thought, well, we'd better not stay too long. So around four o'clock, Don said 'I think we'd better split up into two parties, it's a bit too much, six of us about together!' So three of them decided to go off early, Don went with Ian Hewitt and Dave Perry. And he said 'Give us an hour and then you follow on.' So we said 'Okay'."

MacIntyre, Perry and Hewitt got up, wished them luck and were soon lost to sight as they made their way out of the copse.

"Seeing that the roads were well-patrolled by Nazi troops our plans were

The Fieseler Fi156 'Storch' was an ideal aircraft from which to spot evaders. It had a fairly long endurance, could fly extremely slowly and could land almost anywhere. (via J. Foreman)

made to reach Sweden by an overland route. Using the mountains and woods as protection we travelled east." [44.]

Stevens was not to see them again for over 30 years. He continues his account:

"About half an hour after they'd gone this young lad came running back. He wasn't afraid, he came straight in and we said 'Hello' and he said 'Hello' in Norwegian and started to speak to Pierre Blanchet. Now I couldn't understand, but somehow Pierre could, and Pierre said 'He's offering us some tobacco and cigarette papers from his parents who say they cannot help us, they are working in the field and everybody has to work in the field, but they wish us luck. He's given us the direction to get through to Sweden.' So we thanked him very much and the young lad ran off."

The three of them then discussed what to do, which way to head. They had with them a button compass (a uniform button containing a compass) and decided that they should head due East, in the hope of eventually reaching the Swedish border. Some time later they got up and made their way out of the copse.

Two men, Hjalmar Gjemble and Karsten Granlund, who worked at Støre Farm, remember meeting the three aircrew shortly after they descended from their hiding place in the copse, as Karsten explains:

"We were two farmhands at the Støre Farm at that time. We used to go to 'Bjørkhaugen' (a nearby small hill with a good view) and amuse ourselves when the weather was fine, as it was that evening. (Hjalmar remembers playing his accordion.) When we arrived back at the farm we were met by three men in uniform. At first we thought they were Germans, but they turned out to be English. We quickly got them into the kitchen, because we didn't dare to be seen outside. Ragnhild and Ingemund Myhr, who owned the farm, were out that night. They had gone to a neighbour. There was only one thing to do, that was to warn Ingemund. I ran down to him and warned him. We were told to feed them, and we let them eat well. I got orders from Ingemund that when they had eaten we must show them the direction to Sweden. This was almost impossible, because we didn't speak a word of English, but they understood it anyway."

Following these instructions as best they could, they made their way in a southeasterly direction towards the village of Marka in Markabygda district. The local people have since expressed astonishment that the entire crew of Halifax W1048 'S-Sugar' were able to remain at large, wandering about the countryside for several days, undetected by Quislings (supporters of the Norwegian Nazi Party) and any one of the large number of

Germans who were stationed in the area at the time. Inevitably, they followed a somewhat erratic track. Stevens in particular must have begun to lose interest in their direction, absorbed as he was in the sheer effort of keeping going at all:

> "We walked and we walked - clambered I should say. I scuffed along. I suppose up to the morning I hadn't taken much notice of this pain in my leg. At this point the consciousness came back. It wasn't until I started to walk again that evening, having rested up. I didn't take my boot off because I'd have trouble getting it back on again. Anyway, I dragged my foot along.
>
> "We clambered up these hills, up the track, and so on. It seemed to me I was just climbing all the time and when you get out of breath you get sort of a ball in your throat and I suppose because I was dragging my legs I got a ball of pain behind each knee."

It was evident that Stevens was having increasing difficulty moving, let alone keeping up with his companions, so after a while - it must have been about 10 o'clock by then - they halted. Wilson and Blanchet, with nothing more than a small penknife, made a pair of crude crutches for him. The memory of those crutches makes Wilson and Stevens laugh now. Although they were padded with the few bits of cloth they could lay their hands on, they were very crude and uncomfortable.

> "Come midnight we heard the drone of aircraft and suddenly realised the following night's raid was on. So we stopped and we listened. It was a darkish night but there was a light in the sky. And as we looked across we could see only a speck occasionally of the aircraft going in. And as we watched, we saw two of our own aircraft being hit and going down in flames. One of them just exploded, we heard it, and the other went down in the forest. Anyway, we were a bit subdued, but we went on from there."

One of these aircraft was Halifax W1053 'G-George', which crashed into trees on the far side of Lake Movatn, the neighbouring lake to Lake Hoklingen, killing one member of its crew and injuring others. The second blazing aircraft, which disappeared from sight behind the hills on the horizon, was Halifax W7656 'P-Peter'. After she had been hit, her pilot ditched her in the waters of Åsen Fjord, off Røkke in Skatval.[45.] She sank shortly afterwards, carrying with her two dead crewmen. The remaining crew, one of whom was her wireless operator, Sergeant Gordon Cranstone, managed to get themselves into the survival dinghy. To return to Stevens' account:

> "About 1 o'clock I realised that I was only holding the other two up, there was no place for me here. I suppose the idea was in my mind just to get

away from them more than anything else. I said to them 'Look, I'm leaving you two, and you're going on.' There was quite an argument, they weren't going to leave me, so I said 'The first farm we come across from now on, I'm knocking at that door and from then on you please yourselves.'

"A while after that this farm loomed up on the right and I went over and knocked on the door. It was quite dark, and the door opened, a woman appeared and I didn't even think of what to say to her. I just said 'English flier'. With no more ado she gently pushed the door half to, went back in the house and a man came to the door and gently just got hold of my shoulder and pulled me in and he closed the door not quite to, and we just stood there waiting in the darkness of a wood-panelled hall-way. I suppose he knew as well as I did that there were others."

By a most remarkable coincidence the farm the three men had come across belonged to Johan Gjemble whose son, Hjalmar, they had met earlier in the day. Sundby Farm lay, ironically, a mere four miles from the site of the crew's crash-landing, for they had, to some extent, retraced their tracks. It was then that Stevens realised that his hopes of reaching Sweden were finally over:

"So there came a little timid knock on the door and the door opened and he just brought them (Pierre Blanchet and Ron Wilson) in and went round to make sure there was no leakage of light anywhere. The light came on and in two or three minutes the table was laid. There was a girl there, about our own age, and a lad, and the old chap could speak broken English. I couldn't understand but Pierre got on with him. And Pierre said to him that I'd hurt my ankle; so he said 'Let's have a look at it'. So, for the first time I took my boot off, and then my sock. It was badly bruised, inflamed across the top of the ankle and down the side and he said 'I'm sorry, but you won't make it.' I said to Pierre 'What's he say?', and Pierre said 'He's saying that you can't make it. There's twenty miles (in fact about forty) of mountains to climb over and this time of year there's four feet of snow.'

"They laid a meal for us. The bread was like a thick round pancake, sliced diagonally across the middle with an egg on it, and after about an hour they gave directions to Pierre and Ron and told them to go on the track about 10 miles and they would come to a lake. On the far side of this lake, to the left, there were three huts. They were to go to the middle one and there they would have friends who would give them skis and help them across to Sweden."

Blanchet and Wilson realised that, although it was a course of action about which they both felt most reluctant, they would have to leave Stevens behind. At about 2.15 am. Stevens sadly said goodbye to his companions. It had been comforting to be with them and they had done everything they could to help him. However, he wished them luck as he watched them being ushered out of the house and set on the right path for Sweden and freedom:

"Then the girl showed me the room and the couch they'd made up for me downstairs and more or less put me to bed."

Rough as the last twenty-four hours had been for all the members of the crew, it had probably been toughest for Stevens, tagging along as he had like a lame duck. He fell into the deep sleep of exhaustion.

Magnhild Aabakken was the 'girl' whom Stevens remembers. She recalls that night vividly:

"At that time, my and Hjalmar's father, Johan Gjemble, lived on the Sundby Farm, in between Skogn and Marka. I lived there too with my husband Arnold. We had gone to bed, and it was just after midnight when there was a knock at the door. My father got up and answered the door and let them in. All of us got up when we heard English spoken in the hallway. My mother Nora and myself gave them food and drink. We made up a bed for Stevens so that he could lie down, and he was absolutely exhausted after their long trek. After they had eaten Stevens fell asleep and the other two set out again on the road to Marka in order to walk over the mountain to Sweden. My father Johan and my husband Arnold went with them to show them the way.

"In the morning my father cycled two miles (a Norwegian mile is equivalent to about six English miles) to Åsen where the district doctor lived. His name was Berg Nilssen. But the doctor warned us against keeping Stevens and said we ought to contact Policeman Hoel. The doctor was of the opinion that the whole family could be shot if they got to know that Stevens was with us. My father came back and he spoke English with Stevens and told him what the doctor had said. He agreed that we had to tell Hoel.

Stevens awoke to face the prospect of captivity:

"At 10 or 11 o'clock next morning I woke with a touch on the shoulder and there was a young man there, I suppose about 10 years older than myself anyway, and he said 'I am second-in-command of the area, sheriff of the area, and I have been called out because of you. Because of your condition, and with your permission I would like to hand you over to the Germans. That way we can keep in with the Germans.' I said 'That's alright' - I'd already resigned myself to the fact that I wasn't going to get back. So he said 'The best thing now is to get your coat on, say goodbye to these people and forget them, forget they ever existed, because it's more than their life's worth for the Germans to know that they harboured you. If you get a chance just let it slip, say you were on the second night's raid. If you'd like to say goodbye, I'll take you down to my place.'"

It was not that the *Lensmann*[46.], Ivar Hoel, was sympathetic to the German regime, but rather that he was labouring under a lack of knowledge about the local people. He recalls the difficulty of making his decision:

"I have never forgotten that day in 1942. Sheriff Arne Salberg in Skogn was ill at that time and I had been acting sheriff of Skogn for a couple of weeks when there came a message from Johan Gjemble that I should pick up Victor Stevens. I was a total stranger in Skogn and had no contact with people I knew I could trust one hundred per cent."

Since he had only recently been appointed to this post, Ivar Hoel had not as yet discovered which local people were connected with the resistance. This inexperience gave him little alternative, much to his regret, but to turn Stevens over to the Germans. This action troubled him for over thirty years and, when he was finally reunited with Stevens, he was able to set his mind at rest that no permanent ill had come from his decision. As a captured airman Stevens realised that he would be interned as a prisoner-of-war, but if any of this helpful Norwegian family were caught they would be interrogated, perhaps tortured and possibly even executed. To mislead the Germans for their sake was a grave responsibility for him.

"So I said goodbye to those good people and got in Hoel's car and we drove a few miles down the road to his place. I thought at first it was his home, but it wasn't, it was the local police station, just a house (called Nøysomhet, it lay close to Støre Farm that Stevens had visited the previous day). He introduced me to the employees there. There were two women and another man, and I stayed with him all the rest of the morning plus the afternoon."

When one of the women, Tole Holmen, persuaded her brother Oddmund to come and take a photograph of Stevens they all posed outside the front door of the building. Everything seemed so relaxed and unwarlike, that Stevens could hardly believe what he knew must be about to happen.

Ivar Hoel recalls that:

"A few hours passed before I called the Germans. That telephone call was the saddest task I had to perform during my three to four month stay in Skogn."

Now, all Stevens had to do was wait, but it proved to be a longer wait than he had expected:

"I kept on wondering to myself when are the Germans coming? It was right until 6 o'clock in the evening and he said 'I think we've given them enough time.' I suddenly realised that all this time he'd kept me there for the simple

Above: Outside Hoel's police station at Nøysomhet, near Skogn. (l to r) Yorunne Eide, Edith Salberg, Sergeant Vic Stevens and Tole Holmen.
(O. Holmen)

Right: Vic Stevens with Ivar Hoel outside Hoel's police station, 29th April 1942. (O. Holmen)

purpose of allowing the others a decent time to get going across into Sweden. It was a bit of a shock because I'd been expecting the Germans to come all day. I had to more or less lift the phone up because he was reluctant to do so, and within about half an hour the Germans were there."

Not only had Ivar Hoel given Stevens' companions time to make their way to Sweden, he had also done what he could to make Stevens' story, that he had crashed on the second night's raid, more convincing. There had truly been time for Stevens to be picked up that morning and brought to Skogn, without the Gjembles being accused of harbouring Stevens during the previous day and night.

Stevens continues:

"It was a bit awkward, too: how can you say goodbye in enemy country when people are not supposed to be friendly towards you? So I just waved my hand to them and got in the German car, with armed guards beside me, and we set off then down the road towards Trondheim. Well, I wasn't feeling very happy, I was in pain and the situation was a bit worrying. Anyway I came to with a start, one of the guards digging the elbow in one side, and one in the other, and they both moved their thumbs like that. I bent forward and looked out the right-hand window, and we were going past the fjord where the *Tirpitz* lay. And there was the *Tirpitz* on the far side as if it had never been touched, serenely lying there in the water. The Germans laughed and by this time we were on our way again and I was feeling lower and lower. I thought to myself 'What a waste - all that, and of course the night after'.

"Anyway, we finally came to a *Luftwaffe* fighter 'drome (Værnes). We drove in, the guards got out, beckoned me out. There were all German aircrew sitting around at the tables and chairs out on the lawn drinking German beer, Schnapps, I suppose, and they just sat me down amongst them. The Germans came over, shook hands with me, said 'How do you do?' I said 'I can't speak German', but one or two could speak English. They just chatted to me. For a moment I thought I was back in good old blighty!

"After about ten minutes they took me into a hut and they put me to bed. Come the morning the German doctor had a look at my ankle and he said he didn't think there were any bones broken, but it was badly bruised, so he bandaged it up and I put my boot back on and by this time I could barely put my weight on it, only the heel part. All this time my left foot was getting blistered. That type of flying boots are not made to walk in, they're made to keep your feet warm and that's all. They're fur-lined, sloppy. It's like trying to climb a mountain in bedroom slippers.

"After that a van appeared and they took me off then to the local railway station and they put me on the train then and I found it was a sleeper-train. There were two bunks in this compartment, and on the lower bunk was another companion, an English sergeant with a broken rib, and he was in a bad way (this was probably Sergeant Dennis Butchart, who had been badly injured when his aircraft came down in the trees beyond Lake Movatn during the second raid.)"

And so, at about nine o'clock in the morning of 30th April, the train set off, carrying Vic Stevens on the first leg of the long journey that was to end in a prisoner of war camp in Germany and three years of captivity.

NOTES

42. From a brief, unofficial statement made by MacIntyre, Hewitt and Perry, in Falun, Sweden in May 1942.
43. *Ibid.*
44. *Ibid.*
45. See map page 201
46. A sheriff, or *Lensmann*, is a police official with responsibility for a district.

Chapter Thirteen
Evasion And Capture (I)

When MacIntyre, Perry and Hewitt left the others in the copse near Støre[47.], during the afternoon of the crash, they decided that they would only be able to escape to neutral Sweden by seeking the help of sympathetic Norwegians or even the Norwegian Resistance. The only way to make contact was to choose a house, knock on its door and hope the owner was not only sympathetic to their plight, but also able to feed them and put them on the way to Sweden, perhaps even to make contact with the local resistance group for them. If they chose the wrong house they could find themselves in the hands of the Germans, for a number of local people were Nazi sympathisers. Skirting the lake that lies to the southwest of the town of Levanger, the three men turned east onto a small road leading up into the mountains. They continued up this road until it came to an end at Tingstad Farm, where they decided to take the chance of asking for help.

Paul Øyum was no supporter of the Nazis. As a trainee teacher at Levanger laererskole (teacher training school) he had been one of the students who had gone on strike to show their feelings about what he called the Nazi 'terror regime', thereby forcing the authorities to close down the school. Then, in April 1942:

> "I left my den (digs) and got a job as a servant man at a farm in Frol, a community next to Levanger.
>
> "Only a few days later, early in the morning, I woke from a tremendous bang, but I did not understand the reason why. Later only I learned that an

Allied bomber attacking the German battleship *Tirpitz* had been shot down. "In the evening the farmer, his wife, another servant and I were sitting in the kitchen when we suddenly heard a noise outside the door. But nobody entered. The farmer, P. Hagen, went outside to find out what or who had made that noise. Then I heard someone speaking English. I knew that Mr. Hagen did not understand that language. Nor do I know much English, only a little more than nothing, so I too went outside. And there in the court-yard stood three airmen in uniforms.

"Unfortunately, as I had been on the farm only a few days, I could not give much help. I only could point out the direction to Sweden, and I remember I told the men not to go near the next house, because the farmer and his family there were Nazi sympathisers."

The three men set off in the direction that Paul had given them, following a rough track. Later, they risked calling at another farmhouse. Once again, luck was with them. Moan Farm was owned by Jon and Gudrun Hovdal and, although they had little enough food to spare, they gave the three of them what they could. Gudrun's brother, Harald Slåtsve gives his account of what happened:

"I was staying with my sister and brother-in-law to slaughter a calf, and we had just finished the work when three men came to the farm around 11 o'clock at night. We thought they were Germans and therefore were not too keen to talk to them. But then we saw that one of them had a Canadian emblem on his shoulder and realised that they were refugees.

"They came in and had some food, and later on I took them to Jon Munkeby who spoke a little English. There we were told about the Halifax 'planes and the attack. The three men, MacIntyre, Hewitt and Perry, were completely exhausted when they reached the farm, and one of them actually fell asleep when we were standing talking to them. We understood that they had to go over to Sweden and I promised to help them. I immediately thought of Jens Jenssen - he was used to the mountains and had actually helped people before."

From Jon Munkeby's farm Slåtsve took the men a short way up the track to his own farm, where they were given some eggs and other supplies to take with them. Then they walked on the two miles to Jens Jenssen's farm at Erståsen.

"His wife Mildred was there as well and Jens Jenssen said that they were asleep when they heard the knocks on the door. We asked the men to come in and I gave them a little bit of food and then they went to bed. They stayed the whole of the next day and were moving about quite freely without showing any concern about the Germans. When they were told that there were many German soldiers around and about they got a bit worried, and that evening Jens took them across the mountains. 'I don't know how far he went with them, but he didn't come back until the next day', said his wife." 48.

229

The three men travelled with their guide all night, from Erståsen towards Hoinskinnet and Klonka in Frol-fjellet, then further on to Færsåscn where, as daylight broke, Jenssen turned round and went back, after pointing out the remainder of the route, leaving them to make their own way. He could stay with them no longer without his absence being noted by the Germans.

The twelve-hour march that followed was a testing time for all three of them. The snow was deep and exhausting to struggle through and the rivers, now in full flood, were difficult to cross. Hewitt pulled a muscle in his thigh and went very lame. He was ultimately most grateful for the help and encouragement his companions gave him.

> "We travelled east and arrived over the Swedish border on the night of the 30th. At 11.30 we asked a resident of the area to phone the local police, believing this to be the proper conduct for escaped prisoners of war on reaching a neutral country."

This statement, written by MacIntyre on behalf of himself and his companions after their arduous journey to Sweden, was not written as a description of the operation against the *Tirpitz*, or of their escape from Norway. Its intention was merely to declare to the Swedish authorities that they were 'escapees, not saboteurs dropped in Sweden'. Consequently, although it contains general recollections of their adventures, it gives only part of the story, notably avoiding mention of the help they received and also of what happened when they reached 'freedom'.

They had crossed the border at Mestuga, about fifteen miles north of Storlien, by which time both Hewitt and Perry were struggling. Once again they had knocked on a door to ask for help and again they had been in luck. They were given a good meal, after which the police were called. They were then taken away and handed over to the military authorities who inter-rogated them. Within a short time they were taken by train to Falun to be interned as Allied evaders.

MacIntyre's concern over mentioning to the Swedes nothing of the help he and his companions had received is emphasised by Paul Øyum's recollections of the danger in which local families were placed by giving help to the evaders:

"The morning after the airmen came to Tingstad, the name of the farm where I worked at that time, a German officer came to the farm too. I was working near the house, but the farmer was in the kitchen. I must confess that I was afraid then, but after a while the German left the house. P. Hagen, the farmer, came out and said that the officer had told him to come to the German military camp nearby with potatoes. He had not asked about shot-down planes.

"The reason why I was afraid was as follows. In my home place, Orkland, fourteen Norwegian miles from Levanger, German soldiers, pretending to be Austrian soldiers deserting from the German army, asked for help to run away to Sweden. Some days later Germans came and arrested simple-hearted Norwegians and sent them to Germany. When I met the three airmen, I thought, 'Are they Canadians and Englishmen, or are they Germans in English uniforms?' I had barely spoken to an Englishman at that time, and could not tell whether English was their mother tongue or not.

"A few days afterwards we were asked if we had seen some mysterious men near Hagen's farm, but none of us, of course, had seen anything. We had all gone early to bed that night.

"As you see, I did not give the men much help. My most important contribution to the escape was to keep a secret. But maybe that was a help too, during the hectic days after the incident."

Wilson and Blanchet too, had their share of luck. Before they set off from the farmhouse where they left the injured Stevens, the farmer, Johan Gjemble, gave them directions. Although they were able to follow the gist of these, they found it difficult to take in the details. It seems, however, from the recollections of the local people who took the risk of helping the two of them, that from the Gjemble's farm they walked eastwards up into the mountains, where they continued walking until they descended to the Swedish border, being found by a Swedish patrol only after they had penetrated some miles into Sweden, beyond Skalstugan. They took about three days to make the journey.

Several local people recall being asked for food and directions by a number of Allied airmen seeking the way to Sweden. However, the men did not inform their helpers of their names or where exactly they had crashed or crash-landed, while the Norwegians, for their part, did not tell the airmen who they were or even the name of the farms they visited. While this conspiracy of silence made matters safer for all concerned, it made it difficult for the airmen or their helpers either to make contact with each other after the war, or to reconstruct the desperate journeys they had made years before. This confusion is aptly illustrated by the recollections of a farmer named Petter Trættli:

> "Two airmen came to Markabygda and received a lot of help from Petter Nyborg and Einar Troseth. Two came to Trætli, my family home, which is the highest in Markabygda. They received help and went over the mountains to Sweden the day after. The day after another two arrived, what 'plane they came from we never knew. They also received help to get on the right road. Markabygda is a small parish, but there lived honourable Norwegians and lots of refugees received good help there."

Whether or not Blanchet and Wilson were one of the pairs of visitors to these farms is now difficult to say, for two other pairs of airmen were also on the run in the neighbourhood. These were from the crew who had escaped from the aircraft (W1053:G) that crashed into Lake Movatn after the second night's raid. Exactly what happened is further confused by the fact that Wilson's recollections of so long ago consist of a series of impressions of the journey and memories of meeting several people en route, rather than a sequence of events:

> "We went from the Gjemble's farm - middle of the night. We went straight on again. We knew that Sweden was in the east, and come what may we'd try and go in a straight line for Sweden. They gave us a bit of bread or something - they didn't have a lot themselves, they had less than we had.
>
> "I can remember climbing away from the farm, climbing away, and there wasn't all that much snow about as such. We carried on going until it was daylight, just cross-country through snow. It wasn't so bad there, where we were, it wasn't. It was later on when we got into the mountains. And then we rested that day, because by this time there were aircraft out then, they were small spotter aircraft. They must have known something. So we stopped in the trees for the day - started moving off at night. I remember that part, because that was the worst part, that day. It was cold, for a start, and we couldn't move during the daylight because the spotter planes were out. So we lay up all during the day, and then we got going that night.
>
> "We were quite well dressed really. Only bad thing about it was the flying boots. That was the worst thing about it. I think we had a battledress on, sweaters, long-johns I suppose - we were quite warm. We hadn't got wet in the lake, you know, because we were on the ice, although we might have got wet-footed, perhaps, going through the snow in the trees.
>
> "We were getting higher by this time, higher and higher, and it got colder and colder, and the snow got deeper and deeper, and now we were in a bit of trouble. We had hardly any food, for a start. By this time we were up high

in the mountains, and then when we got higher we stopped again, and it was the next day that we saw the troops - right down in the valley we'd crossed, three or four miles behind us. They seemed to be out looking, though I don't know how long they were there. They must have known that some aircrew were around. By this time the snow was up to our chests, and we were barely moving, just sort of ploughing through, and there was fog about.

"That night we were coming down the side of a hill when we came to a barn - a very dilapidated wooden barn - and when we pushed the door open there was a terrific squeaking and squealing. The door just fell down, open. There was a pit there, and it was full of rats. I've never seen anything like it in my life. It had been a corn barn, or something, and it was full of rats. We got away from there, and went back up in the trees - I remember the place, I can see it now.

"And then we came across another hut. (This may have been Hegglivollen, where Blanchet and Wilson are known to have spent a night during their journey). There were a couple of wooden bunks in there and an old stove. So we flopped down on these bunks, and fell asleep, and we were woken up by two Norwegians - they turned out to be the Resistance. They were in the hut - fire going, and a bit of food, bit of bread, bit of cheese, and that - and they told us to stay there that day, and they'd come back again at night time. So they came back at night time, about four of them, with skis, and food, ski-boots (old ones, not new ones). I'd never seen a pair of skis in my life - Pierre had, in Canada. They showed us how to walk in them, and we put the boots on - they didn't want our boots, they let us keep our own boots. They gave us a knapsack, and off we went. They said they could just take us so far, take us over the mountains. They kept with us all that night, and part of the next day, and they showed us which way to go. They told us to keep going, and gave us a bit of a map, a map you'd get in a school book, to show us which way to go. But it didn't turn out that easily, because we got lost anyhow.

"There was a little lake in the mountains marked on this map, and the Norwegians said, 'Go for that lake. If you find that lake you're on your way.' And that was when we started having trouble, because I couldn't ski. To go down hill I had to take them off and sit on them, like a sledge. Of course I went all over the place, falling off. Actually, it was a good job we were a lot younger then, and could see the funny side of it, because when you fell in the snow you went right in, I mean you went in up to your neck. By this time we were wet, but we went on and on and on, that day and night, and ate our bread and raw bacon, which they'd given us. They had also given us some pipe tobacco - real coarse stuff it was, like wood shavings! We didn't have any cigarette papers, they had just given us some newspapers, and we had to roll the cigarettes in that - the tobacco was so hard it came through the paper! I remember that.

"Eventually, after two days and nights of hard going, we came across a lake. We walked around this lake and we come across a house. Quite a big place it was actually, and we went up there and knocked at the door, had a look around, but the only person we could find was a very, very old lady at a spinning wheel, spinning, and she must have been deaf or something. We were there about half hour when all of sudden a woman came along - I think she was a bit frightened - and we tried to explain what we were 'til a man come along. They couldn't speak a word of English - they were real, country people. I think they just had the fishing - nobody there for miles and miles, and they lived all on their own, in the middle of nowhere. We had some food there and stopped the night, and they pointed us on our way. We kept going and going - had to go over another mountain, I think, and there was a lake there, so we had to go up again to get out of it, and that's when we lost a knapsack. I think it was Pierre who lost his, with a pair of flying boots in it. He lost his when we fell down, went tumbling down the side of a hill - the snow had given way or something - lucky there, I suppose! By this time we were travelling as and when we could - we rested and walked. Of course we couldn't stop for too long because we got so cold - it was freezing cold, because we were up in the mountains and we were partly wet.

"Then, we were sitting down somewhere, and all of a sudden we looked up and we were surrounded by blokes with guns - Swedish soldiers they were! We'd got over the border by then, but I thought they were Germans, that's what I thought they were. They had skiing clothes on, I don't think you'd know the difference, and they'd skis on. They took us to a frontier post where there was a little camp and a soldiers' barracks, and they interrogated us there - asked us what we'd done and where we'd come from. At that point we told them that we were English fliers, come from Norway."

Blanchet recalls that the interrogations were a little uncomfortable, perhaps because the two of them had penetrated quite a distance beyond the frontier before being discovered by the soldiers:

"I wanted to question where we were first, and we were told by signs that we had crossed the border. They didn't believe our story that we had left Norway coming to Sweden. To them we were more somebody who had been dropped there by parachute and were spies. They let us believe that, not wanting to have any trouble with the Germans, they were ready to put us in a car to drive us to a certain place and push us back into Norway! We also realised that going back to Norway, if we had done any damage to their *Tirpitz* they might do something to us because we must have damaged it. So we didn't want to be pushed back into Norway. The questioning was done in a peculiar way, one at a time. First I'd go in and be questioned, and then suddenly somebody would walk in and would stop the conversation and take a paper and say, 'Your friend told us you were flying Halifaxes, do you agree with that?'"

In this way the Swedes tried to find out some details of what had been going on suddenly to produce a crop of evaders crossing the frontier. Wilson and Blanchet were given food there and, after a bath and the first Finnish-style sauna that Wilson had ever experienced, a fresh set of clothes. Then they were taken to a railway station and put on a train to the internment camp at Falun.

The Police Station at Hegra was soon notified of the two aircraft that had crashed near Borås (Halifax W1020 'K-King' and Lancaster L7572 'L-Leather'), also of a third aircraft, which had come down on the Flornesvollen (Halifax W1041 'B-Baker'). It was not long before Germans from *Fliegerhorstkommandantur* at Værnes airfield were on the scene of the two crashes near Borås. Jorulf Nielsen and Rolf Trøite, two clerks at the local police station, were called upon to help. As Rolf Trøite has recorded in his written account of these events:

"Jorulf Nielsen and I helped to recover the thirteen dead aircrew. It was a sad sight that greeted us in Skjelstadmark. Mutilated bodies were found on the ground, in treetops and inside the plane. Twelve were found immediately and the thirteenth a few days later. He had fallen some way away from the crash site.

"The bombs still on the plane had exploded on impact. Parts of bodies and pieces of the plane were spread over a large area at one of the crash sites.

"I can remember that when we were carrying the bodies from the crash by Borås, the farmer's wife, Ingerborg Overrein, stood spruce branches up in the snow and put down smaller ones on the path where we walked. A beautiful sight and thoughtfully done in an otherwise sad situation.

"Of the men from Skjelstadmark who were involved in carrying the dead from the plane at Borås I can remember Johan Hofstad, Tobias Nordvang, Olav Andresen, Nikolai Fossum, and Magne Stavnås. Stavnås was, as far as I remember, a farm worker at Borås West, and he was almost certainly the youngest of the helpers. The dead were brought to Stjørdal and so far as I know later taken to Stavne by Trondheim and buried there. The crews' belongings were taken care of by the parishioners who first arrived at the site. Amongst the possessions that were taken to the police station were the New Testament with English text, maps, watches, family photos from England and English pound notes." [49.]

These two crashes ended tragically, but, when the police at Hegra and the Germans at Værnes reached the site of the crash of the third aircraft, they were surprised to find that there was no sign of any of her crew. Halifax W1041 'B-Baker', crippled and on fire, had been flown by its pilot, Wing Commander Don Bennett, over the same gap in the mountains as the other two aircraft. The mines had been jettisoned near the small settlement of Almo, about a half-mile south of Borås Farm, before the crew abandoned the aircraft and parachuted to safety. The aircraft itself had 'flown' on until it crashed into the mountains of Flornesvollen, a mile south of Flornes. Olaf Horten, a local farmer, witnessed the crash, as Wing Commander Bennett's wife Ly, who met Olaf in 1989, recalls:

"On the night of April 27th, after midnight, he was standing outside his farmhouse on a clear, very cold night. Searchlights were sweeping across the skies when he saw a burning aircraft approaching over the wooded hills, and noted four parachutists in the sky, and immediately before the crash a fifth one jumped out of the blazing aeroplane."

This confirms Bennett's story in his autobiography that 'my parachute hardly opened before I hit the ground'. Olaf continued:

"Early next morning eight Germans came to my house to interrogate me. When they found out that I had seen the aircraft and saw some of the parachutists land on the mountain opposite, they made me lead them to the wreck, which was still burning. On approaching the smouldering Halifax some of the sparks triggered off one of the machine guns and shot one of the Germans in the lower abdomen. The Germans started to inspect and strip the aircraft. The injured German died later in hospital.

"I myself picked up a magnifying glass which I still have. I also took a big blade off one of the propellers back with me as a souvenir. During the next few days the Germans continued to dismantle and search through the Halifax for military information but had to leave one engine as it was embedded at least two metres deep in the ground and could not be lifted out. It is still there now, but inaccessible." [50.]

Another item of equipment that was 'liberated' from the area was a life-jacket found within a couple of days of the crash, as a Mr Roar of Skansen recalls:

"It became quickly known that a British plane had crashed at Flornesvollen on April 28th 1942. I had known this area very well and after a few days decided to go there and investigate. I bicycled from Hegra to Flornes Station and then on by foot to Flornesvollen. I was accompanied by a good friend from Hegra. The place was found south of the hill, and we were not the first ones to have found it. The wreckage was found in proximity to the body of the plane which was still more or less intact. The Germans had arrived before us, removing items of interest for possible use. It was of course quite forbidden to remove anything from the wreckage, and as I had no tools with me, was not able to take anything away with me. According to what I had heard, the whole crew had narrowly escaped, the pilot being the last one to jump before the plane crashed. I assumed that the crew would try to hide some of their equipment before escaping. As there was not a lot of wooded

The wreckage of Wing Commander Don Bennett's Halifax W1041:B near Flornes being examined by interested young Norwegians. Everything of value appears to have been removed. (via M. How)

terrain in the area it was possible to find and track the crew's escape route. I started out from the wreckage site, keeping an eye on the woods down towards Molskdalen where I was convinced the crew must have gone. I cannot remember how far I had gone before I found a life-jacket (on thinking back, it must have been a few hundred metres); my backpack came in very handy and I packed it with my 'find'. As I did not want anyone to know of my discovery, I took a different route home.

"On arriving home I realised that I had to find a hiding place for my discovery. We were very concerned about house searches being conducted by the Germans. Through the duration of the war I was not at home, and my discovery was forgotten. My parents and siblings knew a little about my 'stash', and as soon as the war was over, these things appeared quickly from their hiding place. The parachute and cord was very important and useful to the women who could sew it up into different items. The rest of my discovery was left at home and gradually disappeared.

"When I heard about the Commemoration Event at Åsen in April 1992[51.], I thought about how interesting it would be to have a remembrance of those times, and I found that the life-jacket, belonging to Donald Bennett the pilot of the plane, still existed. My good friend, whom I mentioned before, had done a lot of wandering around the area of Sonvatn and had also found a life-vest which also still exists today.

"I'm sure there are many others who had found different items belonging

237

to the British airmen, but for fear of German retaliation had to keep these 'discoveries' quiet."

There was a set procedure for leaving an aircraft by parachute. In such an emergency both the exit along the port side of the aircraft and the one in the floor beneath the navigator's table were used (the navigator's table and chair had first to be folded away). The crew, already wearing their parachute harnesses, would collect their parachutes from storage places in various parts of the fuselage before moving to their appropriate exit. Sergeant Phil Eyles, Bennett's navigator, was the first to leave through the forward escape hatch of his aircraft. Eyles recalls that he wrenched it open and:

"Out I went - I was the first one out. I don't know how long it takes from the time you pull the parachute to the time it opens, but ever so many things went through my mind, about my wife, my daughter, the things I'd done in my life that I shouldn't have done, the things that I should have done. And the next I knew was as if somebody had given me a terrific kick up the crutch, and something jerked up, and I found myself going slowly down and looking round, beautiful night, moonlit night, and I could see 'pop!' another

The twisted remains of the mid and rear section of Wing Commander Bennett's Halifax W1041:B rears up above its own twisted wreckage. Local people can be seen investigating the remains, which cover a large area. (via Mick How)

Top: Among the finds these locals made, were a parachute, a helmet complete with intercom set and a Mae West. These were found in the vicinity of Wing Commander Bennett's Halifax W1041:B, in the mountains just south of Flornes. (via M. How)

Bottom: (l to r) Reidar Fordal, Patsy Smith and the author. Reidar recovered the life-jacket from the vicinity of Wing Commander Bennett's Halifax within days of it crashing on 27/28th April 1942.
(Stjordalens Blad newspaper, 25th April 1992)

parachute coming out, and 'pop!', another parachute came out, and the plane was still afire, and it was going on. When I got to the ground I was up to my crutch in snow."

In his bemused state at suddenly finding himself away from the noise of the aircraft and on firm ground, Eyles found the job of burying the billowing parachute silk was beyond him. In the direction of what he took to be Sweden he could see a large hill or mountain and he naïvely decided that all he had to do was to cross that to reach safety. So he set off up the hill. As he struggled upwards he was alarmed to see strange paw-marks in the snow and, fearing that they must be wolf tracks,[52] he tried to arm himself with a stick from a tree. However, the stick was rotten and so he climbed on without it, finally reaching a plateau where he saw a hut. However, on approaching this hut he was once more alarmed to see more wolf-tracks and decided he must make his way down from the fearful desolation all around him:

"I couldn't see Sweden, and I couldn't see any lights at all. It was beginning to thaw a bit, and there was a stream going down, so I thought, 'Well, I'm not going to let them smell me!' - they were worrying me, these wolves! So I got into this stream and I followed it right the way down, and when I got down to the bottom there were a couple of houses here and some down there - it was a log-clearing station. I was soaking wet by now, so I knocked at a door and an old boy come down in long pants and he looked at me, and I said 'I'm an Englishman.' So off he went up the stairs again and down come an old lady. Then they told me to come in while they went back upstairs and got dressed. Then they realised who I was, and out they went and sent for somebody else. In the meantime they'd taken my boots off, and my trousers, and dried them."

Despite all the drama surrounding his escape from the aircraft, Eyles recalls a small event of no real significance, but one that still brings a grin to his face even after all these years:

"The old lady made me a coffee and a sort of a pancake cooked straight on the stove, about as big as a plate. Well, I'd no interest in eating, but she was a dear old lady, so when she went out of the room I picked it up and rolled it up and put it in my pocket. When she come back she said 'Ooh!' And she went out and cooked me another one! So of course, when she went out I picked that one up and put that in my pocket!"

And so, his pockets full of pancake, Eyles tried to explain to somebody they had brought up from the log-clearing station what he wanted to do. With the aid of a pencil and paper with which he drew a picture of the sun and the moon, Eyles explained that he wanted to sleep until night-time when the moon would rise and he would then set out again for Sweden.

"So I laid on a sofa and the old lady covered me up, and I went to sleep. Later on somebody came in and shook me, and said, 'Look out of the window!' I looked out of the window - there were some Germans rowing across the river in a boat to pick me up. So I said, 'Why is this?' It was all sign language then, but they knew I was upset about it, and the daughter said, 'Germans. Boom!', pointing an imaginary gun to her head and firing it. Well, it was obvious from what she was talking about that they'd been warned that if anybody was caught harbouring a British airman, and not giving him up, they would all be shot. Now, I don't blame the old lady, I don't blame her husband, I don't blame the daughter, but it was somebody obviously in that Log-Clearing Camp, because there were quite a few houses down there at the village. I've got no recriminations at all, I would probably have done the same thing if I was there, with my family."

There was indeed a Nazi sympathiser living in another house in the settlement who may have been responsible for summoning the Germans. When the soldiers arrived at the Kringberg family home and entered the building, Eyles was ordered to empty his pockets. They were very puzzled when he refused to empty one particular one unless, as he indicated, the Norwegians left the room. When they did the Germans understood the situation as Eyles produced several pancakes, somewhat the worse for wear. They were all still laughing when the old lady came back into the room! Eyles was then taken down into a town where to his astonishment he was given a kind of 'guided tour' by the German officer in his car before being locked into a cell in the ancient fortress of Kristiansten. The 'town' was Trondheim. Here he fell asleep on a straw paliasse, only to be woken by a guard several hours later. It seemed that the area was being bombed by the RAF - in fact the second night's raid on the *Tirpitz* - and Eyles was taken along with some of the civilian prisoners to another cell deeper underground. Some days later he was put on board the train that ran from Trondheim to Oslo, then finally to *Dulag Luft* the Interrogation Camp in Germany. It was six weeks before his wife had confirmation that he was alive but a prisoner of war.

It is difficult to establish exactly where the seven-man crew of Bennett's aircraft landed. However, Rolf Trøite, carrying out investigations in Hegra and Meråker after the war, relying on his own diary notes and a report from Bennett himself, is perhaps best placed to record the likeliest areas in which they landed.

About four miles to the south of the crashed aircraft lay a lake called Sonvatn. Trøite believes that 'the Englishman Flight Lieutenant George (Mick) How, tail-gunner, and the Canadian Sergeant Murray, 2nd wireless operator, came down west of Sonvatn.' Flight Lieutenant How had landed in a tree and became aware that he was some distance from the ground, as he recalls:

"I thought 'Well now look, you're hanging about ten feet up, and there's snow below you, you've got nothing else to do but' I snapped the quick release and dropped into the snow, not hurting myself actually in that way, but going back again on the jump I did gash my knee very badly and cut my forehead open, and I was really in a pretty sorry state.[53.] So, after a little rest in the snow, and thinking I would love a cup of tea - that's one of the first things I thought of! I thought, 'Well I'd better do something about this.' Of course I hadn't any boots, and it was terribly cold, the moon was very, very bright. I started walking, not knowing which direction I was going at this time, just wanting to get away. I took my 'chute off and hid it under the fir trees as best I could, when I almost immediately heard sounds from what sounded like crackling branches, and I thought, 'Aye, aye, there's somebody here, I hope it's not the Germans!' In fact it was Flight Sergeant Murray, and we were so pleased to see each other, of course, at this time,

Flight Lieutenant 'Mick' How.
(M.How)

242

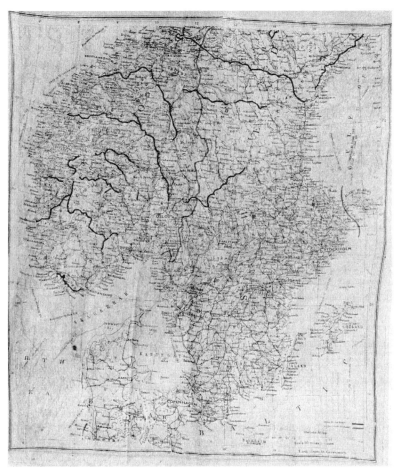

One side of the silk escape map issued to Sergeant Dennis Butchart of Halifax W1053:G that crashed on the edge of Lake Movatn. It depicts the southern section of Norway, including Trondheim. (via Ivar Hoel)

and we hobbled off together, and we said, 'Well what do we do now?' At this time it was freezing, really freezing cold and the snow was hard as ice, and we could walk. Bit forgetful here - we did walk until early light when the sun came up, and it started to get really hot. And then we got our escape kits out and had some Horlicks tablets, I can remember, and looked we did have a printed silk map of the area and a compass, a small round compass, which unfortunately didn't work, and, anyway, we headed off in the general direction of Sweden, not knowing whether we were really on the right track or not, and we marched, or tried to march - having no boots on made it extremely difficult with very, very cold feet. Anyway, during the day the temperature rose so much that the snow melted and we were walking actually up to our waists in snow, and you can imagine how very, very slowly we moved.

"We kept this up all day, and then at night, of course, it started to get freezing cold again, really freezing cold, and we came to a plateau that had, to my amazement, a density of dead trees, barren and absolutely dead. So, we collected a load of wood and we had matches in our Escape Kit as well - and we lit a whacking great fire to try and keep warm for that night. We couldn't go any further, we were totally exhausted, and just clapped out generally. We did really manage to collect a terrific amount of this timber, knowing full well that we'd got to go through a long, cold night, and the moon was full and very bright again, and we did snuggle up and managed to keep reasonably warm. I woke up once, and, to my amazement, Sergeant Murray was actually on fire: the back of his flying-suit was burning. He didn't know, he was asleep. Fortunately I woke up, and rolled him in the snow and put it out. I don't know whether he will remember this, but it was a great point and I thought, 'Christ, you know, I could have lost him!'

"However, next day we plodded on again in the general direction of Sweden. By this time we were very hungry and thirsty, we didn't know whether we were on track, and, of course, again the snow got soft. Now towards that night, to our great amazement, in the distance we did see a little log cabin which apparently, I found out since, is one of the Norwegian's cabins where, if they're caught out, they spend the night there. Fortunately it was open. So we went into this cabin, and of course there were blankets there, no food unfortunately, and we just collapsed on the beds as such and went to sleep.

"At dawn next morning we were awakened by a knocking on the door and the entry of a Norwegian man in his fifties. We got out of bed to greet him, he shook hands and, of course, spoke no English, (he did not bring any much-needed food, by this time we were starving). We couldn't help but notice that he only had one hand, the other was an artificial hand with a black leather glove on it. He then proceeded to pull out a map and a very small compass, and he proceeded to point to where we were, and to the border of Sweden. He seemed to be very nervous and on edge. Again he shook hands and headed off, taking the map with him, but leaving the compass. We thought it was in case he was caught that he took the map, for it could have been traced back to him.

"We looked at each other, very sun-burned, cracked lips, hungry and with only snow for water, and feeling very cold, and decided to sleep a while longer and then have another go to try and reach the border.

"At this time the gash in my forehead was well open and weeping green puss, my leg was very stiff and my ribs hurt like hell. Again, somehow, we managed to sleep.

"Next morning we did feel a bit refreshed, and we thought, 'Well, this is it, chum, we've got to try and get on.' I did omit to say that I did find a very,

The small town of Hegra, with the River Stjørdal running from right to left. The house on the right, on the northern bank (arrowed), is where Flight Lieutenant Mick How and Sergeant John Murray were cared for before being taken captive by the Germans. (via M. How)

very old pair of ski-boots that were leather and were brittle and hard, but they were something I could put on my feet and, with great discomfort, I could manage to walk much better, not having frost-bite - I don't know how or why, and never will.

"We came out of the hut and stood on a sort of a little verandah, the sort of things you see in films, looking. To our amazement, down the hill came a very old man - he must have been eighty, and he had a white, flowing beard and white, long hair. He looked like Jesus Christ. He was, of course, Norwegian, and he knew no English at all. To our amazement he came up to us, he shook hands, and for some reason he gave us both a dose of what I now know to be quinine, a spoonful each, which was horrible. He produced from his bag two hard-boiled eggs which he gave to us, and then, to our embarrassment, he knelt down in front of us and started to pray. Not knowing what to do, we knelt with him, and we prayed. Anyway, he got up and shook hands with us. He vanished, completely vanished, we never saw him again. So off we went again, on track, as we thought, for Sweden. In fact, the compass not working, we walked for about another twelve hours; we did a complete circle, and came back to the same log-cabin again - which is unimaginable. You probably know that if you haven't got a direct bearing, or anything, you do walk in a circle. We just fell on the beds and slept again.

"Next thing we knew we were being shaken up by Norwegians who'd come up with a stretcher and a horse. They'd been sent up by the German police to collect us - they knew where we were. So I was put onto the stretcher (the stretcher was harnessed to the horse) and after several hours, I don't know how long, they took us down to the village of Hegra where the Norwegians were wonderful and very friendly people."

Flight Lieutenant Mick How (with head injury) and Sergeant John Murray resting in the Nielsen's home, shortly before being taken prisoner by the Germans. Jorulf and Margot Nielsen are at the back, with Einer Berg, seated left, at the table. (R. Trøite)

It was Aksel Sonen who came from Sunndal up into the hills with a horse. He and Steinar Nielsen helped to secure How to a simple stretcher, which was then dragged behind the horse, bumping along on the ground, all the way down to the village of Østkil in the Hegra district, from where they went to the home of Jorulf Nielsen (who had helped recover the dead airmen at Borås) and his wife, Margot. The local physician, Dr Aarrestad, came along and, with the help of the Nielsens, as How recalls:

"... dressed my wounds and strapped my ribs up, and they said, 'Look, chaps, we've got to hold you here until the Germans come. If we don't they will shoot us.' So we accepted this fact."

The two men were now recovering somewhat from their shock, but the realisation that they would be taken captive depressed them both. However, Margot fed them and a man named Einar Berg, who dropped in to see these English airmen, was able to talk to them and helped them to cheer up somewhat. They even had several photographs taken!

"Within a few hours the German police came along and took us away. They

Flight Lieutenant How and Sergeant Murray with Jorulf and Margot Nielsen outside their home in April 1942. Note Mick How's fleece-lined flying suit, especially issued to tail gunners.

(via M. How)

took us to a railway station where a German officer said, 'Now we're going on a train journey to Oslo and, if you try and escape, we shall shoot you. If you behave yourselves you will be treated respectfully.' He took us to Oslo where he shook hands with us and put us in a flat with several other prisoners-of-war that they had captured recently (one of whom was Sergeant Vic Stevens from Halifax W1048 'S-Sugar'), and from there they drove us to an airport and flew us in a Junkers 88 to Berlin. From Berlin we were taken to a *Dulag* reception centre where I was put in a hospital bed for a few days, interrogated immensely, but not under any physical torture or anything like that. In the end they gave up on me, and I was despatched to *Stalag Luft III* where I spent three years and one month."

As How remarked at the end of his recollections, 'If it hadn't been for the great airmanship and thoughtfulness of Wing Commander Bennett, I would not have written this account. He undoubtedly saved my life.' Both Murray and How survived the experience of captivity in German prisoner-of-war camps until the liberation, when both returned home, How to England, Murray to Canada.

NOTES

47. See map page 177
48. From a newspaper article checked and corrected by Slåtsve.
49. See also Solveig Skjeldstad's account on page 154-157
50. From Ly Bennett's account of her visit to Norway in July 1989 to meet some of the men who had helped her husband escape to Sweden in 1942.
51. See Chapter Eighteen.
52. In fact there are (and were then) no wolves in this part of Norway. The tracks may have been those of dogs.
53. How had been injured during the attack, his parachute had opened prematurely inside the aircraft and his boots had been lost while jumping out. See page 162

Chapter Fourteen
Evasion

Sergeant Harry Walmsley (second pilot to Wing Commander Bennett) and Sergeant John Colgan (flight engineer) were more fortunate than Eyles, How or Murray. They reached the ground a little to the west of Sonvatn and Harry Walmsley remembers landing in the soft snow there:

> "We were taught to bury the parachutes immediately and despite the warmth it would have given us if we kept them, we did that. I heard the flight engineer calling, 'Hello!' He had seen me coming down ahead of him and we got together and decided on an easterly route through the metre of snow towards, hopefully, the Swedish border.
>
> "The briefing, which is held before a squadron leaves the ground on a bombing operation, includes an instruction to carry an escape-kit. This consists of various things such as a compass, a knife, Horlicks tablets, waxed matches, concentrated chocolate and water-purifying pills. So we trudged along, following the compass and occasionally looking at the silk handkerchief which was another part of the escape-kit and contained a map of the area in which we were operating, including the border region and part of the Swedish terrain.
>
> "We decided to start on the concentrated chocolate which looked quite tempting after fasting for something like nine hours since we left our own country, but heading east we saw a farm (Sonfoss Farm) in isolation in the snow and in the forest, and after much heart-searching we decided to knock at the door and try to obtain some food."

The family inside did not notice the airmen approaching. They were startled by the knock at the door. Lars Langseth, his parents and two sisters were in the farmhouse that morning, none of whom could speak a word of English. The airmen were taken inside, as Walmsley relates:

"A young girl answered the door and we indicated we would like to enter and so after consulting an older man they let us into the house. By our actions we indicated we would like food and we were allowed to sit at the table in the room. Another little girl appeared and an old man, presumably the father, and we were provided with food.

"We got the impression that the old man was very uncomfortable in our presence and may have been thinking of alerting someone. So we left as soon as possible and made our way, not in an easterly direction, but, in order to fool anybody who had been alerted about our presence, we went north. We plodded on through the snow which filled our flying boots."

They were heading towards the small settlement of Sona that lay in the long, deep valley of Sondalen. Some time after daybreak they came across Johan E. Øyan, who lived in the valley. Øyan was chopping wood on his farm at Brobakk when he looked up to see, to his astonishment, two men in British uniforms making their way with difficulty along the snow-choked road leading to his farm. At first he couldn't believe his eyes. Although evidently worn out, they seemed oblivious to the risk they were running of being captured. He waved to them to come over to him. They seemed to be in good spirits, even joking about catching a German plane back to England, but Øyan knew that the Germans were on the alert and had been seen searching the valley. He warned the two airmen that they must be very careful. He recalls what happened that day:

"Two English airmen were walking down along the road to Sondalen. It was very deep snow and I soon realised that if these two didn't get help soon they would fall into German hands. I was able to speak a little English then, as now, and asked them into my house. I gave them some food from the little we had, and they were given some for the coming journey. One of them was injured in the hand and was seen to by my wife. After staying in my house until it grew dark, I took them to Johan Schiefloe, who lived in the telegraph station at Sona, about a mile away in Stjørdal Valley. I knew he could speak English after a stay in America. At the house it was explained to the airmen what they should do further and how to avoid the Germans. They were given more food for their journey, and I myself drew a route for them on a fine map that they had. Schiefloe and myself went with them on the uphill road along the railway to Sweden. This was about 10.30 to 11.00 in the evening."

The route to Sweden that Øyan drew for the two airmen ran past Meråker, a station on the railway line that ran eastwards to the border. He told the two men to follow the railway line, but to travel only at night. He also warned them about the German sentry posts at the railway bridge at Guda. Fortified

Johan Øyan (left) and Harry Walmsley meet again after 47 years, in front of the house in which Øyan lived at the time. The path (on which Walmsley and Colgan had walked) leads on down to Sola.

(via J. Øyan)

with food and once more carrying a food parcel, John and Harry set out with Schiefloe and Øyan, parting from them a few hundred yards along the road at Kilnes Farm. They then continued on their own, keeping close to the railway track that ran along the floor of the valley, walking all night.

Harry Walmsley continues:

> "We walked along the side of the track for a while, but Johan had said that the Germans were manning a bridge at Guda. And so, we avoided that by turning up onto the slopes at the side of the railway and the river which, if I remember, run parallel. This, of course, was another ploy to try and beat the Germans and get through to the next stage of our journey, still heading east, but as soon as we were clear of any sighting from Guda we went back down and followed the railway track."

They kept on walking for hours and, after covering a distance of about 22 miles from Kilnes, they approached a farm. This was Haugen Farm, just near the railway station at Meråker. By now they were very weary and bitterly cold. And so, at about 4.30

am. they entered a small *eldhus* (literally: 'fire-house') that stood near the farm. An *eldhus* is a small farm outbuilding where a fire is made for cheese-making. It is also used for storage and sometimes for living in - a lucky find indeed, as Walmsley recalls:

> "Eventually we came to a house which appeared to be rather isolated - as the first one had been - and we went in a barn. The people must have been in bed, it was in the early hours of the morning. In this barn we were able to make a fire with wood which was available, and using the escape-kit waxed matches, and endeavouring to get warm and if possible dry some of our clothes. We only wore the battledress uniform clothes, and not the full flying kit which was normal on night-bombing operations where we flew at 20,000 feet."

Paula Juliussen, the farmer's wife, remembers this day well:

> "Early one morning, about five o'clock, my husband Herlof was already up and ready to go to work when he noticed some smoke rising from the boiler-house flue. He went to see who was there and found two men sitting on some benches. They were very frightened and asked if we were Nazi, but were very pleased when he said: 'No!' My husband came back and told me and we both went back to see them, and as they didn't speak Norwegian we had to use sign language, of sorts! I brought them into the house and fed them. They were very hungry and tired and wanted to sleep. I didn't allow this because of the number of Germans here in Meråker. They were only 500 metres from us, so it was too risky."

Not only were there Germans in the immediate vicinity, but Paula knew that the farmer in the neighbouring farm was a Nazi sympathiser. Despite the airmen's obvious exhaustion, she felt it would be safer if they did not stay long.

Walmsley recalls some little details of the family he and John had been so lucky to come across:

> "In the house were two women (Paula and her sister Vilma who was visiting at the time), a girl of probably five or six years of age, and a little boy much younger, possibly only two (these were Ruth and Leif). But the ladies made us welcome and being the gentlemen we were we kissed the backs of their hands and asked for food which they supplied. The food was quite good, although it was obvious to both of us that the rationing in England would also be applied in Norway, especially with the German oversight there.
>
> "As we ate the food the little girl was drawing a pig on a sheet of paper and I wrote underneath in English 'PIG', and this caused quite a laugh. Meanwhile the man of the house - of course we didn't know their names for obvious reasons - proceeded to work. No doubt if he had stayed with us the Germans or Quislings may have called at the house to see why he was absent - with dire consequences for the family. He was a very trusting man

to leave two unkempt strangers in his house with his wife and his wife's sister and the two youngsters, and we appreciated his actions.

"There was a map pinned to the wall, strangely enough of England, and I pointed to Leeds and John Colgan, my companion at the time, pointed to London. So at least we conveyed to them where we had come from. We asked the lady in which direction we would meet the Swedish border and at what distance and she pointed out the direction. We checked the compass and bid them farewell."

Paula recalls learning something of her two unexpected guests:

"The pilots had a very good map with them, it was like a silken cloth. We explained the direction that the pilots should take so as not to run into the Germans.

"The airmen told us how they had been shot down by the Germans during the bombing attack on the *Tirpitz* in Fætten Fjord. One of them said that he had been stuck in a tree on the way down. They had walked far, they said, there was a lot of snow up in the mountains as it was still early in the year. They had walked along the railway and had been given food before they arrived in Meråker.

"The two airmen told us their names and where they came from. They were John Colgan and Harry Walmsley. John showed me his ring with J.C. on it, and so I believe that they told the truth.

"They cut some badges from their uniforms and gave them to my sister and myself. I got one with the English crown on (they were the flight engineer and second pilot brevets sewn onto the airmen's battledresses). I remember all this as if it were yesterday, and I remember that I cried when they said 'Goodbye'. The last that we saw of them was when they waved to us before disappearing into the forest here."

The two men decided to follow the route that had been drawn on their silk escape map. The route they were to follow veered northeastwards from Meråker and up into the hills, past a lake called Fjergen and on to another lake called Hallsjøen whose easterly shore lay on the border with Sweden. This was a distance of about 25 miles from Meråker. With a food parcel prepared for them by Paula, Colgan and Walmsley set off into the forest a little to the east of Meråker Station. Although Herlof offered to accompany them some of the way, the two men shook their heads and explained that they could manage with the map.

"We decided to make for the Swedish border but not to go near the town of Storlien. It seemed fairly obvious to my colleague and I that there would be German troops on the border immediately before Storlien. So we made the appropriate adjustment to our compass course, and immediately it started to snow. And there was in fact a blizzard, the sort of blizzard we don't see in England. Our clothes were already fairly-well soaked and the blizzard didn't help in any way, and in addition we were traversing uplands towards the mountain border region and the going was getting pretty tough. We tried sucking Horlicks tablets in the vain hope that we might gain some energy, and finished off the concentrated chocolate."

Their journey took them completely off the beaten track, although in this thinly populated area of Norway few places boasted occupation by more than the odd farm or settlement. The nearest town, Kopperå, Walmsley and Colgan avoided, leaving it far to the south in the Teveldalen, the valley along which the railway ran.

"When we left the house we had asked the distance - I must bring this point up now - and were told it was 'three miles'. And we didn't know that a Norwegian mile is much greater than an English mile. And for that reason we wondered if we were still going in the right direction.

"However, we decided to keep on the same course, plodding on through the deep snow in between the trees and heading for what appeared to be a lake. As the water would be frozen it wasn't that easy to realise whether or not we could cross with safety."

The lake they made their way across was Lake Fjergen, a long narrow lake that stretched some six miles towards Sweden. At the far end of it, isolated in the snowy wilderness, stood a small cabin, Flåmosetra, where a young man, Hans Flåmo, and his fiancée, Dagrun, had come to spend a few days fishing. Walmsley describes what transpired:

"We were met by some people using skis and they escorted us for possibly two or three hundred yards to a hut at the side of the lake. We were given food and allowed to sleep in the bunks in their hut and all our clothes were to be dried while we slept.

"When we had finished sleeping, and incidentally we must have slept for twelve hours, the clothes were dry, especially the boots which were completely sodden when we arrived there. They asked us if we required skis to proceed on to the Swedish border, but neither John Colgan nor I had ever used them and there might have been a serious catastrophe! So we decided to carry on on foot."

Hans and his fiancée set off ahead of them on skis, in order to make tracks the two men could follow, heading for Hallsjøen Lake, that lay two-and-a-half miles away, straddling the border with Sweden. Harry Walmsley continues:

"I believe now that the lake we crossed on the border is called Lake Hallsjøen, part of the lake is the Norwegian side, and part of it is the Swedish side.

"The part of the lake we were at was still in Norway, but because of the care and the food etc. which the Norwegians had provided we gave them the

Sergeant Harry Walmsley, three weeks after his arrival in Sweden. 'The civilian clothes were purchased in Falun, and funded by the British legation in Stockholm. My facial skin shows the ravages of five days trudging across Norway in atrocious weather conditions with insufficient intake of food. Stockholm, 21st May 1942.'

(H. Walmsley)

money which remained in our escape-kit pack, and it amounted to 30 kroner, all that was left of an original 150 kroner. The gentleman took the money and thanked us very much and we proceeded on our way across the frozen lake which was also covered with a thick layer of snow, so that the problem of wet flying boots came back again.

"When we left we were assured by the Norwegians that there were no Germans in that area, they'd never seen any on the border there, and it was quite safe for us to proceed. I think it was a sensible thing to ask and fortunately that is what happened: no Germans appeared. But when we reached a point possibly two-thirds of the way across the lake a Swedish patrol approached in the charge of a corporal - all on skis."

Throughout the journey Walmsley and Colgan never knew the names of the places they passed through or the people they met, until they crossed the Swedish border, when:

"At last we were able to put a name to a person we met. The leader of the patrol was called Oke Myrlov. Oke was a Swede but had been to Oxford in England and spoke perfect English. They took us to their hut in the mountains there and supplied lavish supplies of chocolate and drink and food of all kinds. I asked Corporal Myrlov why he was in the army. He said he was doing his summer training.

"We were then taken to Storlien to the Swedish military authorities there where the inevitable inquisition took place - who were we, and what had we been flying and why were we flying them, and of course we gave the stock answer of name, rank and number. It seemed that the major in charge was not very grateful for the information we gave him and would have liked far more, but he terminated the interview and after a meal we were escorted to the railway station for a journey to the internment camp in Sweden.

"We were joined in the railway carriage by two airmen from number 35 Squadron, which also operated against the *Tirpitz* on the same night, who

255

Trygve Dalanes (in foreground with sleeveless pullover) with his wife and farm workers in 1939. The upstairs room is where Wing Commander Bennett and Sergeant Forbes slept, en route to Sweden in 1942. (via Ly Bennett)

had used skis. One of them was a French-Canadian and one would have expected him to be an expert in the art of skiing!"

The two men were Pierre Blanchet and Ron Wilson who had crash-landed in Halifax W1048 'S-Sugar'.

Before Sergeant Colgan jumped through the aircraft's escape hatch he hooked on Bennett's parachute to his (Bennett's) harness. In the event, Bennett was the last one to leave the aircraft. He left only just in time; his partially-opened parachute only just broke his fall in the deep snow. It was not long before he met up with Sergeant Forbes, his wireless operator. Together they set out from Flornesvollen, where they had landed, in an easterly direction and, after some while, they waded across the Sagelva, a stream swollen with the melt-waters from the mountains. Bennett's main concern at this stage was to make

Mannsæterbakken, Trygve Dalane's farm, in 1939. The deep snow and the pine trees emphasise the isolation and wilderness of this part of the country through which the evaders travelled.

(via Ly Bennett)

sure he and Forbes shook any German soldiers and their tracker dogs off their trail.

Late in the evening they reached Guda Station. They could see a railway official sitting at a table in a room at the station, but did not dare to approach him. A little to the east of the station was a bridge over the river and, at the nearer end, Bennett and Forbes could see a German sentry post. They also believed that they saw a second one at the far end of the bridge. This decided them. They could not risk crossing the bridge and would have to stay, for the meanwhile, on the southern side of the valley. However, feeling very weary by now, and within sight of warmth and comfort, the two of them decided to risk approaching a house on a hill not far from the station. Although the lights were on and the door was open, there seemed to be no one about. This was probably a house called *Loen*, where Agnes and Helmer Hagensen lived. The two airmen crept into a nearby

257

shed where they found a sheepskin and, covering themselves with it, they tried to get some sleep.

Despite the events of the past day or so, and exhausted though they were, they could not sleep for the cold. So they gave up trying to rest and made their way out into the night again. They headed upwards, towards the mountains that lay between them and Sweden. The following day the sun shone a little, but it was still cold up in the mountains as they trudged on. The going, however, was a little easier now. The snow was firm beneath their feet and, when they came across a track used for transporting timber, they followed it. As evening fell they came up to a farm and decided for the first time to seek help. They were exhausted and had survived so far on only the escape rations they had had on them when they had parachuted to safety. They had arrived at Bjørnås Farm in Torsbjørkdalen, where Hans Bjørnås and John N. Dalamo lived. A little girl, Solfrid Torvik, opened the door to their knocking. The family received the two men with some suspicion at first, because John Dalamo:

> "... thought that we might be German 'provocateurs'. Apparently the police were in the district looking for us, and he was frightened that the Germans were trying to trick him, which would have cost him his life or at least a long term of imprisonment." [54.]

When it was realised that the two men were genuine British airmen they were welcomed, given food and allowed to stay the night.

On the following morning a man named Johan Nyheim took them further on up the Torsbjørkdalen valley to Mannsæterbakken, the uppermost farm in the valley. Here lived Trygve Dalanes and his family and it is Trygve who recalls their visit:

> "In the evening Johan Nyheim arrived here in Mannsæterbakken with two British soldiers (i.e. airmen), both in uniform. They had been to Bjørnåsen and brought a message for me from John N. Dalamo with a request to help the British pilots over to Sweden. They arrived late in the evening. My wife Hilma made their beds. Between 4 and 5 o'clock the next morning they were woken up. Hilma had a hash warming and the British had a good meal."

Trygve prepared to take the men towards the Swedish border, despite Bennett's vigorous protests that he was putting his life at risk in accompanying the two of them. In fact, Trygve could not understand a word Bennett said and regarded the forthcom-

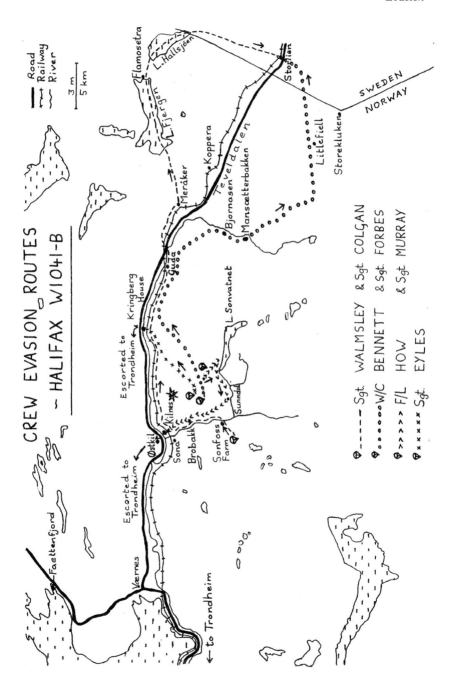

CREW EVASION ROUTES — HALIFAX W1041-B

Road
Railway
River

3 m
5 km

Sgt. WALMSLEY & Sgt. COLGAN
W/C BENNETT & Sgt. FORBES
F/L HOW & Sgt. MURRAY
Sgt. EYLES

Sergeant C. Forbes, wireless operator in Halifax W1041:B, shortly after arriving at Falun, Sweden.

(via Ly Bennett)

ing journey with little concern:

"I organised the skis for the three of us, but the British were no skiers. I skied and they went on foot. I had a gun with a licence to hunt wolves and elks. I brought it in case we should meet any strangers, in which case I would be hunting. It had been a cold night with brilliant hard-packed snow in which we left no tracks. We went towards Vattendalen, and from there to Litlefjell. After that we went to Gilsåfjellet and in the direction of Hårradålen towards the south side of Storeklukken. There I parted from the airmen, but I gave them a piece of paper on which I had drawn the border which could be seen from where we stood. The pilots did not understand anything that I said, nor I anything that they said, but I put my name on the piece of paper. I then went back to Mannsœterbakken where we live. The skiing conditions were still good."

Having covered a distance of about twelve miles with Trygve, Bennett and Forbes walked on the short distance to the border by themselves. They continued well into Sweden, about five miles, before reaching Storvallen, where they gave themselves up to a Swedish ski-patrol led by a Captain Skogh. On the following day, they were taken to the nearby village of Storlien. Here they were handed over to an Air Force officer who escorted the two of them by train to Falun, in central Sweden, where they were interned.

NOTES

54. From *Pathfinder* - Air-Vice Marshal D.C.T. Bennett (Frederick Muller, 1958)

Chapter Fifteen
Evasion And Capture (II)

The aircraft that Stevens, Blanchet and Wilson had seen crashing among the trees was, in fact, Halifax W1053 'G-George'. Struggling to keep in the air, she had flown low over Lake Hoklingen. Then she crossed Movatn, the lake beyond Hoklingen, before crash-landing near the small farm of Elverum. This was on the far side of the lake, where she ploughed a blazing path through the trees. The local inhabitants recall that it seemed as if the pilot was trying to land on the lake only to find his path blocked by a small peninsular. At the last minute he had pulled up and skimmed over this obstruction but, by the time he had put the aircraft down again, he had overshot the lake and had ended up in the trees, the nose of the aircraft resting in a small pond in a clearing. The aircraft came to a halt, its ammunition exploding and flames leaping over 100 feet in the air.

Ivar Hoel, the *Lensmann* for the Åsen District (who had taken Sergeant Stevens to the police station in Skogn), recalls how he became involved with the crew of this aircraft:

"I remember the aircraft crashing on the night after the Halifax (W1048 'S-Sugar') went down at Hoklingen. About three o'clock in the night the telephone rang at my home, and I was told that one English aircraft had gone down at Markabygda in Skogn, and that one airman was badly hurt. I went immediately there and came there before the Germans who also were alarmed (ie. informed). In the aircraft there was a dead airman, and at the nearest farm (Elverum) I spoke to the airman who was hurt. He was very correct and said that he could only give me his name and number. I do not remember the number, but I think his name was Dennis Butshard (in fact

Sergeant Dennis Butchart, the flight engineer). He had broken his upper arm and could hardly stand by himself. After a while the Germans came and took charge of him. The people on the farm mentioned that three or four other airmen had run away. I said to them that they must not say anything about that to the Germans, and I think they didn't, because I never heard about searching after the rest of the crew. Before the Germans arrived at the farm, Mr Butshard gave me a parcel (presumably the escape kit) which contained a silk scarf and some money (Norwegian). I understood that the Germans should not see this parcel. I still have the silk scarf with a map of Norway and the roads to Sweden.[55.] The next day I took a trip up to the aircaft, and when the German guard was sleeping I took a photo of the aircaft."

The mid-upper gunner, Sergeant C.F. Russell, had been burnt to death. His body was taken away for burial at the Stavne Krigskirkegard (War Cemetery) in Trondheim.

Four men had managed to survive the crash-landing without serious injury. Few details of what happened to these four men are known, but it is recorded by Aasmund Vinje, a local historian, that two of them received treatment for minor injuries from the inhabitants of a farm neighbouring the Elverum Farm, before setting out on their way to Sweden, accompanied for a short distance by their helper. Petter Nyborg, Einar Troseth and Petter Trætli, all of whom owned farms on the slopes of the mountains around Markabygda, each recall giving assistance to Allied airmen, but just which airmen was helped by which Norwegian has not been established.

One of these four men was the rear-gunner, Flight Sergeant William ('Bill') Parr. With his partner, he struggled for several days across the mountains, having to stop every so often to try to dry out clothes soaked whenever they fell through the ice and snow. Parr nearly succumbed to exhaustion and was only kept going by his companion slapping him and forcing him out of the icy water into which he had finally fallen.

According to records held at the Air (Historical) Branch in London these four members of the crew became prisoners of war. However, according to information held by the Norwegian Aviation Historical Society, they reached Sweden. It is certain, however, that Bill Parr was taken prisoner, because his widow still has the diary he kept while a prisoner of war.

Ivar Hoel's illicit photograph of the rear section of Halifax W1053:G in the woods near the lake at Movatn. (I. Hoel)

The other aircraft that was shot down that night was Halifax W7656 'P-Peter'. After she had been hit, she lost height rapidly and crashed in the waters of Åsen Fjord, off Røkke in Skatval, a few miles south of the *Tirpitz*. The wireless operator, Sergeant Gordon Cranstone, who has vivid memories of surviving the ditching of his Halifax, was the first man to climb out of the aircraft after it had hit the water. Within seconds he was joined by Sergeant Price who calmly set about releasing the dinghy. This first appeared as a square package popping out of its stowage in the wing, which Cranstone kicked about a little to help it inflate. Cranstone, in fact, was the first man to climb down into it. He recalls looking up at the stricken bomber wallowing in the water:

"I always remember Petley who was walking back from the front of the kite, and you'd have thought he had just got out of a taxi in Picadilly because he was a very calm man, one of those kinds of blokes. He said, 'I'm sorry about that fellows, damn bad show' or something like that, and he stepped down into the dinghy as if he was Lord Muck! By this time Price had joined us.

Unfortunately we never saw Evans who was a New Zealander, never saw him, and we never saw Columbine the observer. George Pomroy, the rear-gunner joined us, and this all happened very quickly, but I always admire George. In fact I'd have thought if there was any medal going it should have gone to George, because he went back in the kite. He was very fond of Columbine, but he'd have gone back anyhow. We remonstrated with him, but he went back in. He wasn't in there more than 30 seconds and he realised the water was coming up fast, because those kites don't float more than a couple of minutes. Well, he did try to rescue Columbine but he had to come out. We were lucky that he did because he got out only just in time.

"The dinghy was attached by an automatic cord, and we were trying to get away from the aircraft when all of a sudden it took its final dive. I've never seen a ship sinking, don't want to, but it's the same thing, suddenly the kite stood up on end, momentary pause, and then went under, and you could still see all the flames from the wing that was on fire as it went down. I always remember pulling old George Pomroy's leg, 'cause he was a Geordie, you know, and he could half swear like a Geordie, and I said to him, I said, 'George, when we get back to England you'll be put on a charge.' And he said 'Why the --- ?' And I said, 'You left the light on in the rear turret!'

"Yes, the kite was gone, and there we were."

The four men drifted in the dinghy in the cold and the silence for about three hours, until about four o'clock in the morning. The currents in the icy waters of the fjord swept them first one way and then another. They found the dinghy hand-paddles totally inadequate for them to actually propel the dinghy anywhere. Cranstone continues:

"It was kind of semi-light all the time, and then suddenly we saw a rowing boat come out which turned out to be a couple of Norwegians. I thought that we were going to be very, very lucky, because they eventually managed to throw us a rope, because we weren't getting anywhere although we had the paddles. Anyhow, they threw us a rope which we got hold of, and they gradually, slowly, towed us into shore. Now I thought we were possibly in the hands of the 'underground', but they turned out to be 'Quislings'. I suppose we should have twigged because when we pulled the dinghy up on to the beach, all stones, I remember we said to them, 'Look, we'd better destroy this lot.' They said, 'No. Leave everything as it is, it'll be picked up later'. - words to that effect. They conned us. Mind you, I suppose if we hadn't just had that experience a few hours earlier we might have seen through it, but I think, when you've been through that experience you don't always think straight. Anyhow, we left it, and then they led us into the woods, and I thought they were going to take us to the 'underground' (the resistance).

"All of a sudden we came out into an opening: it was a German camp! And as they led us out into this opening they started yelling their heads off, these two Norwegians, and from nowhere Germans came running. And that was it. They took us on to a disused tennis court, which was part of this camp, and they put us at one end and then they marched on at the other end a load of German 'Goons'. And I hadn't twigged at all. But Pomroy, the rear gunner, his knees must have been knocking. He nudged me and said, 'They're going to shoot us!', because the soldiers lined up these men at the other end. But then on came this German officer - he had a cloak on his shoulders, a big cape, but he walked the intervening distance of the tennis court and in perfect English said, 'I suppose you are hungry, would like something to eat?' And we, in a slightly squeaky voice, said, 'Yes.' And he called his sergeant over and he just said, 'Take them away and give them something to eat.' And that was all it was. This particular drama only lasted about a minute, but we all thought for one moment that we were going to be shot."

From this camp Cranstone and the other surviving members of his crew (both Sergeant A. B. Columbine the navigator and Sergeant A. Evans the wireless operator had been killed either in or before the ditching) were taken and put on a train bound for Oslo. Here they were housed in a large building for a few days and briefly interrogated before boarding a Junkers 52 for Germany.

No doubt the large building in which Sergeant Cranstone was held was the one that was to become familiar to Sergeant Stevens (the flight engineer with the badly sprained ankle from Halifax W1048 'S-Sugar'), who arrived here on the afternoon of 30th April. The train journey from central Norway had been a lengthy and, at times, a tedious one, as Stevens recalls:

"The train set off, fast to start with, and after a time it stopped at one or two main stations. It stopped at a biggish station, and there were the equivalent of the German Red Cross nurses walking up and down the platform. I think they were passing chocolate to the people inside. They came up towards us at our end, and there was a bit of a commotion. I said to one of the German guards, 'What's the trouble?' He said, 'This is a hospital train. It's full up with injured from your night's raid. Those nurses were passing chocolate along, but I don't think you're going to get any. I don't think you're very popular!'"

After travelling south for most of the day, the train finally pulled into Oslo Station. Stevens' travelling companion, Sergeant Dennis Butchart (suffering from severe injuries sustained when his Halifax, W1053 'G-George', crashed by Lake Movatn), was taken off to hospital, while Stevens was taken by vehicle to a large building in the centre of Oslo. Here he was brought before an officer who asked him the routine questions to which Stevens replied with his name, rank and number. Then a guard was called. He was taken to:

"... another big building which was a massive hotel at one time. It was a rectangular building about three or four storeys high and I suppose it would be about the third storey. They'd turned one of the rooms into a guard room with a raised, sloping section of floor along one side. They gave me a blanket and I slept on the floor.

"After a week there were six of us they'd captured. There was a squadron leader, two pilot officers and another two sergeants like myself (Stevens didn't recognise any of them). Anyway, on the Sunday the German guard on duty there - he had a desk and a chair (by the way, they brought good meals to us, including some meat) - said to us, 'Tomorrow you fly to Germany, Junkers 52.'

"In the morning we got up and they took us outside, a lorry turned up and they took us off to the airport. We all climbed aboard this Junkers 52. There was a long bench on one side and a long bench on the other side, and when we got in I was the front one on the port side and right opposite me was the Canadian pilot officer, and then the others on my right and on his left. On his right was the German *Feldwebel*. (sergeant). The guards got in and they just laid their rifles down higgledy-piggledy in the back of the aircraft, on the floor.

"We took off and after about a couple of minutes or so, settling in the run, by eye language I saw that this pilot officer wanted to speak to me. So I leaned over and all in one breath, and it was pretty fast I can tell you, he said to me, 'I know you've got a gammy leg, and you can't walk properly, but all I'm asking you to do is to throw yourself at the navigator of the aircraft (who was in his corner with his instruments) and stop him getting his gun (his gun was on a hook). I'm knocking this geezer out on my right and I'm taking over this aircraft and we'll crash-land in Sweden.'

"I suppose I had a bit of a shock, because I thought to myself 'Who, me?' So I leaned back and I weighed this navigator up, weighing up exactly how I'm going to launch myself at him, and I looked at the German next to the Canadian and I looked at the Canadian, and I looked at the German again out of the corner of my eye, casually, and my eye dropped and all of a sudden an electric shock ran through me because I could see straight through his holster. His holster was empty, and I knew darned well where his gun was, his gun was in his hand and his hand was in his battledress. I suppose he'd done all this before, knew exactly what could happen and what could not happen. I must have signified this shock to the Canadian because we both leaned over together and I said to him, 'Don't you dare. His holster is empty and his gun's in his hand and it's pointing straight at you. You wouldn't have a chance.'

"I leaned back and relaxed and after a time he leaned forward again, looked to his right, leaned back and wiped his hand across his forehead.

"But this gave me a reaction, you know. I was all tensed and it was like an anti-climax which is worse than having to carry it out. I disappointedly looked down then at the Swedish coastline just disappearing behind us. Anyway, after a time I came to terms with it and we carried on. We stopped at some God-forsaken aerodrome and they seemed to have run out of oil and they filled up with oil and we set off again, and we landed again at Copenhagen, and then we went on to Berlin."

Stevens was now a prisoner-of-war and as such he was to remain for the duration of hostilities in Europe. He had no way of knowing at the time that he was one of a total of eighteen aircrew from the raids who had been captured and would remain behind barbed wire until May 1945, when he, and many other prisoners-of-war, would be flown home to England.

Those aircrew who made their way to the safety of the Swedish border did so on foot. But Bjørn Rørholt, the Norwegian agent, was able to travel, at least for part of the way, in some style. Having reported on the RAF attack on the *Tirpitz*, he had left Trondheim by train in the early hours of the morning of 28th April, with a ticket for the town of Formofoss, en route for the Swedish border:

"As I came on the train to Stjørdal Station there was quite a lot of talk about this raid, and there was some talk about several aircraft having crashed and that most of the British airmen were dead, but some had been rescued and that the great question was to find them. Who would find them first: the Resistance or the Germans? Of course the Resistance had the edge, being locally acquainted with the terrain and so on, but the Germans spared no effort.

"So when I came off the train at Formofoss Station two German police soldiers converged on me, each holding a Luger 9mm, fully unsecured and so on, and came straight on to me. Why me? - I never found the answer but it probably was because I did wear a tweed jacket, which indeed was made in England but I don't know how two ordinary private German police soldiers would recognise that. Anyway, they converged on me, and I had the radio apparatus and two pistols on my body and I was not very keen on being searched. So they asked for identification, and of course there was absolutely no chance trying to get away - you know I could have used my right hand, taken my pistol, and I thought the chances of that were absolutely zero, and the chances on my identification card couldn't be worse than that. So I took out my identification card and showed it to them, and they talked and they asked me questions: they said, 'Where do you come from?' I said, 'I come from Oslo, I'm an insurance salesman, I have papers to show you, I'm an insurance salesman,' (and it said 'Agent' on my identification card!). So finally after talking for a little while they just said, 'Okay.' And I went away - and sat down on a bench. I won't say my knees buckled under me but it was a pretty close thing, you know. And this man, my contact-man that I should meet there, who incidentally posed like a German sympathiser, came up to me and we connected and the thing went on, and I tried to ask him and he said that probably the only explanation you could find was that they suspected that I was one of the British airmen who had managed to get into civilian clothes and had gone by the railway. And it was a natural thing, really, perhaps to do.

"But then we made our way - it took two days before I crossed the border - I crossed the border the night before the 1st of May. We tapped the German lines. They had a party line and the man who was hiding me was part of the Export Organisation (ie. the Resistance) but he was also tied into this party line so we could listen and there was a lot of talk in German about these airmen, you see. And I thought, but I later found out that it was not the case, I thought that those who were to accompany me over the border had been diverted to help some of the British. But it turns out that this probably is not the case - this was just an impression I had at the time because I had to cross the border all alone, nobody was with me, but anyway I have a fairly good sense of direction so I got there."

For the evading and escaping aircrew the dangers were over, to be exchanged for the boredom and tedium of life in an internment camp with no certain date for the return home. Not far away, however, on the German-occupied side of the border, the Norwegians were still at the mercy of a frustrated and angry enemy. The German police simply could not understand how four of the crew from the Halifax that had crashed at Flornesvollen had simply disappeared. Not long after returning from guiding Wing Commander Bennett and Sergeant Forbes to the Swedish border Trygve Dalanes suddenly found himself in danger:

"When I got back I had a rest, then in the evening when we were eating, the dog began to bark and we saw a troop of Germans. In all, there were thirteen of them. The leader spoke good Norwegian and said that they had followed the tracks of the two English pilots to the house. I denied there had been any pilots here. The Germans searched the shed and grounds, but not the house. I opened the window in the room where the pilots had stayed because in there were bandages that smelt of petrol.

"Fortunately for us, the Germans were satisfied with the search, and carried on in the direction that we had gone. They said that they were going to Størdalens Kapell. (In fact, Trygve believes to this day that the German officer in charge did not carry out a particularly thorough search because he did not condone the cruelty of shooting Norwegians who helped Allied airmen escape captivity). The day after, I received a telephone message to say that the airmen had arrived safely in Storlien. I don't know who telephoned me, I had no time to answer. The day after, a big search was carried out throughout Bjørkdalen by people on foot, and in cars and motorbikes which drove up and down the whole valley. But the Germans found no British airmen here in the valley. They had got to Sweden a long time previously."

But this was not the end of the affair, as Rolf Trøite comments:

"In Hegra the Germans must have understood that the pilots could not have got away without help. I heard that they had had a furious row with the policeman Brenne because of his unsuccessful investigation into what had happened to the crew. Would it not be possible to find the guides, who must have helped the crew? Yes, it was me that handled the search and me that should have been hauled over the coals. According to my diary notes, I used a whole day. On Tuesday 5th May is written, amongst other things, 'difficult journey to Sona-Sundal. Asked about Englishmen. Home 10 o'clock.' If the investigation was bad or not I haven't noted down. However, I remember questioning old Lars Langseth on Sonfossen. It was then that Lars said, 'You have to write what needs to be written.' Lars was taken by the Germans for questioning in Trondheim, but was soon back. His explanation was good enough, apparently."

There were no more arrests following this escape, but the Germans had certainly not forgotten the episode. When Nils Trøite was questioned in the prisoner-of-war camp at Falstad in 1944, he was accused of helping the English pilots over to Sweden in 1942. But Nils had a cast-iron alibi; he was in Oslo at that time and could, amongst other things, prove a conversation with a well-known N.S. (the pro-Nazi National Samling Party) man at a horse show in Bjerke. He did not mention that he had also had an important conversation with *Milorg* [56.] boss Erik Gjems Onstad.

And so, despite the risks that some of the Norwegians took, none of them suffered unduly for helping allied airmen on their way to the freedom of Sweden.

NOTES

55. See photograph on page 243
56. *Milorg* was the Norwegian Resistance Movement.

Chapter Sixteen
Internment And Return

The aircrew who had made it to Sweden, however, were still far from home. At the small town of Falun in central Sweden lay the internment camp in which all those who had sought refuge in Sweden from German-occupied countries were held.

Harry Walmsley recalls the joy of seeing familiar faces on his arrival at the Falun Internment Camp:

> "On entering the camp the first persons we saw were Wing Commander Bennett and Sergeant Forbes the wireless operator. It was marvellous to meet again, but the remainder of the people on the camp were a Polish submarine crew, who had been sailing out of Gdynia in Poland to escape from the Germans in September 1939. They had to put into Gothenburg through lack of fuel and they'd been in the internment camp since September 1939. But they seemed well aware of the female population in the local town!"

The two officers from W1048 'S-Sugar', Pilot Officer MacIntyre and Pilot Officer Hewitt, were interviewed here by a Lieutenant in the Swedish Army named Hansen. In the report made by the British Interrogation Officer, Wing Commander S.D. Felkin, on 22nd June after MacIntyre and Hewitt's return to England, the two men stated that Lieutenant Hansen:

> "... appeared to be an experienced and resourceful interrogator. He had a suave manner, and did not press his questions, but endeavoured to obtain answers by skilful indirect approaches. He frequently made claims which he hoped would call forth counter-claims and supply the answers he wanted."

The two men reported that they 'did not satisfy his curiosity'. They added:

"The interrogation took the form of a pleasant social reception, and W/Cdr Bennett was shown into the room and joined them."

Repatriation of aircrew who crossed over the border to Sweden was governed by rules that turned on the definition of the refugees' status at the time of leaving German-occupied Norway. If they had been captured by the Germans and had contrived to escape, they were technically 'escaped prisoners of war' and, since they had thereby lost their 'belligerent' status they were entitled to immediate repatriation. If, on the other hand, they had managed to avoid being captured by the Germans, then they were technically 'evaders' and as such had no rights of repatriation. The opportunity to 'bend the truth' so as to ensure a speedy repatriation was quickly taken up by Wing Commander Bennett, who felt unable to sit idle in Sweden while the war went on without him. At his interrogation on reaching Sweden he claimed that he had been captured by a German soldier, from whom he had later escaped. The official statement made by Bennett and Walmsley, in England on 29th May 1942, states:

"Shortly after landing, Wing Commander Bennett was taken prisoner by a single German on skis. Soon after he had surrendered the skier went away to round up some of the others, thus leaving him alone. He took full advantage of the opportunity and made off in the direction of Sweden."

The statement goes on to include the claim that Sergeant Walmsley and Flight Sergeant Colgan also managed to escape successfully from the custody of some German soldiers.

So, Wing Commander Bennett claimed that he was an 'escaper' and should be repatriated forthwith. Within a few hours of his arrival at the camp, Bennett was telephoning the British Legation in Stockholm. The assistant Air Attaché with whom he spoke was not very encouraging, but Bennett managed to get parole to enable him to visit Stockholm. Here he had an interview with Count Bernadotte, head of the Swedish Red Cross with responsibility for all internees. After some very persuasive discussions Bennett managed to get the Count to agree that his repatriation could take place.

It seems clear that the 'escapes' recorded in Bennett's and Walmsley's statement to the Air Intelligence officer in England at the end of May 1942, were fabrications concocted to ensure a swift return to England, for they are not mentioned in either

Don Bennett's published memoirs or in Harry Walmsley's recollections.

News of the safe arrival in Sweden of some of the aircrew who had failed to return to base after their attack quickly reached their squadrons, as Sergeant Charles Harrison of 10 Squadron recalls:

> "About a week after the April attacks the tannoys on the 'drome announced that W/C Bennett and Sgt. Forbes (W/OP) were safe in Sweden, and sometime later they announced again that Sgt Walmsley and Sgt Colgan were safe in Sweden."

Both Bennett and Walmsley stayed in the camp for only a fortnight and, as Walmsley explains:

> "At the end of that time I went to Stockholm with a railway warrant, completely unescorted, on a train. The Swedish authorities had apparently agreed to repatriate English fliers on a basis of two at a time, and Bomber Command when advised of this insisted that pilots should be released first. I was sent to the British Legation in Stockholm who provided accommodation for me locally to wait for a 'plane from Stockholm across the Skaggerak to the aerodrome at Leuchars in southern Scotland.
>
> "For five days we (Bennett and Walmsley) waited, but eventually we were flown home in a Lockheed Lodestar civil aircraft flown by two Free Norwegians (the pilot was Arvid Piltingsrud). We landed at Leuchars on the 26th of May 1942, which was approximately four weeks from the time we had left England at the start of the raid.
>
> "The usual interrogation took place with MI5 or MI6 about what we had seen of the Germans, if anything, in Norway or any activity of theirs on the railways etc. in Sweden. I was then told they were sending me for six weeks leave, but would not be returned to operations as was the custom with returned escapers or evaders."

On his return Bennett immediately took up his command of 10 Squadron and, within weeks, was appointed to command the Pathfinder Force, 8 Group, which developed techniques that dramatically improved the ability of the bomber force to bomb with increasing precision and accuracy for the remainder of the war.

MacIntyre and Hewitt reached England on 15th June, three weeks later than Bennett and Walmsley. As Hewitt points out:

> "The normal drill was exchange, and we were exchanged for a corporal and two Airmen. The Germans had airman pilots, and so on, and they were going from Norway to Finland or Finland to Norway and crash-landed in Sweden in the fog, so they had three bods to set off. If they'd had six then probably Perry and Wilson would have come along with us, but they only

had three, so they had to wait. There were more of us than there were of the Germans."

Flying home was not without its dangers. Bennett recalled that his flight over the Kattegat took place in broad daylight, a most unnerving experience, while MacIntyre recalled that, during their flight home, they became lost and sent out an SOS, before discovering their position and landing safely in England.

As the aircrew from the raids on the *Tirpitz* soon learned, the camp provided a very loose form of internment. Supervision of the inmates was quite relaxed and, after a period of time, some of those for whom repatriation was to be delayed were able to find work in the locality and even to live outside the camp in the local town.

Wilson recalls that he and Blanchet were treated very well. They not only received money from England but were also given an allowance by the Swedish authorities. They were able to rent a flat in the nearby town because they had found work in the neighbouring brick-kilns. Later they worked in the forests felling trees. They never lacked for money or necessities, for they were told they could charge the British Legation for anything they bought - Wilson recalls with a laugh, 'You can be sure we made the most of it!' For men who had just come from the strictly rationed England, the choice and availability of goods in Swedish shops came as something of a pleasant shock.

About a year after they had been shot down, Wilson and Blanchet were sent unescorted by train to Stockholm to report to the British Legation there. They then spent about a week there, really living it up, while waiting for seats on an aircraft flying to Britain. Finally they were put on board a Lockheed Lodestar, which flew them over the North Sea to land at Lossiemouth. The other internees from the raids, Sergeant Forbes, Sergeant Colgan and Sergeant Perry, also returned home safely later in the year. All the aircrew who returned to Britain before the end of the war went on to serve as Instructors, or in Air Sea Rescue work, or returned to operations abroad, in North Africa or South East Asia.

The battleship *Tirpitz* continued to be, however, a most potent force. It was a sleeping giant that might awake at any moment. A variety of very courageous and ingenious attempts were carried out to destroy her, the 'Lone Queen of the North', with varying degrees of success, from that spring of 1942 to the autumn of 1944. A thwarted attempt by the British Navy to sink her using human torpedoes ('Chariots') took place in October 1942 and later, midget submarines succeeded in severely damaging her at Alta Fjord in Northern Norway, during an attack of astonishing daring and bravery in September 1943. She was attacked a number of times by the Fleet Air Arm in 1944, with some success. Finally, lying in Tromsø, Northern Norway, immobilised by damage, *Tirpitz* received two direct hits from *Tallboy* bombs dropped from Lancasters of 9 and 617 Squadrons, which attacked her on November 12th 1944. The remaining bombs caused her to capsize in the shallow water. Seven hundred men, nearly half her crew, lost their lives.

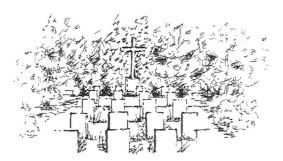

Chapter Seventeen
In Memoriam

When peace came, most of the participants who had survived the raids on the *Tirpitz* in 1942, and who had lived through the remaining three years of the war, wanted nothing more than to pick up their lives that had been so suddenly interrupted and so irrevocably changed by the conflict. The *Tirpitz* lay, a rusting, twisted hulk, in the shallow waters of the fjord at Tromsø, much

The capsized Tirpitz, now being dismantled by Norwegians for scrap.
(via J. Øyan)

HRH the Queen Mother meets the crew of Halifax W1048 'S-Sugar' at the opening of the new Bomber Command Hall at the RAF Museum, Hendon, on 11th April 1983. (l to r) Vic Stevens, Ron Wilson, Pierre Blanchet and Dave Perry. The mid-section of their old aircraft can be seen behind them. (via V. Stevens)

of her fabric removed as scrap. As the years went by so the memories of all those things that had happened to the participants in the drama receded. Nobody, it seemed, wanted to remember what had happened to them. Like Halifax W1048 'S-Sugar', which settled deeper and deeper into the soft mud at the bottom of Lake Hoklingen in Norway, so their memories too became buried under the activities of normal everyday life.

The last Halifax to fly took to the air in 1952. By then virtually all of them had been scrapped. Immediately after the war several ex-aircrew associations were founded, in particular the RAF Escapers Club and the Ex-PoW Association, and many aircrew tried to trace the brave men and women who had befriended them on foreign soil and risked their lives in helping them to escape the Germans. But apart from that, most of the participants just got back to making a living while the past became a personal memory that was difficult to share with those who had had no part in it.

After 42 years, Vic Stevens meets Ivar Hoel outside Ivar's home in 1984. (Leif Knutseth)

In 1973 the news that from the bottom of a lake in central Norway an old World War II aircraft had been raised to the surface and brought back to England, generated a wave of interest across the nation. It reached the national media and soon it seemed that everybody had heard about it. When the six men who had flown her on that last, now historic, flight, were reunited once again, the imagination of the public was caught and, much to the general surprise and even dismay of those men, each became something of a celebrity. As far as they were concerned, they had just been young men doing their job. They had no wish to be singled out above all the thousands of other young men in the RAF at the time, many of whom had not survived the war.

The discovery of Halifax W1048 'S-Sugar' must, in part, have been responsible for a resurgence of interest in the activities of the crews of Bomber Command. Memories, often painful ones, had become sufficiently distanced in time from the events of the war for them to be recalled without too much pain, even with pride and gratitude. A trickle turned to a flood as ex-RAF Associations sprang up. Men who had last seen each other in uniform met to recall old times. Memoirs, although a few had been published in the years since the war, began to appear in increasing numbers; it seemed that these airmen were the repositories of history. Public interest in their exploits, especially among those too young to have been participants of the conflict, continued to grow.

In 1983 Halifax W1048 'S-Sugar' was placed on permanent exhibition in the Bomber Command Hall at the RAF Museum at Hendon. The new wing that contained her was opened that April by the Queen Mother, who met the six men who had flown the aircraft over the *Tirpitz* 41 years before. The following year Vic Stevens, as so many other members of the armed forces have done both before and since, returned to the scenes of his most vivid wartime experiences. Other participants of the raids also made a pilgrimage to Norway, some meeting their Norwegian helpers for the first time since the drama of those days.

The Norwegians themselves have never forgotten the events of 1942. Reminders of the attacks on the *Tirpitz* and of the presence of the Germans in their district, are not far from the minds of the older people. Only just below the surface of their land can still be found the detritus of war. In 1986 the remains of the engine of Pilot Officer Gimson's Spitfire was recovered from the lake into which it had crashed. The spinner had flattened itself onto the engine with the impact and the remains of the metal propeller blades were twisted and bent. The engine itself was in remarkably good condition and is now on display in the Royal Norwegian Air Force Museum.

Opposite page, top: The remains of the propeller of Spitfire AB307, flown by Pilot Officer Peter Gimson. Bottom: The remains of the engine. (via Asbjørn and Gudrun Heggdal)

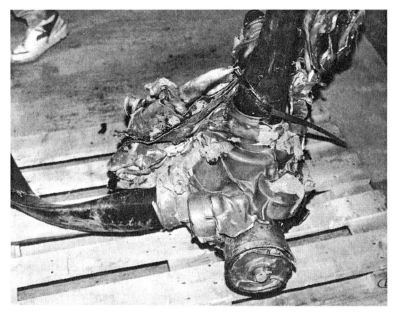

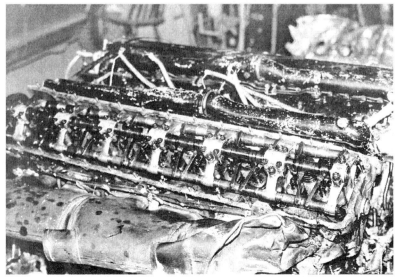

On the farm at Elverum, where Flight Sergeant Roe's Halifax
W1053 'G-George' crashed after over-shooting Lake Movatn, are
a number of objects recovered from the wreck and preserved.
Local people out walking amongst the hills and forests still
come across aircraft remains and, at all of the crash sites, it is
still possible to find pieces of aircraft and their equipment
hidden by the undergrowth, but lying where they fell nearly
fifty years ago.

For some, however, the remains constitute a hazard. Erling
Ulvik, a farmer living and working on the shores of the Frosta
peninsular four miles from the site of *Tirpitz's* berth, has good
cause to know this. Fifteen drums, leaking chemicals, were
found on the beach at his home, Vagen Farm, in the summer of
1989. He recalls that in the Autumn of 1941 the Germans began
to use Åsen Fjord for mooring and exercises with their ships. It
was at this time that they began to position smoke-producing
apparatus at various places in the area. This apparatus
consisted of a group of two or three large drums of a size similar
to 40-gallon oil drums, connected to a gas cylinder. The
chemicals in the drums, activated by the gas in the cylinders,
released vast quantities of smoke. The apparatus was sufficiently dangerous for the Germans working with it to wear
rubber suits and gas-masks. These 'smoke-pots' were mounted
on specially constructed platforms (now almost entirely vanished with the passing of time) at strategic points along the
shores of the fjords and in the hills. They were also placed on
boats that could be anchored offshore, or manoeuvred into
suitable positions on the water. Forty such drums were brought
to Vagen Farm at the time.

The placing of the smoke-pots here on Frosta, some distance
away from Fætten Fjord, is evidence that a very large area was
prepared by the Germans in which to conceal their ships under
the protection of a smoke screen. Ulvik recalls the smoke-pots
being activated on a number of occasions, including the times
when the RAF attacked the *Tirpitz* at the end of April 1942. He
believes that the whole area between Frosta and Langstein (just
to the south of the *Tirpitz*) was completely obliterated under a
vast pall of chemically-produced smoke.

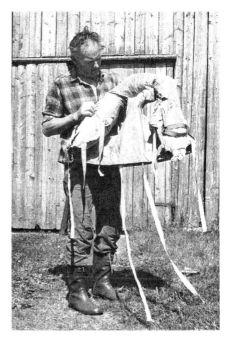

Einar Stormo in 1973 with a Mae West recovered from the wreck of Halifax W1053:G that crashed near his farm at Elverum (S. Usher)

Among the hills, in the woods, and by the lakes, where young airmen from the RAF met their deaths while attempting to destroy part of the occupying German might, are raised simple, stone markers in their memory. At the site of Flying Officer Malcolm's crash in the mountains of Forbordfjellet stands a small stone memorial with parts of the engine of his Spitfire mounted at its base. Near the farm at Borås, where Lancaster L7572 'L-Leather' and Halifax W1020 'K-King' crashed on the night of 27th April 1942, stands a large stone surrounded by a number of smaller ones. On the stone is inscribed the names of each member of the crew who died when their aircraft crashed in flames nearby. Each one of the smaller stones represents one of those who lost his life.

Magnar Hassel, who, as a young boy of fourteen years, witnessed the last moments of the life of Pilot Officer Peter Gimson, whose parachute failed to open after he baled out from his burning PRU Spitfire over the waters of Hammarvatnet, has this to say:

"I have often thought of this young pilot, and why he has no memorial at the site of the crash of his aircraft. After all, he gave his life for Norway. Some years ago I revisited the area where we found the pilot. I had trouble finding the exact spot, because the road had been reconstructed. By chance I was able to learn the pilot's name, thanks to Skaugstad Diving and Historical Research in Trondheim this year (1986). He is buried at Stavne War Cemetery in Trondheim. His grave has been visited every 17th of May (our national day) since then by one of the boys who watched his fight for life on a spring afternoon in 1942."

Stavne War Cemetery is the last resting place of the crews from Halifaxes, Lancasters, Spitfires and Beaufighters who lost their lives over the *Tirpitz*, a place of pilgrimage for Norwegians and returning ex-members of the RAF alike.

The battleship herself, hiding in parts of Trondheim Fjord for many months during 1942 and 1943, cannot be forgotten. Even today, where the *Tirpitz* lay moored to the side of Fætten Fjord, there remain the two large concrete abutments against which she was secured. Still set in the concrete, the massive mooring bollards used by the great battleship and even a number of links of her anchor-chain, remain as mute testament to her presence and what it meant for the local inhabitants in the dark days of the war. Five hundred yards away there now stands a granite plinth. On the top of it, mounted on three links of the *Tirpitz's* giant anchor-chain, rests one of the mines that was carried across the North Sea by a Halifax over forty years earlier. The inscription on one face of the monument reads, in both Norwegian and English:

> **FOR FREEDOM**
> **IN MEMORY OF THE ALLIED AIRCREWS**
> **FROM THE ROYAL AIR FORCE**
> **KILLED IN ATTACKS AND RECONNAISSANCE**
> **ON THE GERMAN BATTLESHIP TIRPITZ**
> **IN THE FÆTTENFJORD 1942**
> **IN GRATITUDE AND VENERATION**
> **TO THOSE WHO GAVE THEIR LIVES**
> **FOR OUR COMMON CAUSE**
> **ERECTED BY LOCAL PEOPLE 1985**

Chapter Eighteen
Closing The Circle

Sunday April 26th 1992.

Into the still air over the small, isolated, upland farming community of Borås rise the notes of the Hegra Brass Band, echoing through the scattered trees that cover the summit of the hill that looks over a single standing stone embedded in the grass on its slopes. The Norwegian and British national flags hang in the stillness under the bright blue skies as a slight figure approaches a microphone that stands near the stone. In clear, beautifully intoned English, Solveig Skjelstad brings into the hearts and minds of all those present a moving moment from her childhood, fifty years earlier:

"Welcome to the ceremony.

"We are now standing in the area where the two aircraft crashed on that terrible night in April 50 years ago, when the RAF was attacking the *Tirpitz*. The Halifax was shot down a hundred metres east of this memorial stone. The Lancaster crashed further to the west.

"Early that morning fifty years ago, all the people in the area came up here to look - me too. I was wondering why one airman was sitting straight up and didn't turn to look at me as I approached the aircraft. Then I realised: he had passed away. No one had survived. Let us remember the Halifax crew: Pooles, Henry, Rarity, Wilstrop, Hill, Booth. The crew from the Lancaster were brought into my Grandfather's house down there (you can see the gate at the end of the building). I remember Germans on duty, keeping watch while men from the neighbourhood made wooden boxes to serve as coffins, before they were taken away.

"Let us remember the Lancaster crew: Mackid, Underwood, Tree, Marshall, McDermott, Bennett. Some days later they found another body from the Lancaster crew: Raymond Day. Let us remember him. He was brought into my Grandfather's house as well. My sister and I gathered branches from the pine tree behind the building, and laid them in Raymond Day's coffin, as is our custom.

Ever since the memorial stone was raised in 1979 Solveig has made an annual pilgrimage every April to Raymond's grave in the war cemetery at Stavne, Trondheim, placing a wreath composed of branches from that same pine tree on his grave.

This simple, moving ceremony, during which a wave of old griefs and sorrows seemed to rise up the hill, and free themselves in the bright sunlit skies over the distant snow-capped mountains, was the culmination of a pilgrimage made to this spot by many people - some of whom were the veterans, both Norwegian and Allied, of the attacks on the *Tirpitz* in 1942.

In the short period of four months from January to April 1992 the people of the country district of Åsen in Nord Trondelag made preparations for an influx of visitors from overseas. Embassies and airline companies were contacted. High-ranking officers of the Norwegian Military forces and local dignitaries were invited to attend. Members of the Åsen Historielag (Historical Association) talked and planned and organised a series of events. The Norwegian Air Force and pilots of the local aero club rehearsed the flypast that was to be part of the opening ceremony in Fætten Fjord. A major event, to be recorded on television film, was in full preparation.

Most of the overseas visitors had arrived in a Braathens jet that flew into Værnes Airport on Thursday evening, to be whisked away by the local families who had generously offered to accommodate them. By Saturday morning they had begun to get used to the traditional Norwegian breakfast of bread, cheese and fish, with English tea made with individual tea-bags. Despite the difficulties of the language barrier much had been talked about between visitor and host and many places in the area had been visited. One man was shown the exact spot where one of his 4,000lb bombs had fallen and some were taken to the spot where their aircraft had crash-landed. Everyone was beginning to be familiar with the landscape - its woods and hills and lakes.

At the head of Fætten Fjord, on the grass near the stony beach against which the water lapped, a large crowd had

A Guard of Honour before the comemmorative monument during the ceremony. (via Johan Øyan)

gathered in front of a temporarily erected covered bandstand. Some fine music was performed by the Åsen Band until, at about 2pm a distant roaring brought everyone's attention towards the fjord, where pinpricks of light could be seen high in the sky against the backdrop of lowering clouds. With rain in the wind, a formation of about twelve light aircraft droned steadily up the fjord at about 1,000 feet. They were com-memorating the original flight up this fjord 50 years earlier, but inevitably there were differences. The aircraft were single-engined light aircraft, some owned by private individuals, some from the military flying school at Værnes Airport. They were flying at about 100mph, not 210 mph. They were not being attacked, but they were flying at a greater altitude than had the Halifax bombers, since permission to fly at 300 feet had not been granted 'for reasons of safety'. Nevertheless it was a most impressive and moving sight as these reminders of the past flew overhead and on up the Åsen valley. The final aircraft, a sea-plane, struggled to keep up with the others, slowed down by the wind resistance put up by her floats. Her pilot was the son of Bernhard Bergersen, a most remarkable man who had had the original inspiration for this whole event and who at this time was among the crowd, co-ordinating the fly-past by radio. The flypast had been his idea and it gave him deep satisfaction to see it occur so successfully, despite the somewhat grey, drizzly weather. During the early afternoon, speeches were made by several people, including Trygve Lian the Chairman of the Åsen Historielag (the Local Historical Association), Wing Commander J. Marshall (the Defence and Air Attache from the British Embassy in Oslo), a representative of the Norwegian Air Force, Bernhard Bergersen, and Don MacIntyre (the pilot of Halifax W1048 'S-Sugar' that had crash-landed on nearby Lake Hoklingen in 1942).

Early that evening, more speeches were made at a splendid banquet that took place at the Åsen Community Hall. Several hundred quests listened to beautiful renditions of a wide variety of Norwegian music, performed by the local band and choir, then they watched a fine slide show presented by Trygve Lian.

The author of this book gave a speech to welcome and introduce all those veterans who had travelled from over the sea to be in Norway for this occasion. Men (and their wives) had travelled from Australia, Canada, the United States of America and the United Kingdom, men who had corresponded with the author during the previous five years of research. Here too were the relations of several of the airmen who took part in the raids, in particular Ly Bennett, wife of Air Vice-Marshal Don Bennett, who survived the loss of his Halifax W1040 'B-Baker', Jackie Gimson whose brother Peter was killed on reconnaissance over the *Tirpitz* in 1942 and Arthur Day and his sister, whose brother Ray was killed in the Lancaster that crashed at Borås. Two unique gifts were presented to Ly Bennett and Jackie Gimson. Parts of the aluminium recovered from the wreckage of Don Bennett's Halifax and from Peter Gimson's PRU Spitfire had been moulded into scale replicas of these two aircraft and were presented to the two ladies by the local aircraft enthusiasts who had conceived the idea and carried it out so beautifully.

Bernhard Bergersen spoke of his memories of the dark days of the war in Norway.

The Mayor of Levanger, commenting on the bravery of the RAF pilots of fifty years earlier, said:

> "Maybe we have difficulty in understanding such willingness (as shown by those pilots) to sacrifice their lives. Every man and woman had to go though worse ordeals and trials than peaceful everyday life demands from us now. We in Norway are lucky to have such good neighbours in the West who came to our support and rescue. Let us hope that the good will in co-operation, that we notice today, will continue."

The Parish pastor, Gustav Danielsen, spoke briefly of the question of the presence of evil in human beings:

> "This desperate question is to be found between the lines of the song 'Where have all the flowers gone?' It is a question many people have struggled with, especially those who have experienced war. I do not think there is any explanation. Man's evil is neither to be explained away, nor to be excused. It is to be acknowledged.
>
> "'Where have all the graveyards gone? Gone to flowers everyone'. The singer has a hope. Even the darkest of the dark will be turned into a new beginning. The hope is, however, conditional. We feel an evil circle: 'When will they ever learn?' The Jews who were to suffer more than most people during the last World War, have an old book telling about the beginning of all things. A Jew who lived at the beginning of the reckoning of our time did not give an explanation of all things; even so, he gave the hope that death would be no more one day, nor would grief, anger or pain. His hope shares the hope of the song, but it is hope without reservation, unconditional: 'Man shall come to an end, because of horror and pain coming to the earth. The strength of heaven shall shiver. When this happens, lift your heads, because your salvation is near'."

Don MacIntyre spoke eloquently of the young men with whom he flew fifty years earlier:

> "On April 27/28th 1942, in bright moonlight, 43 bombers of the RAF attacked the *Tirpitz*. In Trondheim Fjord the ship was found and bombed. Five aircraft were lost. On April 28/29th 33 bombers returned. Two were lost. Just two entries in a long list of air battles against German targets.
>
> "To the RAF crews that flew those missions, they meant much more. The *Tirpitz* was a major threat to Atlantic shipping and the Royal Navy. No sacrifice was too great to contain this large battleship from the seas. The risks were high but the prize was great. Brave men knew their flight plans and carried them out with skill and disregard for the great dangers.
>
> "Fifty years after, it is with pride we salute these airmen. They could not have done more. They brought honour and respect to their service. They helped win the war. It was for freedom that these men flew and it was for freedom that many of them died. It is their valour we must remember. We will remember.
>
> "The Norwegian Friends who honoured these brave men with graves and

memorials have shown their respect for this sacrifice. The RAF crews thank you. It is an honour to salute a very renowned group on their 50th Anniversary of the Raids on the *Tirpitz*."

Wing Commander J C W Marshall, RAF, Defence and Air Attache remarked, too, on the courage of the war-time crews:

"With my experience of modern aircraft with their modern sophisticated avionic and navigation systems, of modern weapon systems, and my flying experience in Harriers in Norway, I know only too well the difficulty of flying in this sort of mountainous terrain. To have done so in the types of aircraft you had to fly in with rudimentary dead reckoning navigation and bombing systems, possibly at night, in and out of cloud, took courage indeed. As a professional military pilot in the modern RAF I salute you."

He also spoke of his admiration and gratitude for the Norwegian people:

"... who had to endure the occupation of their land - who spied on enemy movements - who passed back vital information - who helped in guiding aircraft to their targets - who helped surviving crews to escape - who showed great care and sympathy for those who were killed by finding and caring for their bodies and giving them a decent burial.

"Thus, this weekend is not just about a particular attack on a particular target, but is a commemoration to the courage and exploits of people. For many, this weekend will clearly be a closing of the circle. For the aircrews a chance to see and remember once again those eventful days of long ago - for the families, to see something of what their loved ones had to go through, and for some to pay homage to their loved ones who fell in battle while defending freedom - for Norwegian people, to meet after all these years those crews and their families who helped in liberating their country."

As the guests left the hall around midnight they passed a display of photographs and original pieces of equipment concerning the raids and, out of the doors, passed an almost complete rudder recovered from the remains of the Lancaster that had crashed at Borås. This rudder had been brought down from the hills only a day or so earlier.

The second (and final) day of this commemoration event began, after an early breakfast, at the doors of the Åsen Community Hall where two large coaches waited to take everyone on a sight-seeing tour of the area and a trip to Trondheim. The two coaches travelled around the Frosta Peninsular, passing Lofjord - one of several secluded fjords where the battleships of the German *Kriegsmarine* had been moored - and the residential home specially built for German officers.

The party stopped in some bleak woods to visit a monument to those men who had been put to death in secret at the Falstad Concentration Camp. The woods stood silent and the day felt dark, despite the bright sky and the sunlight piercing the trees. The coaches went on to Markabygda where Halifax W1053:G had crash-landed, then on to Lake Hoklingen, the site of the remarkable recovery of Halifax W1048 'S-Sugar' in 1973. Then, turning from small country roads up onto lanes that were little more than rough tracks for the logging vehicles to carry their loads from the woods to the nearby port of Levanger, the visitors were taken to Borås where they honoured the crews of the Lancaster and the Halifax that had come to rest so high up in the hills, listening to the short speech given by Solveig Skjelstad.

En route for Borås the leading coach stopped briefly. The guide descended and disappeared into the woods at the side of the road for a moment, emerging with what looked like a piece of dead wood; in fact, an unexploded shell. The detritus of war lies very close to the surface in rural Norway.

The final stopping point of the journey was the Stavne War Cemetery in Trondheim, where a short, moving service was held before both a Norwegian Guard of Honour and a very special Guard of Honour composed of those veterans who had fought the enemy above and within the Norwegian landscape.

By midday the following morning many of the visitors from overseas had once more taken to the air over Norway, winging their way home over a land of ice and snow, mountains, rivers and lakes. Finally, the memories that had surfaced so powerfully during the two days of commemoration, had been laid to rest. The monuments to past sacrifice stood alone once more, at one with the land. Time had healed much and there had, in truth, been a final closing of the circle.

Appendix I

Memories of a Young Girl

Excerpts from an interview between the author and Solveig Skjeldstad, with her husband Lars, in London in the Autumn of 1992, some months after the 50th Anniversary Commemoration.

"When the Memorial Stone up at Borås was raised in '79 I had Raymond Day's brother and wife to visit us. They were my guests. And his (her husband Lars') committee responsibility was for the Stone Memorial, and it is due to him that there is a Memorial Stone there. And since '79 I have brought spruce branches to Stavne. Some times I do like that. Every year since then.

"But you see, the speech I held at the Memorial Stone (in April 1992) was nothing, I think it was the way I put it that affected the people. I get, as Arthur Day said, a bit emotional. But I really want you to make a flowering story because I remember the war - well it wasn't that harmful to us. The Germans didn't do any harm to the farmers up there. They walked past Borås and they popped in and warmed their fingers and my Grandfather had been to America and spoke English to them and a bit of Norwegian, and a little bit of German, and they passed to Skei again and many mornings I remember Mother woke up: 'Solveig! Come and have a look.' And there were Germans everywhere in the garden.

"So we got used to them, and sometimes we got sweets and an apple, and I had never seen them before. And my sister played the organ as well. They were young soldiers, and nothing happened. But we were not allowed to have celebrations, dances and cinemas - nothing! Everything was closed, school as well. So when something happened it was entertaining. So the Germans provided a bit of entertainment. So when you write a little bit about this I don't want you to make it too dark.

"But we had no food, just milk; and we grew corn, but the Germans just stood there and said to Grandfather, 'Well, this corn you can have but this is for the German's horses, and this grass we will have for hay for the

German's horses.' So they took half the crops. So the children sometimes got free from school to go into the forest to break branches to feed the animals, because the Germans took the grass, took the corn, and we had no coffee. But Grandmother burned peas, and when she boiled it she got a colour like tea, and it served the purpose! And I remember Mother took some animal fat and mixed it with home-made flour and made cakes and biscuits - it was everything we had. But on the farm at least we had something to eat, and I even remember the Germans came to buy some eggs, fresh farm eggs, and some bacon - they hadn't enough at the camp. And we very often travelled by train, and I remember Mother had a pink piece of paper, like this, and it was a picture of Mother and she handed it to the Germans - it was like a passport. We girls, we hadn't anything. But you see we travelled by train a lot of times, to visit Grandfather.

"Sometimes it was impossible to get back to Steinskjerrigan (where we lived), so we had to join the school here, one English mile. So we went to school here and when we were allowed to go by train again we went back home. So I was staying at my Grandfather just that very night, the 27th of April. This Memorial Stone - anyone else could have told you about what happened here. But, because we spoke English we were told 'There is an Englishman coming, can you give him hospitality, because you speak English?' And I said, 'Oh yes, that's okay.' And so we gave Arthur Day hospitality, and he stayed. And I think it is due to him that we became involved. And later on a lot of military groups came visiting, and I would get a phone-call: 'Can you come up to the memorial stone and tell the story?' So I have been up there and telling stories a lot of times. And now again at that Fifty Years Anniversary I was asked, 'Can you have a little ceremony?'

"I remember my Grandfather risking his life: he had a horse and a sledge, and he fetched ammunition from a boat - a British boat, I think - and on top of it he put wood for the fire, some logs, and he passed the Germans and he passed Borås and he went up to Hegra Fort with ammunition. He risked his life; but he said, 'I am so old', and the same night when the Halifax crashed, and the Lancaster crashed, Grandfather said, 'I'm so old, if it's determined that I'm going to die tonight, let me die in my bed, so I won't go down to the basement.'

"May I tell you a story? Up here was the Halifax. And the fuselage was quite whole, and all the farmers they hadn't anything because there wasn't anything to buy in the shops. So they brought back pieces from the fuselage to repair their houses, and glass from the cockpit. We made this knife, and from the wheel I had stocking-supports! You see it was so marvellous, and from the parachutes I made a blouse, because we hadn't clothes, we hadn't shoes."

Solveig's husband Lars recalls:

"During the war, I was there on the same morning when the planes had crashed and I saw the pilot sitting just as Solveig has described, and we took parts from the 'plane just to use them for things we were short of. So a lot of things are still kept around on the farms. And some of them are more valuable, like a propeller, a wheel, a motor, you know."

Looking at a map of the district he also explained how he believes the Halifax approached Borås:

"The Halifax came in from the southwest; it came this way, and came back here; people saw the Halifax coming, they didn't see any fire at all, it was quite alright. And it was shot at by these batteries, and it went back and crashed. And I think this is something new, it hasn't been brought out.

"And here is a hill, and you can find parts from the plane all over this area. So it must have come that way. But looking at the trees here, there is a forest here, and here is a moor. I looked at the trees and it seems that the plane came in the air and straight down.

"The only thing I can think of is the fuel tanks blew up, for this is an area that couldn't be reached by any gun batteries."

Appendix II
The Impossible Mission?

A View Of The April Raids - 50 Years On
(i) A Pilot's Viewpoint

On September 1st 1991, Bernhard Bergersen, who during 1942 had kept a secret watch on the *Tirpitz*, took off from Jons Lake, near Trondheim, on a unique flight in his light float-plane. He and his son set out to re-create the flight that the last Halifax, 'S-Sugar', had made over Norway on the night of 27th April. They followed the flight plan as recorded in the debriefing that S-Sugar's pilot and navigator, Don MacIntyre and Ian Hewitt, gave on their return to England in June 1942. Bernhard explains the conclusions which, as the first pilot to fly that exact route for nearly 50 years, he has now reached:

"After my flight on September 1st 1991, following the exact route which the Halifax 'S-Sugar' followed from entering the Snillfjord after having crossed the Norwegian coast, until it crashed on Lake Hoklingen after attacking the *Tirpitz*, I came to realize that this was a raid representing something very special. But it was only after having seen my own video film of my flight, that it dawned on me what had really happened, and why it went wrong.

"Let me first explain that Fættenfjord is a real death trap for a heavy bomber flying at 300 feet. On both sides and at the head of the fjord there are steep hills rising to between 2,000 and 4,000 feet. The river entrance to the valley itself is very narrow and twisted for the first 2 - 3 miles and cannot be flown, even by a small plane. The only way to get into the more open part of the Åsen valley therefore was close to the hillside on the left side, which meant planes flying at 300 feet had to pull up violently, turning to the left, and climbing to some 600 feet.

"In his de-briefing Pilot Officer MacIntyre stated that, after releasing his mines at 300 feet, he made a left turn and then climbed into the Åsen valley, exactly the way I have just described. Why did he do so? The answer is simple! He was well away to the starboard side of the *Tirpitz*, probably in the centre of the fjord, and consequently had to turn to the left and climb to get into the valley.

"The pilot had, in fact, no choice. Flying over the target at 300 feet was impossible, as he then would be too close to the hillside. He therefore did the only possible thing, to follow the only track which could save the plane and its crew, in other words in the centre of the fjord!

"There is another aspect to the question: the mines probably had to be released at 300 feet, not higher. If so, they would have disintegrated hitting the water or the ground (not in fact so, see below). But on the other hand, if flying at 600 feet - which was the logical height - this would have taken the planes right over the target - and further on straight into the valley, without climbing or turning. But this would probably have taken them right into an impenetrable barrage from the battleship itself. One should remember that the vessel was covered by smoke, in other words blind! The gunnery control was placed on a hilltop, giving the signal to fire when enemy planes approached the vessel. All her smaller guns then fired with fixed barrels into the air. Planes flying right over the ship then were bound to be hit.

"As the planes came up the centre of the fjord, the *Tirpitz* was, in fact, not shooting at them. So when 'S-Sugar' was hit in its starboard wing, this was most certainly from guns on the south side of the fjord, or perhaps on the hill tops. Without the smoke screen the *Tirpitz* could no doubt have put up a tremendous and accurate fire. The smoke saved the battleship, but also many of the bomber crews, strangely enough also because they were flying too low.

In 1961 Bernhard visited Germany and while there he hired a light aircraft and flew over the Mohne and Eder dams made famous by the 'Dam Buster' raids mounted by 617 Squadron. He circled the dams for a while, considering the famous attack that had taken place there in 1943. Bernhard is well placed, then, to consider the *Tirpitz* attacks of 1942 in the light of this later operation:

"Apart from the attack on the Mohne/Eder dams I cannot remember any other RAF heavy bomber low-level attack during the war - the mine dropping operations against German canals and coastal waters not taken into account. The Mohne/Eder attacks by 617 Squadron were of course daring, especially because of its spectacular low flying across Germany and back again. But the target was not so heavily defended, and the area not very hilly. Squadron Leader Guy Gibson was in fact circling the lake at low level for a considerable time, directing the attacking bombers.

"The *Tirpitz* attacks were pressed home against perhaps the most concentrated and heavily defended target during the whole war, through a blinding smoke screen and into a death trap with its steep hills on all three sides. To survive, the planes had to make a hair-raising pull-up, climbing out at tree-top level with the wingtips dangerously close to the hillside. The attack on the Mohne/Eder dams went down in history because it was successful - the squadron even being given a name: 'The Dam Busters'. The *Tirpitz* raids were total failures - and are therefore forgotten. But if the *Tirpitz* had been hit - and even only slightly damaged - then this attack, in my opinion - would have gone down in history as perhaps even more daring and audacious than the Mohne/Eder attack. Having followed in the path of these brave men, my feeling therefore is one of admiration - beyond any description and words!"

After landing on Lake Hoklingen after his historic re-creation of 'S-Sugar"s flight, Bernhard and his son took off to return to Trondheim. They flew back down the Åsen valley and decided to land on Fætten Fjord to rest for a while, not far from the mooring place of the *Tirpitz*. And it was there that Bernhard considered what must have happened at that spot, nearly fifty years before. Bernhard's thoughts on that Autumn morning were recorded at a reunion at the Royal Air Force Museum, Hendon, in 1991:

"We were there on the seats of the light float-plane, just looking, and it was a beautiful morning, the sunshine, everything was quiet, everything just wonderful, and my thoughts went further, and suddenly I could hear the Merlins, you know, the Halifax coming screaming up the fjord, pulling up, standing on its tail to get over the hill and then everything was quiet. Then, we were sitting there, and suddenly two or three seagulls came, you know, screaming and splashing down, just near the plane. And so I switched on the intercom, and said to my son, 'What do you make of it, what do you think?'. I think he had exactly the same thoughts as I had, because he said, after a while, 'Well, Dad, it was madness, sheer madness.' And I think that was the word for it.

"By then we had drifted nearly up to the moorings, so we had to get away. I contacted Trondheim Control, we took off and flew back to Jons Lake.

"But I have something more to say. Every year since the war, in early May, early spring in Norway, I go to the British War Cemetery in Trondheim at Stavne, and I walk around on my own, you know, saluting every one of those boys lying there. Some of them I know; I know their story; I talk to them, really, and now I know the story of those people, those young lads who were involved in the *Tirpitz* attacks. I want you to join me in a minute's silence, honouring those who gave their lives, for me to take with me back to Trondheim. And I'll go to the Cemetery next week, talk to the boys, and tell them they're not forgotten."

(ii) An Analysis

So, what happened in Fætten Fjord at the end of April 1942 and why were the attacks so unsuccessful?

The whole purpose of the raids was to deliver the specially modified mines close up to the *Tirpitz*. As the briefing notes say:

"One mine directly under the stern will damage propellers and rudders, thus making it necessary to tow the battleship back to a major naval depot for repairs - a battleship in tow would be a set-up for our air and naval forces. 25% of the mines down close to the ship between it and the shore would sink it."

To give the mine-carrying aircraft a chance of releasing these mines with the necessary accuracy they were to attack from a very low level. To help prevent the defences hindering this low-level attack, the mine-carrying aircraft were to be preceded by a force of bombers whose purpose was to disable these defences by bombing the ship and the shore batteries.

This first force of bombers, consisting of Halifaxes and Lancasters, was to drop 4,000 lb H.C. (blast) bombs and 500 lb and 250 lb general purpose bombs from a height of 6,000 feet, firstly on the target and then on the anti-aircraft gun emplacements that surrounded the fjord. They were then to make way for the force of mine-carrying Halifaxes to carry out their bombing runs, by ceasing their attack five minutes before this second force was due over the target. It was stressed at the operation briefing that strict adherence to timing was essential; aircraft of the first wave were not to drop their bombs after a specific time, to ensure that they would not bomb their colleagues flying below them.

The sequence of the attack by the low-flying mine-carrying Halifaxes of 10 and 35 Squadrons was to be as follows:

From Salt Island they would fly for about twenty seconds up Fætten Fjord at over 200 mph (the Briefing Notes suggest 210 mph) hugging the sides of the rising ground to port and flying at 150 feet above the water (note: the altitude planned for the March raid had been 300 feet above water level). Three or four hundred yards short of the target they would each release their four mines at intervals of one hundred feet. They would immediately pull up and climb directly over the battleship, to reach a height of 600 feet in time to avoid the high ground that blocked the exit from the end of the fjord. To clear the ground that continued to rise (although less sharply) from the steep sides of the fjord, they would then make a steady 180 degree turn to port and fly on to re-trace the outward route and so home to the North of Scotland.

The reasons that this plan did not, and could not, work are as follows:

The aircraft were unable to fly close enough to the cliffs on the western side of Fætten Fjord to keep in line with the stern of the battleship. Therefore they could not release their mines to sink close enough to the target, for the mines had to be released in a trajectory that would take them directly into the water next to the hull of the vessel. Although mines released from aircraft flying above 600 feet could be dropped in the correct trajectory, the additional height reduced their accuracy.

The climb out of the steep-sided fjord to reach 600 feet in a few hundred yards was extremely dangerous in a 22 ton bomber, particularly if it was still carrying up to one and-a-half tons of mines if some or all of these had hung up, or not been released, over the target. The natural inclination was for the pilots to run up the fjord at a greater altitude in order to avoid the cliff at the far end.

The presence of a very effective smoke-screen surprised some crews and all the crews found that their bombing-run was severely hampered by it.

So what seems to have happened is this:

Most of the bomb-aimers found themselves releasing their mines blind as they approached a target that lay hidden somewhere beneath a dense pall of smoke that filled almost the entire valley to a height of several hundred feet. On the first night none of the crews from either 10 or 35 Squadrons reported seeing the target at all. Only four crews of 10 Squadron reported seeing it on the second night. However, some of the airmen who were shot down remember catching glimpses of the *Tirpitz* masts and upper superstructure through the eddying smoke and indeed the *Tirpitz* crew themselves realised that their ship had not always been totally invisisible during the attacks. In general then, many of the aircraft had to rely on a bomb-run timed from the last identifiable landmark: Salt Island.

The only aircrew to report that they were able to release their mines on a visual sighting were aboard four Halifaxes from 10

Squadron on the second night. From these aircraft one mine was seen to burst beneath the stern of the ship, two undershot, one burst very near the ship and two struck the bank, while a third aircrew claimed that, 'The mines were seen to fall between the battleship and the edge of the fjord, and two columns of water shot up.' This crew, incidentally, had released its mines from 600 feet, the lowest 'safe' height. The crew in the fourth aircraft reported seeing nothing of the results of their attack.

None of the aircraft that flew between the planned height of 150 feet and 600 feet could have flown over the *Tirpitz*, for had they done so they would have hit the hillside that sheltered the battleship. So instead they were forced to fly more or less up the centre of the fjord, passing by her starboard side. There are a number of reports in the *Tirpitz* log of aircraft passing to starboard, while a smaller number are reported as passing overhead at an unspecified height.

Although the 35 Squadron Operations Record Book does not give the height at which any of their aircraft attacked, the heights at which all the aircraft from 10 Squadron attacked was recorded. Thus the following summary can be given:

Only five aircraft of 10 Squadron attacked from below 600 feet (the lowest being the remarkably brave crew of Flight Sergeant Rochford, who ran up the fjord and attacked at 250 feet on the first night, and 200 feet on the second). The remainder released their mines from between 600 and 1,500 feet, the average being 750 feet. The only record of a 35 Squadron aircraft's height of attack is that of W1048 'S-Sugar'. Pilot Officer MacIntyre stated in his debriefing that he had attacked at 300 feet at 260 mph., so it may be presumed that some others from 35 Squadron did likewise.

Those that attacked from above 600 feet were high enough not to be troubled by the cliff at the end of the fjord. They were able to turn to port and climb out of the target area with some confidence. Those that attacked from a lower altitude were still able, as it turned out, to pull up in time and to make the necessary steep climbing turn to port in order to leave the valley, but only because they must have flown down the centre of the fjord.

Many of the aircraft were hit by *Flak* as they flew into the attack and a total of seven were shot down during the two nights. S-Sugar's pilot recorded that his aircraft was hit in the starboard wing 'a fraction of a second' after she had released her mines, almost certainly by a land-based gun on the south-eastern side of Fætten Fjord. Despite a burning starboard wing, she managed to climb over the cliff at the end of the fjord, turning to port as she did so (further proof that she was not in fact flying over the battleship). Unable to gain much more height, certainly not above 1,000 feet, she struggled along the Åsen valley that continues the line of the fjord into the surrounding hills and, within a few minutes, crash-landed on Lake Hoklingen.

A number of the crews recall that the ferocity of the defences in Fætten Fjord was greater than that of any other target they attacked throughout the remainder of the war. Indeed, at least one crew was prevented by the intensity of the barrage from flying their aircraft into the fjord at all. Many crews reported 'intense and accurate *Flak* from both sides of the fjord', but none mentioned any firing from the *Tirpitz* herself. The *Tirpitz* fired approximately 2,200 rounds of ammunition during the entire two nights of attacks. The reason for this remarkably low number of rounds is explained in the *Tirpitz* log; the battleship's gunners were unable to fire because the smoke screen was so effective. And so it was the shore-based batteries that kept up an almost continuous bombardment against the incoming aircraft. They shot down most, if not all, of the aircraft that failed to return and damaged many of those that did manage to limp home.

Several 'gunnery control' or 'aircraft warning' posts were set up on the nearby hills overlooking the fjord. From here, during the attacks, German observers telephoned details of the speed, height and direction of the approaching bombers to the ship- and shore-based gunners. The ship's gunners would have had their weapons trained vertically upwards and at a signal would have stood on the firing pedal, launching an impenetrable barrage of explosives into the air over the ship. Any aircraft passing directly over the vessel would have been hit. But few aircraft did pass over the ship and, of those that did, their mines failed to do any damage. Most of their mines landed in the water, while some landed harmlessly on the wooded slopes above the target, giving rise to the presumption that these mines were intended to roll down the side of the hills and land alongside the ship. Given the nature of the terrain - rough, rocky and tree-covered - it is most unlikely that crews were given orders to drop their mines onto the cliff-face with the intention of them rolling down onto the battleship. There is no mention of this tactic in the briefing orders given to the crews before take-off.

And so, not only did the smokescreen save the *Tirpitz* but, by effectively reducing the number of anti-aircraft guns in action, it also saved the lives of many airmen too.

So, it seems clear that the plan of attack was fatally flawed. Despite the detailed maps and aerial photographs that were available to the planners, the fact that there was insufficient air-space for an aircraft to approach the *Tirpitz* directly from astern, so as to accurately aim its pay-load, seems to have been ignored. The aircraft were expected to follow a precise flight path during their bomb run, at a very low altitude, despite the fact that the hostile terrain, the likelihood of a smoke screen and the inevitability of a spirited defence, indicated that they would not be able to manage it.

Had the bomb-aimers been able to deliver their mines (from whatever height they managed to release them) right up close to the hull of their target, how effective would that have been? The size of weapon to be used in the attacks was limited by the capacity of a Halifax bomb-bay. Consequently the Mark XIX mine was chosen because it could be modified to fit into this space. The eight mines recovered after the attacks by the Germans in the Fjord were dated between 13th and 16th March 1942. The original mines had therefore been modified in only six weeks. This modification more than doubled their original explosive potential, as Wing Commander J. A. MacBean, an authority on British air-dropped weapons and the co-author of *Bombs Gone*,[57.] explains:

"The original mine, weighing 290 lbs., contained about 100 lbs of amatol (or TNT). When the guts were removed for air use it was filled with 770 lb of minol (amatol plus aluminium powder to increase blast). The conversion was set to go off at a depth of 14 feet when a hydrostatic pistol operated under water pressure. The general feeling was that this was not deep enough to get at the vulnerable hull, and in any case to get the desired effect the mine would have to be much more powerful to achieve any significant damage." 58.

A comparison of the destructive power of these modified mines with that of the sea-mines that were struck by the *Scharnhorst* and the *Gneisenau* during *Operation Cerberus*, their celebrated break-out from Brest in February 1942, is most revealing. The sea-mines contained 1,500 lbs of high explosives, causing both vessels that struck them to be holed, the engines being damaged in both of them and navigational equipment in one of them.

The *Tirpitz* herself was damaged by an underwater device that was deposited beneath her hull by one of the *X-craft* (midget submarines) that carried out an attack on her when she lay in Kaa Fjord in 1943. The explosive 'side cargo' caused considerable damage, containing, as it did, 2,000 lb of Amatex.

The crew aboard the *Tirpitz* reported that no damage or casualties resulted from enemy action. The near misses recorded by the crews of several aircraft must therefore have either failed to explode, or have simply done no damage.

So, the mines dropped in Fætten Fjord had insufficient explosive power to damage the vessel significantly, even if detonated beneath the water, next to her hull. They could not have been any more powerful because they could not have been constructed any larger for, as it was, the Halifax bomb-bay doors could not close over them. The mines needed to have at least twice the explosive power they actually had. They also needed to be detonated alongside the vessel deeper than the fourteen feet at which they were set to explode, for them to achieve useful damage. This fact was put to use later in the war when 600 lbs of the more powerful explosive Torpex was used in the design of *Highball*, intended for attacking ships from low level. 59.

There is, therefore, a feeling of desperation, an implication of haste, about the whole four-month affair. A need for something to be done about this menacing vessel. Within days of first sighting the *Tirpitz* an attack was planned and carried out (albeit abortively) and, within six weeks, a weapon had been specially modified, tested and used on a second (largely abortive) operation. Four weeks later two concentrated attacks were carried out with great bravery using the same weapon, and then the attempts to sink her by air attack were abandoned for many months, after which bombs, not mines, were used.

There was, perhaps, a belief that if enough aircraft dropped enough mines over the target area, then one, just one of them, might be lucky enough to do the trick. And on this fervent hope RAF aircrews were despatched on an operation whose planning was fatally flawed, with a weapon that, although it was the best weapon available, was in fact inadequate for the purpose.

The *Tirpitz* was to prove indeed a very hard nut to crack. It was to take two more years before the ship was sunk - and then it was by much more powerful bombs than the mines that were used in Fætten Fjord in 1942 and dropped from a high altitude with the aid of a more sophisticated bomb-sight.

The terrain of Fætten Fjord, the defences and the smoke-screen, ranged against small forces of heavy bombers carrying out a flawed plan with an inadequate weapon gave little chance of success for the RAF. However, the experience gained from these, the first attempts to sink Germany's largest battleship, was no doubt a contributory factor in the planning and execution of the attack that successfully destroyed her in 1944.

NOTES

57. Bombs Gone, by Wing Commander J.A. MacBean and Major A.S. Hogben (Patrick Stephen Ltd)
58. In a letter from J. A. MacBean to the author.
59. *Highball* was an airborne mine developed from Dr. Barnes Wallis's 'bouncing bombs' used by 617 Squadron in the celebrated Dams attack. During tests against obsolete cruisers, it passed straight through the armoured target without exploding!

Appendix III
Photographic Reconnaissance

Richard Cussons added the following details to his recollections of flying operations in a PRU Spitfire over the *Tirpitz*:

> "The early versions of Spitfires adapted for reconnaissance work had only a short range and only 8" focal length cameras in the wings, but gradually the P.R. Mk IV was evolved and this was the Mark which we used in 1942. We had an extra 65 gallons of fuel in each wing leading edge in place of guns (these were known as 'D' type wings) and two vertical cameras of 14-inch, 20-inch or, later, 36-inch focal length mounted behind the pilot's seat. The camera compartment was heated by warm air ducted from the engine as otherwise they froze so that the shutter and wind-on mechanism wouldn't

PRU Spitfires. A Mark IV with a Mark XIX behind it, probably over Oxfordshire.
(R. Cussons)

work. These cameras were operated by a control box mounted in front of the pilot (in lieu of a gun-sight); this box had one dial to control the interval between exposures which was set, by the pilot, according to the speed and height of the aircraft so that a 'strip' of photos could be taken by each camera which overlapped by 55-60%, thus giving a 'stereo-pair' of every point on the ground. The two cameras were slightly tilted relative to each other so that they took two parallel strips overlapping by about 10% at 30,000 ft. When the pilot switched on, the cameras automatically tripped the focal plane shutter and wound on the film at whatever intervals the pilot had set, until he switched off again.

"In the case of the 36-inch cameras, the film magazine held enough film for 500 photos, each about 9" x 9", so one sortie could bring back 1,000 pictures; from 30,000 feet one photo covered about 1 square mile and on a clear day one would be able to see people walking in the street. It is worth noting that this type of camera was a British development, using Ross lenses (not Zeiss!).

"Aiming was a bit tricky and required a lot of practice; when the target was located, the aircraft had to be banked very steeply (about 85 deg.) towards the target and when it was just about to disappear under the nose, straighten out and turn on the cameras until one judged it had passed under the tail when one switched off again. It sounds a bit hit-or-miss but after practice it was surprising how accurate one could get.

"Low oblique shots were taken with a separate camera looking through the side and controlled by a button on the throttle lever. There was a separate sighting mark on the side of the cockpit hood and another on the wing trailing edge; the aircraft was flown low beside the target and when it appeared behind the wing one pressed the button. The whole technique of low obliques was quite different from the normal P.R. high altitude verticals, and I personally only did one such sortie."

Appendix IV
The Raising of Halifax
W1048 'S-Sugar'

In 1971 Peter Cornish, an experienced amateur diver, recovered the remains of a World War II Beaufighter from the sea off Mousehole in Cornwall. In carrying out this recovery he came to know the Keeper of Exhibits at the RAF Museum at Hendon and one day he received a telephone call from him, telling him that he had just heard of a very interesting 'find'. Peter Cornish:

"The story had come out of Norway [60.] through to the British Embassy, then hence to the RAF Museum, that a 'three-engined British bomber' had been located in a fresh-water lake called Lake Hoklingen, about 25 miles north of Trondheim, and it was being pillaged by the local divers, and were they (the Museum) interested? Well of course the answer to that was they were tremendously interested. Now, I was the only person he knew who had any experience of recovering sunken aircraft, and so he asked me whether or not I would be interested in going to have a look at it. Having said that, of course he had already alerted the Royal Air Force Sub-Aqua Association whose members are amateur divers within the Royal Air Force, and part of the British Sub-Aqua Club.

"And in early October 1972 a mini-bus left RAF Wyton with six men on board, five RAF personnel and me, and we drove to Newcastle, went across on the ferry to Stavanger, Bergen, then overland, which was a long journey - 24 hours solid driving - to end up in Trondheim where we met the local Norwegian divers who were responsible, largely, for finding the sunken aircraft."

The team discovered that a young Norwegian lad, living with his parents in their home right on the shores of Lake Hoklingen, had decided to take up diving as a sport. He had joined Draugen Froskemannsklub, the local diving club in Trondheim ('Draugen' being Norwegian for the 'Old Man of the Sea').

"His father always said to him 'In that lake out there is an aeroplane, 'cos I remember seeing it coming down in the war, and it lay on the ice and then fell through.'

"He and a couple of other fellows, over a period of about 18 months, apparently, using a rowing-boat dropped a grapnel down, hooked it into anything, and anything it hooked into they'd go down with very rudimentary simple diving torches to find out what was down there. And they found tree-trunks and God-knows-what, I hate to think what they found!

"It took them about a year to fifteen months I think before they actually found this aircraft. And they hooked into the aircraft and pulled it up tight and put a buoy on it and sent a man down with diving equipment and of course he landed on an aeroplane. And it was what they called a 'twinned-tailed three-engined British bomber' because it had a great roundel on.

"Now there's no such thing of course as a 'three-engined bomber'. It had to be a four-engined, having lost one, and it could therefore only effectively be a Lancaster, a Halifax or a Stirling, of which all overflew Norway sometime during the war."

Much as they would have liked to, the Norwegians felt unable to carry out the recovery, as Bjørn Olsen, who at the time was a member of the board of the Norwegian Aviation Historical Society, explains:

"The existence of the Halifax was first brought to our notice in 1968, when the aircraft was found by a local diving club. We did, at the time, want to recover the bomber ourselves and restore it for display here in Norway. However, it soon became clear that to do such a job would be impossible for us, both technically, financially and in question of manpower. The N.A.H.S. is a small body, dedicated to the collection and recording of Norwegian aviation history, and, even if we have later restored two aircraft, one of them a Norwegian pre-WWII built Tiger Moth, it would have been far beyond our capabilities to recover and restore a four-engined bomber which had been on the bottom of a lake since 1942."

Before leaving England Peter Cornish had carried out some research. He discovered that a number of raids had taken place during the war against the German battleship *Tirpitz* when she lay in Trondheim Fjord and some aircraft failed to return. The plan he and Mick Glover of the RAF Sub-Aqua Association came up with was to inspect the wreck that had been discovered to see what it was and if it was worth recovering.

Each member of the team could only dive once a day for twenty minutes, so cold was the water in which the aircraft lay at a depth of 90 feet. It took them two or three days to establish

Peter Cornish in consultation with other divers during the recovery.
(S. Usher)

that this was indeed a Halifax bomber, with the number W1048 rather badly painted onto the side of its fuselage.

"There was a lot of damage to the starboard wing. We actually took a piece of rope and measured the distance from the end of the port wing-tip to the end of the tailplane, and we did the selfsame thing over on the starboard wing. That confused us because they weren't the same length! But when you swam along the wings they looked perfect. We knew that the starboard wing had suffered a lot of damage, and in reality what of course had happened is that the wing-tip outboard of the starboard outer engine had actually moved forward a bit, like a broken bird's wing. So the wing-tip was a slightly different length from the tail-plane.

"We knew that the wings were roughly about the same length, three engines, starboard outer gone, nose, tailplane, bomb-doors open and nothing in them, so the bomb-bay was empty and open, no tail-wheel, the tail-wheel was missing; I could stand in about six inches of soft mud and the tail-wheel position would have been about a foot above my head. It was stuck in like a dart with the wing-tips level with the top of the mud, its nose buried. You could lay in front of the front turret gun on the mud, thick cloggy mud, and you could stick your hand down and touch the point about two foot six down inside the mud where the barrels of the two .303 Brownings went up into the turret, into the mounting, 'cos they were pointing down, but you could actually reach the point where they just went through that perspex screen - the front turret - which was well-buried.

307

"She was W1048, code letters TL-S, 'S for Sugar', an early Merlin-engined Mark II Series 1 Halifax. We had brought enough evidence to pinpoint not only which aircraft it was, which was a 35 Squadron aircraft, but also what her crew was.

"We did an analysis while we were there of putting forward the proposition of recovery, 'cos that was what was in everybody's mind."

By the end of the year plans had been put forward to Strike Command for the recovery of the aircraft. A team of sixteen RAF personnel, ostensibly taking part in 'expedition training', set off for Norway from RAF West Drayton, with Peter Cornish (the only civilian), in a C-130 transport aircraft from RAF Brize Norton. The expedition, led by Sergeant Dave Walker, was severely constrained by the RAF's limit of 28 days of expedition leave and Peter's need to return to his job within 21 days. The plan, thought through and worked out with great attention to detail, was a simple one, based on the use of 40-gallon oil drums made freely available by Norske Shell. Teams of divers would fill empty oil drums with water, sink them down to the wreck where they would secure them to strong-points on the aircraft's structure. They would then blow out the water from the drums with compressed air and, when a sufficient number of buoyant drums were attached, the aircraft would rise from the bottom of the lake.

"We planned to lift the aircraft within about Days 14, 15, 16, 17, and then get it out. After Day 7 or 8 we'd rigged up all the heavy lifting-points, put lots of drums on, and the aircraft was actually changing attitude; the aircraft was stuck in tail up, so we knew the thing was moving."

Although working in 90 feet of pitch black water was difficult and dangerous, gradually drum after drum was attached in the necessary sequence:

"Slowly these drum structures all built up and we knew the aircraft was moving. Still no one had got into the cockpit; it had been penetrated inside by going through the door in the bottom of the fuselage but a lot of the fixatives had fallen away and they were all hanging down like a derelict house, and it was very dangerous. You know, the idea of getting inside there and getting hooked up and never being able to get out again was not conducive to going too far in."

The operation went ahead so fast and so successfully that by Day 11, with 47 drums attached, the aircraft began to relinquish its grip on its resting place. The diving crew were instructed that, if they happened to be on the aircraft when it

Top: The blunt prow of the Halifax breaks the tranquil surface of Lake Hoklingen. (via Author)
Lower: Delicately, 'S-Sugar' is towed ashore, having already lost part of her starboard wing. (via Author)

started to come free from the suction of the mud on the bottom of the lake, they were to hang on. And that is precisely what happened to one diver who had the ride of his life as this great wreck surged upwards and broke the surface of the waters of Lake Hoklingen on 30th June 1973.

She was gradually towed towards the shore, where a cradle made by local carpenters from trees cut down from the neighbouring woods, was placed within the bomb-bay. A local tractor-driver brought along his tractor and, with the help of steel tracking laid on the bank, Halifax W1048 was dragged inch by inch from the watery tomb which had embalmed her for 31 years.

Bjørn Olsen, who spent as much time as he could at Lake Hoklingen during the recovery operation, commented in a letter to Vic Stevens:

> "I need hardly tell you that it was the moment of my life when I saw the old Halifax safe and sure on the beach. It meant, for me, the end of several years of work with the project."

She was in remarkably good condition, more or less complete apart from the missing outer starboard engine and the lack of some of her guns. Although the perspex windows in the gun turrets and the fuselage were opaque with age, the single layer of camouflage paint still adhered to most of the surfaces. Amazingly, when a battery was attached to the electrical circuits some of the light-bulbs actually glowed! She was dismantled without undue difficulty into the main components from which she had been assembled, then lifted onto a low-loader. When it was found that the load was too high to pass under a railway bridge that crosses the small road to the nearby port of Levanger, local goodwill came to the rescue. The trains were stopped, overhead lines were cut, and a crane hoisted the load over the bridge, then back onto the low-loader waiting on the other side. From Levanger she was ferried by a tank landing craft to Ipswich Docks in England and thence to RAF Henlow for stabilising and refurbishment.

The decision to return her fabric to its original appearance was only reversed after her front turret had been refurbished, by which time it had become apparent that so much of her was in a fragile condition that a full refurbishment would leave little

Top: *The fresh water lake allowed the bomber to be recovered in a quite remarkably well preserved condition. (via Author)*
Lower: *'S-Sugar' today, displayed in the Bomber Command Hall at the RAF Museum, Hendon. (Author)*

Halifax W1048 'S-Sugar at RAF Henlow shortly after her arrival from Norway in July 1973. Note the front turret still in its original state, the perspex still in place, and the remains of her paintwork. Her flight engineer Vic Stevens stands in front with his wife Gwen. (via Author)

of her original metal in place. It was decided to leave her in the condition in which she had been found, retaining in her appearance the evidence of an aircraft that had been to war and had suffered as a consequence. Eleven years later she was finally placed on permanent display in the new Bomber Command wing at the RAF Museum at Hendon.

The only other sizeable aircraft remains from the raids is part of the cockpit section of Halifax R9371. This 10 Squadron aircraft was part of the force that flew to Lossiemouth in the second week of March 1942, to take part in the raid that was aborted, the aircraft returning to base within four days. She skidded on landing, tore off her undercarriage in a drainage ditch, and never flew again. The remains of her cockpit section is to be refurbished and used as part of the Yorkshire Air Museum's rebuild of a Halifax bomber.

NOTES

60. Via Bjørn Olsen of the Norwegian Aviation Historical Society, whose article *Norwegian Finds* was published by Neville Franklin in his magazine *Control Column* in August 1969. The British Embassy only became involved when permission to survey W1048:S was being sought. (Information from Bjørn Olsen in 1993).

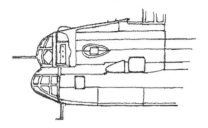

Appendix V

The Manufacture of Halifax W1048 'S-Sugar'

Halifax W1048 TL-S is the only surviving virtually complete example of a Handley Page Halifax B Mk II Series 1 four-engined heavy bomber. She was built by the English Electric Company at their works at Preston in March 1942, one of a batch of 181 Halifax Mark II bombers (at a time when they were producing about 36 aircraft a month) and she flew her only operational flight in April 1942 with No 35 Squadron, as described in the pages of this book.

Halifaxes were very strongly built and, as is attested by many of the men who flew in them, they were able to withstand a considerable battering on operations. They were built to a high standard by men and women who now look back with pride on this period in their lives. It was a desperate time of dedication to work, and the exhaustion of long shifts, as Charles Pallett, who worked at the Preston factory, recalls:

> "It was nothing to work 36 hours at a 'stretch' - through the day shift, the night shift, another day shift - go home exhausted and back in for the day shift. ... 40 hour week? I, like others, was lucky if I could keep it down to 100! My favourite story: a little boy had been prepared for bed and looked again at the photograph on the mantlepiece - 'Mummy, who's that man with you?' Reply - 'Sonny, that's your daddy, and one day when he can get away from work you'll be able to meet him!'"

Harry Jacques, who built Halifaxes at Preston from the very beginning - from the time the Hampden bomber was phased out - points out that the workers, in addition to their long shifts,

AIRCRAFT

A.M. Form 78.

Air Ministry Form 78 records the movements of Halifax W1048 to 102 Squadron, then to 35 Squadron and, finally, her failure to return from her first operation. (via author)

carried out other duties of great importance to the life of the community, as Special Policemen, Firemen, Air Raid Wardens, etc. Many of the women who worked there (about one third of the work force in 1942) had families and homes to care for as well.

The English Electric Company was originally engaged in producing locomotives, buses, tram cars, etc., before a small team was temporarily transferred to the Handley Page works at Cricklewood in North London, 'to learn and bring back to Preston the knowledge of aircraft assembly ...', as Harry Jacques, who was a member of this team, recalls. One of his fellow team members, David Milne, remarks that 'little did we think that we would eventually establish the English Electric as a world leader in the design and construction of military aircraft'. Harry Jacques goes on to make the following comments:

"During the early stages we had relatively little difficulty in obtaining skilled operators, be it without any previous knowledge or aircraft assembly experience. Finally, we had to [train] ... people from all walks of life: cotton operators, other trades than engineering, shop-keepers, housewives, etc.

"Full credit must be given to the Designers for an aircraft not only functionally good, but also straight-forward to work on from a product point of view. In relation to numbers of aircraft and quality produced at Preston, the numbers, when related to operators and space occupied, more than compared favourably to any other company. That, also considering we had only as a basic background a Heavy Engineering Company and work force completely strange to aircraft assembly."

It is a great credit to the energy and effort of the skilled and unskilled workforce at Preston that they were able to produce so many excellent aircraft. In such an environment, and under such circumstances, Halifax W1048 was built and assembled in March 1942 - that she survives to this day is no small reflection on the quality of the work of her builders.

The Halifax B Mk II Series I bomber was 69' 9" in length, with a wingspan of 98' 8". It could fly at a maximum of 261 mph and, with a full load on board, could reach 22,000 feet. It had a range of about 1,860 miles carrying a bomb load of 5,800 lb, although on shorter flights it could carry a bomb load of up to 13,000 lb.

The fixed armament consisted of two .303 Browning machine guns mounted in Boulton Paul C Mk II turrets in the nose and on the mid-upper fuselage, and four .303 Browning machine guns mounted in a Boulton Paul E Mk I turret in the tail. The fuselage was constructed of light alloy.

There were four Rolls Royce Merlin XX engines, each one powering a Rotol compressed-wood three-bladed propellor with a turning diameter of thirteen feet.

An interesting feature of the Halifax was its system of split assembly, a system developed by Handley Page, by which the aircraft was divided into convenient pieces for transport and repair, and to enable more people to work on each stage, thus increasing the speed of production output.

Altogether, nine different marks were designed and produced (Mk X never left the designing board), from October 1940 to November 1946, by which time a total of 6,176 had been built.

Opposite page: Brand-new Halifax Mark IIs at Warton Aerodrome, Preston, awaiting delivery to squadrons. In the upper photograph the engines of one aircraft are being run up. (British Aerospace)

The last time a Halifax flew was in March 1952, but a small, final postcript must be added. H.E.('Batch') Batchelder, the pilot who ferried W1048 'S-Sugar' to Linton-on-Ouse on 9th April 1942, recalls being told in 1987 that:

"... some of her engines had been cannibalised for spares for the Merlins used by aircraft of the Battle of Britain Memorial Flight. Two camshafts were removed, one of which was in a state where it could be used immediately after cleaning, the other had to be treated but is now in use.[61]

And so, although no airworthy Halifax exists, parts of 'The Last Halifax' have been pressed into service to help keep one of the last Lancasters in the air. Poetic justice indeed for the many admirers of the Halifax!

NOTES

61. In a letter from H E Batchelder to the author.

Appendix VI
Failed to Return

**The fate of the aircrew from the 18 aircraft that
failed to return from operations against the *Tirpitz*
January - April 1942**

10 Squadron

Halifax W1043:F 30/31 March	Sgt Hague	Died
	Sgt Hall	Died
	Sgt Hall	Died
	P/O Leney	Died
	F/L Stevens-Fox	Died
	S/Ldr Webster	Died
	F/Sgt Wheatley	Died
Halifax W1044:D 30/31 March		
	P/O Blunden	Died
	P/O Day	Died
	Sgt Eastwood	Died
	F/Sgt Franklyn	Died
	Sgt May	Died
	Sgt Henman	Died
	Sgt Richards	Died

Halifax W1037:U 27/28 April	Sgt Annable	Died
	Sgt Curran	PoW
	Sgt Gregory	PoW
	F/L Miller	PoW
	Sgt Roberts	PoW
	Sgt Ryder	PoW
	Sgt Stott	Died
Halifax W1041:B 27/28 April	W/C Bennett	Evaded
	F/Sgt Colgan	Evaded
	Sgt Eyles	PoW
	Sgt Forbes	Evaded
	F/L How	PoW
	Sgt Murray	PoW
	Sgt Walmsley	Evaded

Total Died: 16

35 Squadron

Halifax R9438:H 30/31 March	F/Sgt Buckley	Died
	F/Sgt Bushby	Died
	Sgt Meredith	Died
	Sgt Peach	Died
	Sgt Powell	Died
	Sgt Usher	Died
	Sgt Wood	Died
Halifax R9496:L 30/31 March	F/Sgt Archibald	Died
	Sgt Francis	Died
	Sgt McLaren	Died
	Sgt Murray	Died
	Sgt Nelmes	Died
	Sgt Palmer	Died
	Sgt Staff	Died

Halifax W1015:P 30/31 March	P/O Brown	Died
	Sgt Campbell	Died
	Sgt Cowan	Died
	Sgt Dunlop	Died
	F/Sgt Goodrum	Died
	Sgt Meade	Died
	F/Sgt Steinhauer	Died
Halifax W1020:K 27/28 April	Sgt Booth	Died
	P/O Henry	Died
	F/Sgt Hill	Died
	F/L Pooles	Died
	Sgt Rarity	Died
	Sgt Wilstrop	Died
Halifax W1048:S 27/28 April	Sgt Blanchet	Evaded
	P/O Hewitt	Evaded
	P/O MacIntyre	Evaded
	Sgt Perry	Evaded
	Sgt Stevens	PoW
	Sgt Wilson	Evaded
Halifax W1053: 28/29 April	Sgt Butchart	PoW
	Sgt Morrison	PoW
	F/Sgt Parr	PoW
	F/Sgt Roe	PoW
	Sgt Russell	Died
	Sgt Williams	PoW
Halifax W7656: 28/29 April	Sgt Columbine	Died
	Sgt Cranstone	PoW
	Sgt Evans	Died
	F/L Petley	PoW
	Sgt Pomroy	PoW
	Sgt Price	PoW

Total Died: 30

76 Squadron

Halifax L9581: 30/31 January	Sgt Marwood	Rescued
	Sgt Patey	Rescued
	Sgt Petch	Rescued
	F/Sgt Roche	Rescued
	F/Sgt Scott	Rescued
	Sgt Smarden	Rescued
	Sgt Young	Rescued
Halifax R9453:K 30/31 March	P/O Bowsher	Died
	S/Ldr Burdett	Died
	Sgt Cadger	Died
	Sgt Davis	Died
	Sgt Fletcher	Died
	Sgt Hanson	Died
	Sgt Martin	Died

Total Died: 7

97 Squadron

Lancaster L7572:L 27/28 April	Sgt Bennett	Died
	Sgt Day	Died
	F/L Mackid	Died
	Sgt Marshall	Died
	Sgt McDermott	Died
	P/O Tree	Died
	P/O Underwood	Died

Total Died: 7

248 Squadron

Beaufighter X 27/28 April	W/C Hyde	Died
	F/Sgt Paget	Died

Total Died: 2

1 PRU

Spitfire AA810 5 March	P/O Gunn	PoW
Spitfire AA797 3 April	F/Sgt Jones	Died
Spitfire AB307 10 April	F/O Gimson	Died

Total Died: 2

---

534 airmen took part in the *Tirpitz* Raids

from January to April 1942

18 became Prisoners of War in Germany

9 evaded captivity by reaching Sweden

7 were rescued from the seas off Scotland

64 (12%) lost their lives

Index

People

RAF Personnel And/or British

Acott, F/L R. 1 PRU   94
Allen, P/O. 1 PRU   91, 153
Annable, Sgt E. 10 Sqn   158, 211
Archibald, F/S W. 35 Sqn   88
Balderson, W.   127
Baldwin, AVM J.   19
Basson, F/S 15 Sqn   48, 53
Batchelder, P/O H.
   102 Sqn   97, 318
Bell, P. 10 Sqn   76
Bennett, L. 236,   248, 286
Bennett, W/C D. 10 Sqn   106, 117, 118, 130, 160-2, 184, 204, 235-9, 242, 247, 249, 256-8, 260, 268, 270-3, 283, 286
Blanchet, Sgt P. 35 Sqn   99, 128, 220-2, 231-4, 256, 261, 273, 276
Boggis, S/L, P. 15 Sqn   41
Booth, Sgt, H. 35 Sqn   283
Brown, P/O, P. 35 Sqn   90
Buckley, F/S J. 35 Sqn   84
Burdett, S/L. 76 Sqn   87
Bushby, F/S J. 35 Sqn   83, 84
Butchart, Sgt D. 10 Sqn   226, 243, 261-2, 265
Carr, AVM C.R.
   AOC 4 Gp   109, 116, 117, 119, 120, 205
Cartridge, S/L. 248 Sqn   136-7
Charlton, F/S C. 10 Sqn   73, 74, 194
Churchill, Sir W, PM.   18, 20, 31, 33, 116, 119, 188
Clack, F/S K. 76 Sqn   145-7, 182-3
Clear, F/S. 10 Sqn   195
Colgan, Sgt J. 10 Sqn   162, 249, 251-6, 271-3
Collins, P/O T. 76 Sqn   200, 202
Columbine, Sgt A.
   35 Sqn   196, 264-5
Cantillion, P/O A. 1 PRU   94
Cook, S/L. 235 Sqn   134-5
Cornish, P.   305-308
Coton, F/L. 97 Sqn   76, 146
Craine, F/S. 76 Sqn   83

Cranstone, Sgt, G.
   35 Sqn   78, 103, 126, 196, 221, 263-5
Cribb, S/L P. 35 Sqn   129, 185-7, 193
Crow, P/O. 235 Sqn   135-6
Curran, Sgt. 10 Sqn   211
Cussons, F/O R. 1 PRU   22, 23, 24, 60, 91, 94, 303
Day, P/O G.C. 10 Sqn   90
Day, Sgt R. 97 Sqn   156, 157, 283-4, 286, 290
Day, A.   286, 290-1
De Puysselyr, P/O, J.
   1 PRU   121, 176
Dempsey, P/O, 10 Sqn   195
Dugdale, S/L. 97 Sqn   186, 190
Eadie, F/L 210 Sqn   124
Elizabeth,
   Queen-Mother   117, 276, 278
Ellison, F/S P. 10 Sqn   14, 71, 152-3
Eunson, J.   85, 86
Evans, Sgt A.   264-5
Eyles, Sgt P. 10 Sqn   161, 238, 240-1, 249
Fairley, P/O R. 210 Sqn   127
Falkoski, F/S.   149, 151
Fane, F/L P. 1 PRU   22, 23, 24, 25, 37, 79
Felkin, W/C S.   270
Fink, P/O D. 15 Sqn   40, 44
Finney, LAC.   86, 87
Forbes, Sgt 10 Sqn   256-7, 260, 268, 270, 272-3
Gardiner, F/Sgt G.
   35 Sqn   80, 83, 148, 180, 193, 200
Gibbons, Sgt B. 10 Sqn   118, 149, 151, 188, 200, 205
Gibson, G.P.   294
Gifford, Sgt 10 Sqn   195
Gimson, Jackie   286
Gimson, F/O P. 1 PRU   91, 92, 93, 94, 278, 281, 286
Glover, Sgt M.   306
Godfrey, P/O T. 10 Sqn   149, 151, 191, 205
Graham, G/C S.   77, 80, 106, 117, 119, 122, 199
Gregory, Sgt 10 Sqn   211
Gribben, Sgt M. 10 Sqn   153

Grierson-Jackson,
P/O W. 35 Sqn   84, 100, 104, 191, 193
Gunn, P/O   64-6
Hague, Sgt A. 10 Sqn   88, 90
Hallows, F/O B, 97 Sqn   76
Harris, AM A.T.
AOC-in-C BC   12, 33, 64, 199, 202, 204, 206
Harrison, Sgt Charles
10 Sqn   70, 71, 87, 90, 272
Harwood, Sgt 10 Sqn   47
Henry, P/O C. 35 Sqn   101, 283
Herbert, Sgt 35 Sqn   46
Hewitt, P/O I. 35 Sqn   99, 101, 110, 120, 128, 130, 132-3, 163-4, 166-8, 170-2, 174, 214-15, 219, 227-230, 270, 272, 293
Hill, F/S F. 35 Sqn   283
Hill, F/L A. PRU   22
Hogben, Maj A.   302
How, F/L M. 10 Sqn   160-2, 242, 245-9
Hutcheson, P/O 1 PRU   91
Hutton, W/C W.H.   127
Hyde, W/C E.L. 248 Sqn   136-7
Ismay, Maj-Gen H.   31
Iveson, F/L. 76 Sqn   36, 46, 82, 83, 145
Jacques, H.   314-5
Jeffs, W/O D. 15 Sqn   38, 40, 41, 45
Jones, F/O, 35 Sqn   195
Jones, F/S. 1 PRU   91, 131, 149
Kenwright, Roy PRU   60
King George V.   116, 117
King, P/O. 15 Sqn   44
Lamb, W/O, 44 Sqn   189
Lane, P/O R. 35 Sqn   80, 204
Lawes, Sgt W. 76 Sqn   146-7, 181
LLoyd, W/O 10 Sqn   195, 205
MacBean, J. W/C (Rtd)   70, 300, 302
Macdonald, W/C J.C.
15 Sqn   36, 38, 48, 49
MacIntyre, P/O D.
35 Sqn   98, 99, 100, 101, 102, 105, 106, 109, 116, 118, 120, 128, 132, 164, 166-174, 185-7, 215-16, 218-19, 227-230, 270, 272-3, 286-7, 293, 298
Mackid, F/L J. 97 Sqn   283
Mainland, J.   84, 86, 87
Malcolm, F/O F. 1 PRU   94, 95, 281
Marks, W/C J. 35 Sqn   100, 103, 129, 204
Marshall, Sgt W. 97 Sqn   283
Marshall, W/C J. 286,   288
McDermott, Sgt. E.
97 Sqn   283

McMurtrie, G/C I.   86, 87
Meredith, Sgt R. 35 Sqn   85, 86
Merifield, F/L J. 1 PRU   79, 81, 177
Miller, F/L G. 10 Sqn   46, 130, 158-9, 176, 209-12
Milne, D.   315
Morrell, Sgt E. 76 Sqn   145
Murray, P/O. 10 Sqn   195
Murray, Sgt J. 10 Sqn   242, 244-7, 249
Nesbit, R.C.   63
O'Connor, Sgt R. 10 Sqn   151
Osborne, W/O. 44 Sqn   130, 189
Osbourne, Sgt. 248 Sqn   136-7
Paget, F/S J. 248 Sqn   136-7
Pallett, C.   314
Parr, F/Sgt W. 35 Sqn   262
Peach, Sgt A. 35 Sqn   84, 85, 86, 87
Perry, Sgt D. 35 Sqn   98, 99, 128, 219, 227-230, 272-3, 276
Petley, F/L. 35 Sqn   103, 104, 192, 196, 263
Pomroy, Sgt G. 35 Sqn   264-5
Pooles, F/L. 35 Sqn   101, 154, 177, 283
Price, Sgt. 35 Sqn   197, 263
Rarity, Sgt D. 35 Sqn   283
Renaut, P/O M. 76 Sqn   82, 200, 207
Richards, F/S. 10 Sqn   73
Richards, Sgt R.G. 10 Sqn   90
Roberts, Sgt P. 10 Sqn   210-12
Rochford, F/S. 10 Sqn   195, 298
Roe, F/S J. 35 Sqn   190, 192, 196, 280
Russell, Sgt C. 35 Sqn   262
Ryall, I. 15 Sqn   43
Ryder, Sgt J. 10 Sqn   210-12
Saunders, Cpl R. 10 Sqn   42, 43, 106, 108, 118
Schofield, E.   125
Sellick, S/L B. 15 Sqn   44, 45, 49
Seymour-Price, S/L
10 Sqn   119
Siebert, Sgt P. 10 Sqn   153
Sinclair, Sir A,
Minister for Air   116
Smith, LAC G. 10 Sqn   106, 107, 108
Smith, Sgt S. 15 Sqn   41, 48, 52
Smith, N & P.   239
Smith, F/S J. 97 Sqn   76
Steinhauer, F/S G.
35 Sqn   83, 90
Stevens, Sgt V. 35 Sqn   99, 102, 103, 110, 119, 120, 128-9, 131-3, 163, 166, 168-9, 172-3, 214-16, 218-19, 227, 231, 247, 261, 265-7, 276-8, 310, 312
Stevens-Fox, F/L. 10 Sqn   90
Stobbs, Cpl A.D. 15 Sqn   40, 48

Stott, Sgt H. 10 Sqn	211		Dalamo, J.	258
Stott, W/O. 44 Sqn	142		Dalanes, T & H.	256-8, 260, 268
Strachan, R.A. 15 Sqn	40, 43, 52		Danielsen, G.	287
Swales, F/O I. 15 Sqn	40, 41, 42, 44, 47,		Eide, Y.	225
	49, 50, 51		Flåmo, H & D.	254
Tait, W/C J.B. 10 Sqn	119		Fordal, R.	239
Taylor, F/L.	86		Fossum, N.	235
Thompson, S/L. 10 Sqn	74, 147, 183		Fossum, A & R.	170-1
Tree, P/O T. 97 Sqn	283		Gjemble, H & J.	220, 222-4, 226,
Trenchard, MRAF				231-2
Lord H.	116		Granlund, K.	220
Tuck, W/C 10 Sqn	38, 46		Grønn, B.	55
Underwood, P/O R.			Hagen, P.	229, 231
97 Sqn	283		Hagensen, H & A.	257
Usher, Sgt. 35 Sqn	84		Hassel, Magnar	281
Waite, P/O W. 76 Sqn	124, 126, 133,		Hassel, Magne,	56
	145-7, 181-3		Hernes, B & K.	28, 58, 61, 152,
Walker, P/O J, 210 Sqn	125, 127			155
Walker, Sgt D.	308		Hoel, I.	223-6, 261, 263,
Wallis Dr. Barnes	302			277
Walmsley, Sgt H. 10 Sqn	19, 74, 161, 202,		Hofstad, J.	235
	249, 251-5, 270-2		Holmen, O & T.	224-5
Warne, F/S H. 15 Sqn	40, 48		Horten, O.	236
Warner, T. RAF Padre	86		Hovdal, J & G.	229
Watt, A.	84, 86		Høgsve, J & G.	56
Watts, F/O J. 10 Sqn	71, 74, 130,		Huseby, M.	92
	149-51, 162, 191,		Jenssen, J & M.	229-30
	205-7		Juliussen, P & H.	252-3
Webster, S/L F.D. 10 Sqn	87, 90, 91, 93		Kringberg	241
Whittles, E.	84		Langseth, L.	249, 269
Whyte, F/S. 10 Sqn	73		Lian (Tirpitz watcher)	56
Wigmore, S/L, 235 Sqn	136		Lian, T.	286
Wilding, S/L. 35 Sqn	149, 195		Lovtangen, O.	28
Williams, Sgt R. 76 Sqn	180-2		Mossing, S & N.	215-16
Wilson, S/L. 15 Sqn	44		Munkeby, J.	229
Wilson, Sgt R. 35 Sqn	99, 128, 132-3,		Myhr, R & I.	220
	166-9, 172, 214,		Myrlov, Cpl O.	255
	219, 221-2, 231-4,		Nielsen, S.	246
	256, 261, 272-3,		Nielsen, J & M.	235, 246-7
	276		Nilssen, Dr. B.	223
Wilstrop, Sgt A. 35 Sqn	283		Nordvang, T.	235
Windle, Sgt D. 10 Sqn	153		Nyborg, P.	232, 262
Wood, Sgt. 10 Sqn	153		Nyheim, J.	258
Wright, W/O. 44 Sqn	130, 189		Olsen, B.	306, 310, 313
Wyatt, Sgt. 10 Sqn	72, 73		Onstad, E.G.	269
Young, W/C D. 76 Sqn	37, 38, 46, 80, 131,		Overrein, I.	235
	189		Øyan, J.	250-1,
			Øyum, P.	228-230
Norwegian			Roar, Mr.	236
			Rørholt B.	20, 54-8, 66,
Aabakken, A & M.	223			137-8, 267
Aarestad, Dr.	246		Salberg, A & E.	224-5
Andresen, O.	235		Schiefloe J.	250-1
Baardvik, R.	58		Skjeldstad, S & L.	154-5, 248, 283-4,
Berg, E.	246			289, 290-1
Bergersen, B.	58-9, 179, 285-6,		Slåtsve, H.	229
	293-5		Sonen, A.	246
Bjørnås, H.	258		Sonstad, B.	216
Brenne (policeman)	269		Stavnas, Magne	235
Dahm, J.	22			

Stormo, E. 281
Thorsen, B. 22
Torvik, S. 258
Trætli, P. 232, 262
Trøite, N. 269
Trøite, R. 235, 242, 269
Troseth, E. 232, 262
Ulvik, E. 280
Vinje, A. 262

German

Gerhard, Lt D. 65-7
Hitler, A, Reichsführer 18, 19, 30
Huppertz, Oblt, H. 92, 94, 95

Knoke, Lt H. 64-5, 67
Kuhnen, E. 178
Raeder, Admiral 19

Other Nationalities

Bernadotte, Count 271
Hansen, Lt. 270
Hauch, Photographic Interpreter 24
Piltingsrud, A. 272
Skogh, Capt. 260
Stalin, Josef 18
Aalesund, Nor 110, 113, 134, 136,

Places

139
Aasfjord, Nor See Åsen Fjord
Aaviksaune Farm, Nor 153
Aavikstykket, Nor 28
Aberdeen, UK 48, 50, 76
Agdenes, Nor 55-6
Almo, Nor 161, 236
Alta Fjord, Nor 274
Archangel, Rus 14, 18, 68
Åsen Fjord, Nor 23-24, 26, 47, 110-112, 121-122, 142, 150, 164, 167, 176, 178, 184, 196, 200, 209, 212, 221, 261, 280
Åsen, Nor 47, 92, 112, 137, 141, 142, 154, 170-171, 191, 192, 196, 223, 237, 261, 284-6, 288, 293, 295, 299
Ausetvatnet Lake, Nor 154
Bergen, Nor 22, 305
Berlin, Ger 123, 247, 267
Birmingham, UK 86
Bjerke, Nor 269
Bjørkdalen, Nor 269
Bjørkhaugen, Nor 220
Bjørnås Farm, Nor 258
Blekpynten, Nor 153
Bogen Fjord, Nor 75, 202
Bonn, Ger 88
Borås Farm, Nor 154, 155, 156, 235-6, 246, 281, 283, 286, 288-92
Brake, UK 84
Brekkstad, Nor 91
Bremanger Island, Nor 46
Brest, Fr 16, 19, 31, 32, 40, 301
Brobakk, Nor 250

Buckie, UK 49, 110
Burghead, UK 110
Bynesset, Nor 138
Carnoustie, UK 40
Copenhagen, Den 267
Copinsay Island, UK 94
Cricklewood, UK 315
Dortmund-Ems Canal, Ger 102
Dunkirk, Fr 100
Eder Dam, Ger 294-5
Edo, Nor 90
Elgin, UK 42, 76
Elverum Farm, Nor 261-2, 280-1
Erståsen, Nor 229, 230
Essen, Ger 52, 99
Faana-landet, Nor 92
Falstad, Nor 10, 269, 289
Falun, Swe 227, 230, 235, 255, 258, 260, 270
Farnborough, UK 88
Færsåsen, Nor 230
Fætten Fjord, Nor 19, 21, 24-26, 28-32, 35, 56-9, 60-1, 64, 68, 75, 79, 92, 110-112, 141-142, 144, 149, 150, 164, 177, 179, 183, 189-91, 193, 198-9, 202, 204, 253, 280, 282, 284, 293, 295-7, 299, 301-2
Filey Bay, UK 71, 72, 101
Firth of Forth, UK 118, 121
Fitful Head, UK 84, 85, 86
Fjergen Lake, Nor 253-4
Flåmosetra, Nor 254
Flornes, Nor 162, 236-7
Flornesvollen, Nor 236, 256, 268
Forbordfjell, Nor 94, 95, 164, 281

Formofoss, Nor 267
Forres, UK 74, 119
Frol, Nor 228
Frol-fjellet, Nor 230
Frosta, Nor 164, 176, 280, 288
Gaulosen Fjord, Nor 142
Gdynia, Pol 270
Gilsåfjellet, Nor 260
Gothenburg, Swe 270
Gregness, UK 48
Guda, Nor 250-1, 257
Hallsjøen Lake, Nor 253-4
Halten Light, Nor 126
Hammarvatnet,
    Lake, Nor 92, 281
Hårradålen, Nor 260
Harrow, UK 87
Haugen Farm, Nor 251
Hegglivollen, Nor, 233
Hegra, Nor 235-6, 242, 245-6,
    269, 283, 291
Heim, Nor 90
Hendon, RAF Mus, UK 276, 278, 305,
    311-12
Henley, UK 22
Herdla Aerodrome, Nor 134, 138, 139
Herma Ness, UK 109, 132
Hindrem, Nor 164
Hitra, Nor 88
Hjelte Fjord, Nor 138
Hoinskinnet, Nor 230
Hoklingen, Lake, Nor 13, 15, 171, 187,
    193, 196, 213, 216,
    221, 261, 276, 286,
    289, 293, 295, 299,
    305, 309-10
Hopleelven Fjord, Nor 209
Ipswich Docks, UK 310
Jons Lake, Nor 136, 137, 293, 295
Kaa Fjord, Nor 61, 301
Kaldadammen, Nor 146
Kiel Canal, Ger 19
Kilnes Farm, Nor 251
Kinnairds Head, UK 47, 90
Klonka, Nor 230
Kopperå, Nor 254
Kristiansten (fort), Nor 137, 241
Kristiansund North, Nor 90, 134, 163, 176
La Pallice, Fr 32
La Rochelle, Fr 32
Lade Aerodrome, Nor 64, 65, 92, 113,
    134, 136, 191, 203
Laksåvika, Nor 88
Langfjord, Nor 136
Langstein, Nor 146, 155, 280
Leeds, UK 253
Lerwick, UK 84, 85
Levanger, Nor 57, 216, 228, 231,
    289, 310
Lista, Nor 19

Litlefjell, Nor 260
Lofjord, Nor 93, 112, 116, 122,
    145, 154, 176, 181,
    189, 190, 288
Loire, River, Fr 75
London, UK 204, 253, 262
Lorient, Fr 102
Malvik, Nor 157, 211
Mannsætterbakken, Nor 258, 260
Markabygda, Nor 220, 223, 232,
    261-2, 289
Meråker, Nor 242, 250-3
Mestuga, Swe 230
Moan Farm, Nor 229
Mohne Dam, Ger 294-5
Molskdalen, Nor 237
Montreal, Can 99
Moray Firth, UK 106, 117, 118, 121
Mousehole, UK 305
Movatn, Lake, Nor 192, 196, 221, 232,
    243, 261, 263, 265,
    280
Murmansk, Rus 18, 68
Narvik, Nor 75, 202, 210
New Brunswick, Can 99
Newcastle, UK 305
Norviksundet, Nor 62, 199
Nøysomhet, Nor 224-5
Oban, UK 125
Orkedal Fjord, Nor 142
Orkland, Nor 231
Orkneys, UK 20, 91, 104, 109,
    110, 128
Ørland, Nor 91, 113, 203
Oslo, Nor 211, 241, 247,
    265-7, 269, 286
Ostend, Fr 100
Østkil, Nor 246
Outer Skerries, UK 110
Outer Hebrides, UK 70, 71
Oxford, UK 255
Perrig Heim, Nor 30
Port of Ayr, UK 102
Preston, UK 314-16
Quendale, UK 84
Reykjavik, Ice 68
Rinnleiret, Nor 203
Røkke, Nor 196, 221, 263
Romford, UK 99
Ruhr Valley, Ger 40, 104, 204
Sagelva (river), Nor 256
Salt Island, Nor 28, 30, 31, 56, 110,
    141, 146, 148, 153,
    166, 179, 296-7
Saltøya, Nor See Salt Island
Scapa Flow, UK 20
Seagull Isle, UK 102
Shetlands, UK 46, 54, 80, 83, 84,
    85, 86, 91, 109,
    110, 128, 132, 133,
    161

Skalstugan, Swe,	231	Teveldalen, Nor	254
Skansen, Nor	236	Thorney Island, UK	63
Skansund, Nor	199	Tingstad Farm, Nor	228, 231
Skatval, Nor	94, 196, 221, 263	Tipito, Nor	30
Skei, Nor	155, 290	Toft, Nor	138
Skitten, UK	63	Torsbjørkdalen, Nor	258
Skjeldstadmark, Nor	154, 161, 235	Tromsø, Nor	274-5
Skogn, Nor	218, 223-6, 261	Trondheim, Nor	10, 19, 20, 22-23,
Smøla, Nor	88, 142, 163		30-32, 46-47, 53-8,
Snill Fjord, Nor	163, 293		60, 62-4, 81-83,
Sola, Nor	251		88, 90-91, 94, 111,
Sona, Nor	250		117, 121, ,126,
Sondalen, Nor	250, 269		132, 135, 136, 137,
Sonfoss Farm, Nor	249, 269		138, 139, 142, 145,
Sonvatn, Nor	237, 242, 249		148, 150, 156, 158,
St. Nazaire, Fr	19, 75		164, 176, 184,
Stavanger, Nor	305		190-1, 203-4, 211,
Stavne War Cem, Nor	90, 93, 156, 157,		212, 226, 235, 241,
	235, 262, 281-2,		243, 262, 267, 269,
	284, 289-90, 295		281, 284, 288-9,
Steinskjerrigan, Nor	291		293, 295, 305
Stettin, Ger	24	Trondheim Fjord, Nor	19, 22, 26, 28,
Stjørdal, Nor	94, 162, 235, 162,		30-32, 42, 47, 56,
	267		58-60, 62, 64, 66,
Stjørdal River, Nor	245, 250		88, 90-92, 109-110,
Stjørdalens Kapell, Nor	268		126, 137, 142, 147,
Stjørdalselva			149, 151, 157, 163,
(stream), Nor	94, 135		164, 168, 180, 184,
Stjørdalsfjord, Nor	164		189, 191-3, 198,
Stockholm, Swe	57-8, 255, 271-3		209, 216, 282, 287,
Stokken Island, Nor	134		306
Støre Farm, Nor	220, 224	Vagen Farm, Nor	280
Støre, Nor	218	Væna-Sund, Nor	62, 199
Storeklukken, Swe	260	Værnes Aerodrome, Nor	47, 75, 76, 79, 113,
Storlien, Swe	230, 253, 255, 260,		121, 122, 134, 135,
	269		136, 142, 146, 186,
Storvallen, Swe	260		190, 191, 198, 203,
Storvatnet (lake), Nor	164		226, 235, 284-5
Stranden Fjord, Nor	189	Vattendalen, Nor	260
Strensall, UK	101, 102, 103	Vest Fjord, Nor	74, 75
Strindfjord, Nor	142, 164	Vududalen, Nor	28
Sullom Voe, UK	127	Whitby, UK	73
Sumburgh Head, UK	80, 87	Whitehaven, UK	102
Sumburgh, UK	124	Whitley Bay, UK	38
Sundby Farm, Nor	222-3	Wilhelmshaven, Ger	19, 20
Sunndal, Nor	246	York, UK	76
Sunndalsra, Nor	64	Ytterøya, Nor	92
Terningen LH, Nor	90	Prinz Eugen	16, 40, 60, 93, 94,

Ships

Admiral Hipper	60, 94, 122, 168,	Arthur	54-5
	194	Bismarck	18, 30
Admiral Scheer	59-60, 93, 94, 112,	Feie	54
	116, 122, 145, 168,	Gneisenau	16, 19, 40, 301
	176, 189, 194	King George V Class	18
Altmark	94	Lützow	24, 112, 116, 122

	145, 158-9, 168, 186, 189, 194, 210-12		141-2, 144-6, 148-150, 152, 154-5, 158, 161, 166-9, 175-7, 179-81, 183-4, 188-190, 192-4, 196-200, 202-3, 205-6, 215, 226, 229, 234, 241, 253, 255, 263, 273-5, 278, 280, 282-4, 287-8, 293-303, 303
Scharnhorst	16, 19, 40, 301		
Sea Wolf, HMS	66		
Tirpitz	10-12, 14, 15, 18-26, 28-32, 34-38, 42, 45-49, 52-64, 66, 68-70, 73-77, 79-82, 92-94, 96-98, 101, 102, 104-106, 109-112, 114, 116, 118, 122, 126, 131, 133, 135, 137, 139,		
		Victorious, HMS	74

Miscellaneous

RAF BASES			312
Alconbury	40, 50, 51	Manston	100
Benson	22, 23, 24, 61, 199	Marston Moor	97
Brize Norton	308	Medmenham	61
Dalton	97	Middleton-St.-George	38, 206
Dishforth	97-98	Mildenhall	36, 38
Dyce	47	Peterhead	47-48, 50-53
Henlow	310, 312	St. Eval	23
Kinloss	47, 74-75, 79-80, 83, 99, 105-106, 109-110, 116, 118-119, 121, 204, 218	Sumburgh	22, 24, 63, 83, 84, 86, 94, 190, 194
		Tain	75, 76, 80, 82-83, 90, 105-106, 116, 121, 124, 126,130-131, 139, 182, 204, 206
Leeming	38, 43, 70-71, 75-76, 88, 106-107, 117, 119, 205-6	Topcliffe	97
Leuchars	60, 91, 272	Waddington	206
Linton-on-Ouse	71, 97-102, 104-105, 206, 318	West Drayton	308
		Wick	22, 23, 24, 46, 50, 60, 63, 65, 80, 82, 83, 94, 121-122, 182
Lossiemouth	36, 38, 40-53, 60, 73-77, 80, 82-83, 88, 105-108, 110, 118, 121, 122, 124, 130, 180, 183, 193-4, 204-5, 273,	Woodhall Spa,	76, 206
		Wyton	38, 41, 45, 51, 305

Armed Forces Units

1 PRU	22-3, 37, 60, 63-6, 93, 111, 177, 206		200, 204-6, 272, 296-8, 312
9 Squadron	274	35 Squadron	71, 75, 77-78, 80, 83, 85, 88, 90, 97-98, 100-101, 105-106, 109, 111-114, 116, 122, 124, 126, 131, 147-49, 154, 180, 187, 190-191, 193, 195, 204, 206, 255, 296-8, 308, 314-5
10 Squadron	14, 19, 36, 38, 41-42, 45, 68, 70-71, 73-77, 83, 87, 88, 91, 105-106, 111-114, 116-118, 124, 130, 147, 149-153, 159-160, 183-184, 188, 191, 193-195,		

42 Squadron	64
44 Squadron	69, 105, 114, 124, 130-131, 142, 180, 184, 188-189, 193, 206
48 Squadron	126
76 Squadron	36-38, 46, 75, 77-78, 80, 87-88, 90, 105, 114, 116, 123-124, 126, 131, 145, 147, 180, 184, 189-191, 193, 200, 206
77 Squadron	205
97 Squadron	68, 76, 105, 114, 124, 154, 184, 188, 190, 193, 206
102 Squadron	97, 98, 102, 315
149 Squadron	36, 38, 45, 53
15 Squadron	36, 38, 40, 41, 44, 45, 48
210 Squadron	124, 126, 134
217 Squadron	63
235 Squadron	134, 190

248 Squadron	136, 138
416 Squadron	47
603 Squadron	47
608 Squadron	126
617 Squadron	274, 294
883 Squadron	180
45 MU	106
77 MU	79
1652 HCU	97
Central Interpretation Unit	22, 24, 118, 122
3 Group	34, 36, 38
4 Group	34, 36, 38, 97, 100, 108-109, 110, 116, 120-121, 206
5 Group	97, 106, 109, 121
8 (PFF) Group	272
18 Group Coastal Cmmd	113, 133
Strike Commd	308
9./Jagdgeschwader 5	92
Fliegerhorst-kommandantur	235
Sperrwaffenkommando	179
XXXIII Armeekorps	64

Miscellaneous

Halifax W1048 'S-Sugar'	13, 15, 97, 98, 99, 100, 101, 102, 103, 105, 113, 128-9, 131, 142, 148, 163-4, 166, 168, 170-2, 178, 185-7, 196, 215, 220, 247, 256, 261, 270, 276, 278, 286, 293-5, 298-9, 308-12, 314-16, 318
Mines, Naval Mark XIX	69, 76, 77, 114, 124, 300
Shetland Bus	54-6